Scene and Hird

Thora Hird

My Autobiography
Volume 1

Fount
An Imprint of HarperCollinsPublishers

Fount Paperbacks is an Imprint of
HarperCollins*Religious*
Part of HarperCollins*Publishers*
77–85 Fulham Palace Road, London W6 8JB

First published in Great Britain in 1976 by W. H. Allen
Published in 1995 by Fount Paperbacks

3   5   7   9   10   8   6   4

Copyright © 1976 Thora Hird

Thora Hird asserts the moral right to be
identified as the author of this work

A catalogue record for this book is
available from the British Library

ISBN 0 00 627929–5

Typeset by Harper Phototypesetters Limited
Northampton, England
Printed and bound in Great Britain by
Caledonian International Book Manufacturing Ltd, Glasgow

Dedication

I have written this book, basically, for my dear American grandchildren, Daisy Ann and James Scott Tormé, so that when they are older they can read it and learn all about *me* . . . from *me*.

I would also like to use the book to show my sincere gratitude for having been blessed with a wonderful mother and father, who not only taught me most of what I know about the precarious business known as the theatrical profession but who between 'em bestowed upon me a sense of humour that has sustained me sufficiently to remain in it!

For a super brother and a good man, Neville, who could make me laugh more than anyone I've ever known.

It's also for Scottie . . . my husband, who escorted me out of the Wesleyan Chapel, my arm firmly through his (to make sure he didn't get away) thirty-eight years ago . . . for better or worse. Poor soul! It's been an endurance test but he says he's getting used to it now.

For my daughter, Janette, the most loving and charitable person I have ever met, who apart from being a splendid wife and mother manages to be an excellent Sunday School teacher, works for the blind babies, helps to save the mustangs and the whales, supports the Schools for Red Cloud Indian children, works for free spaying for animals, teenagers with emotional problems, is on the board of the Haemophilia Foundation and helps to save the Wilderness mountain regions and wildlife and uses white toilet rolls in each of her six toilets because, apparently, coloured paper poisons the fish! Dearest Jan . . . don't ever change!

Phew! And that's the first page done.

Contents

I give a great many interviews each year on TV, radio and in the press. The most often requested stories are tales of my early years. I am delighted that HarperCollins wish to share some of these with you, by this reprint of my 1977 autobiography *Scene and Hird*.

1

Overture and beginners, please!

I was born on a Sunday, when the church bells were ringing. My brother Neville was born on a Sunday, when the church bells were ringing. He was born just before Morning Service and I was born just before Evening Service – not on the same Sunday of course. He appeared one year and nine months prior to my arrival.

Knowing him as I do I think he was born twenty-one months before me so that he could look the world over, approve of it and make sure it was 'safe' for 'Our Kid', 'George' or 'Horace'. These are the names he always called me – I can't think why, as I am very proud of being extremely feminine!

I remember the love and devotion that shone in my mother's eyes when she recalled the church bells; it was such that, as a little girl, I liked to feel that they had rung *because* Neville and I had been born. There was no feeling of conceit about this, and if there had been it would have been daft because we were *chapel* not *church*.

I used to swank at school about the church bells bit, not in a 'clever clogs' way, but in a rather grateful way. I know I used to feel privately sorry for any of my school chums who'd had the misfortune to be born at five-to-one on a Tuesday or twenty minutes past three on a Saturday.

There was something else I rather enjoyed swanking about at school – it was that my mother's birthday was in April, my own in May, my dad's in June, my sister Olga's in July and my brother Neville's in August!

That statement was always received with open-mouthed amazement, and many times I was requested to 'Go on, Hirdie, and tell So-and-So about the birthdays at your house!' Whereupon I would oblige, with pleasure. Encouraged sufficiently I would tell 'em about the church bells as an encore!

My childhood, my home life, and my parents can sincerely be headed or entitled The Happiest in the World – and that *is* swanking, so I'll settle for *one* of The Happiest in the World. But I adamantly stick to that!

My mother, Mary Jane Mayor, was the daughter of a fisherman. He had a trawler and, along with my uncles, trawled for shrimps in Morecambe Bay.

My mother was born in Morecambe so comes under the heading of a 'Sandgrown 'un' – and because I was born in Morecambe, so do I.

She had a really beautiful mezzo-soprano voice and always sang the solo 'I know that my Redeemer Liveth' when *The Messiah* was performed at the Green Street Wesleyan Chapel.

When she was seventeen, she bravely left the Milliners and Drapers where she was employed and 'went into the business', as the theatrical profession is so often called (*another* profession has been called 'the business' but thank heavens they now refer to that activity as being 'on the job'!).

However, as I was saying, my mother went into the theatrical profession with the good wishes of all and the blessing of the Wesleyan Minister.

The choir presented her with a really lovely wooden trunk, decorated with embossed leather. In addition, the Minister presented her with some advice; he also assured her that if ever, during the precarious life she was about to embark on, she was in any trouble, she could always return home – and sing in the choir! I am happy to report that when she did return to Morecambe to live, it was neither because she was in trouble nor because she had led a precarious life. It was because in the years between leaving and returning she had met, fallen in love with and married James Henry Hird.

James Henry Hird was born in Todmorden, the town which boasted that half of its Town Hall is in Lancashire, the other half in Yorkshire. My father's personal boast was that he was born on the Lancashire side.

I am like my father in many ways, one in particular being my true love of Lancashire. I, too, am proud of being a Lancastrian – yes, even prouder of that than the church bells incident!

Although James Henry was born in Lancashire his forbears came from Fifeshire, and as my mother's family were believed to have descended from Viking stock, I'm not sure what that makes me and my brother Neville. But I don't wonder the church bells rang – perhaps they were sounding the alarm!

Prior to Miss Marie Mayor and James Henry Hird marrying, they had met in a touring company. In those days, artistes performed 'one night stands', and were on tour for many months. When I think of the work involved during these touring seasons, I feel I can never grumble about my own work.

I don't think there was a county in the British Isles in which my parents had not 'played'. As my brother and I grew older in school years, we would sit around the fire with our school chums, drinking cocoa and eating my mother's apple pie or currant pasty, while Marie Mayor would relate witty, pathetic and interesting stores of when she and Dad were 'on tour'.

We never wearied of these tales, which my mother told so well – about the business manager 'doing a bunk' and leaving them stranded without money; or about the young dandies who would crowd the stage door waiting for the girls, with bouquets of flowers. In fact, my mother swore that my father would never have proposed had it not been for the fact that one young gentleman waited for her at the stage door for four nights in succession, *avec* flowers!

I used to love the expression on her dear face as she came out with the 'curtain line' – 'so, on the fifth day, your father took me on a picnic and during our meal, he *proposed*.'

Good old James Henry, he showed 'em. You don't compete with a lad from Todmorden and get away with it, especially if he's born on the Lancashire side of the Town Hall!

Playing for real

I wasn't born in a trunk, a theatrical skip or hamper, I was born comfortably and snugly in bed. However, I did make my first appearance 'on the boards', 'on the green' or in everyday parlance 'on the stage', at the tender age of eight weeks old!

My mother was appearing in a drama at the Royalty Theatre as the young heroine who had been 'done wrong' by the Squire's son, I played the 'unfortunate result!' My father was the director. I had no audition. I was cast as the result of three short words which were directed at my mother by my father, 'Take *HER* on!' The *HER* was me – my first and only engagement I ever got through influence! According to records I didn't over-play, cry, or wet myself – I slept during the entire proceedings!

But eventually my parents decided to stay put, and made a permanent home for themselves in Morecambe. My father always had a fair share of initiative and was never afraid of hard work. Consequently, he was able to get a job which enabled him and mother to start a home of their own instead of the continual 'digs' they had lived in on tour.

Being a splendid swimmer, when offered the job of

manager and swimming instructor at the appropriately named Bare Bathing Pool he 'dived in at the deep end' as you might say!

Determined to better himself, his next job was stage manager on the West End Pier, and then with a foot on the next step of the ladder, he ascended one rung higher still when he became stage manager at the Alhambra, which in those days presented most of the biggest variety turns outside London.

From the Alhambra he moved onwards and upwards again to become stage manager of the Royalty Theatre. As stage manager of the Royalty, the house next door at Number 6, Cheapside, went in with his wage. Of course, up to this juncture I wasn't even a gleam in his eye.

I still smile when I recall my mother telling me how, after six years of marriage, they were *delighted* to discover a baby was on the way. That was Olga. And how, fifteen months after Olga was born, they were *delirious* to discover that another baby was on the way. That was Neville. And how, twelve months after Neville was born, they were *demented* to discover there was yet another baby on the way. Yes, that was *ME*!

3

Just Cheapside

Thora Hird, 6 Cheapside, Morecambe, Lancashire, England, Europe, The World. That is what I would write on my very own very personal possessions – such as the flyleaf of my Schoolgirl's Diary, my Sunday School prizes which were always books, the inside flap of my leather school bag, the bottom of my varnished wood pencil box and on many other very private and very personal possessions too numerous to mention.

Mind you, I grew out of the 'Europe' and 'The World' bit by the time I was about nine, but I'm quite sure it was only because I would have been satisfied – no, more than that, *proud* to have gone through life with the one word after my name. *Cheapside*!

I enjoyed the sound of the word. In fact, I was so proud of it, I swanked about it, defended it, scrubbed half of it (which I'll come to in a minute) and sincerely loved every inch of it, even the warm coloured *Yorkshire* stone flags that were used as a pavement – and that's praise indeed from a Lancashire woman!

Cheapside. Not Cheapside Street or Road or Avenue or Drive or Crescent – just Cheapside.

The word needed no embellishment to me. I always felt that there was a great sound of authority about it –

added to which there was the number of our house. Six.

Now you must admit that Six, Cheapside, has a bit of a musical ring to it – well, what I mean about Number Six is, it *goes* with the word Cheapside better than any other number.

For instance I would have been deprived of a lot of private pleasure had I been born at, let us say Number Two or Eleven or Twenty-eight or Thirty-one.

Our side of Cheapside – get that bit, *our side*; anyone would think reading this that we owned the whole of one side of Cheapside. Please don't misunderstand; the side of Cheapside we lived on was the one with even numbers – but more than that, our side was the three front steps and bay window side. The residents of the other side, the odd numbers, poor unfortunate souls, had only one small step and a flat ordinary window.

Now at this point, in fairness to readers, I must be my age and admit that it *was* a street. That's all, just a street. But a street that housed many, many wonderful, good and kind people.

We all knew and cared about each other in this street; and one of my greatest pleasures, even now at Christmas time, is receiving cards from dear elderly neighbours who knew me from my birth and who I knew as young women. The sad but inevitable thing is that each Christmas I receive fewer cards because the young women I knew have grown into old women and have passed on to an even more important place than Cheapside.

Running across the top of Cheapside was Market Street – so named, of course, because there was a red and yellow brick covered market in it.

Market Street also boasted the front entrance of The Royalty Theatre.

Turning into Cheapside, the side of the Royalty ran down the left hand side (our side) for about 50 yards. There were the exit doors of the Gods, then the exit doors of the balcony. Next, there was a little stretch of lovely stone wall, then the Pit exit doors and the Orchestra Stalls exit doors. Then came the exciting bit, the Stage Door – or Doors. They were double doors, but of course everyone always says 'the stage *door*', singular, don't they?

After the Stage Door there were the Scenery Doors, the bottom of which were about five feet above the pavement over some dressing room windows – and these afforded us untold – and I really mean untold, until now – pleasure. When all of us kids were 'playing out' in the street after tea, the dressing room lights would be on, and the windows slightly open to allow the artistes a little fresh air. They couldn't see us peeping in, but we could see *them* – changing or making up, and well, er! – other things.

Talk about the Permissive Society – crumbs! – I recall one week there was a very good looking actor (well, *we* thought he was, we were very young y'know – all of us) using the dressing room with the window which had the best view through the slit where it was open, and it didn't seem quite normal to we very unsophisticated young Lancastrians that he walked about the dressing room without clothes on – or as we called it, bare. What a week! We never played hop scotch, or rounders or marbles once! It was 'Window on the World Week'.

We started off by taking turns to peer in at his assets, but before long we were shoving and pushing each other out of the way. Add to this the fact that we had to keep dead quiet or he would have heard us and – tragedy – he would have shut the window, or worse still put some clothes on!

I remember what agony it was not to titter when he displayed his manly form, so the drill was that if we couldn't keep our titters in, we had to creep quietly away with our hand over our mouth and let our titter burst forth when we were out of earshot of the window.

It's amazing when one thinks back, that most of the peepers, including myself, had brothers. We'd all seen them on bath nights and knew how they were made – but this good-looking actor wasn't the brother of any of us – and a free look at a non-relative's piece of equipment was not to be missed. Anyhow he sang 'Roses are blooming in Picardy' whilst he was walking about nude and that was an added attraction. According to the dictionary the word 'equipment' is described as: 'Soldiers accoutrements' – well in this case it was 'Actor's accoutrements!'

To this day – and it's a long time since then – I can remember feeling guilty when I went indoors for my supper each night and I had no answer when my mother enquired, 'What have you been doing – your nose and forehead are all covered in black dust?' But however young you are you can *think* – and I was thinking, Why don't they wash the dressing room windows at the Royalty?

So much for the week of Abandoned Excitement. It never happened again. The following week the room was occupied by a very respectable character actor, and when he was off stage all he did was sit in the dressing room, smoke a pipe and read. Although we had all taken our positions and reminded each other to keep our titters in, it wasn't worth bothering about to get our noses and foreheads black. So we played hop scotch under the street lamp on the opposite side to our house until one of my friends exclaimed, 'Hey, there's some more dressing room windows up that passage next to your house, Hirdie.'

The Charge of the Light Brigade had nothing on us. Phfft! We were across the road quicker than I've written it – but our bunch halted at the entrance to the passage – or ginnel – and then quietly tip-toed the rest of the way only to discover no less than eight windows.

Pshaw! None of 'em open and on top of that they'd been painted all over with whitening! Each face registered disapproval and then we all let our titters burst forth. That's the great thing about being young – a disappointment doesn't last long.

Speaking of the passage, it was the next bit of the Theatre and also next to our front door. It hadn't always been so; from the time I was born to the time I was about five years old, there had been another house, Number Four.

Well, I say a house, but that isn't quite correct. The front of it was exactly like ours but only the ground floor was lived in. The first and the top floors were used as dressing rooms for the Theatre, so although the entire front of Number Four was in harmony with the rest of the houses on 'our side' it was really only habitable on the ground floor because it had no staircase.

The front bedrooms were approached by a staircase from the back of the theatre stage.

This was something that afforded my brother and me great fun – I'll tell you how.

When my mother was playing at the theatre or maybe visiting someone in one of those dressing rooms and we were in bed, she could literally be in the next room. My bed was next to the wall, and Neville's a bit further along, also next to the wall. We would lie in bed and wait for the exciting bit. It always came.

Suddenly, right next to either my head or Nev's, we would hear it – Pom tiddly-om-pom, *pom, pom* banged on the wall. Scuttling out of the bedclothes we would kneel up and reply with our Pom-tiddly-om-pom, *pom, pom* – I can remember even now how it hurt my knuckles. Then, clear as a bell, mother would say, 'Aren't you two asleep yet?' and we would chorus 'No-o-o'; and then she would say, 'Well, settle down, I'll be home in a few minutes!' and we would shout 'All right – good night and God Bless' and mother would reply 'God Bless.' And that was the end of the exciting bit!

Not a moment to be recorded in history perhaps, but all the same, I don't suppose I shall meet more than a hundred people tomorrow whose mother spoke to them through a wall, when *she* was in a Theatre and *they* were in bed?

Not long afterwards, Number Four became part of the Theatre building, so the passage or ginnel that had been on the other side of Number Four was then moved up next to us. This didn't alter the top of Number Four; the dressing rooms were still on a level with our bedrooms.

It was quite a few years after that that they scrapped those dressing rooms to make the back of the stage into a scene dock, so the hurt wasn't so bad. Nev's room was at the back of the house by then and although I had the big front bedroom to myself we were both in our teens and too 'grown up' to play at knocking on walls.

Or were we? Neither of us was madly sophisticated – of course, we *thought* we were – but I know now we weren't. Even though it wasn't long after that time that I was wearing my long hair plaited and coiled into two flat saucers called 'earphones', and I endured the agony of plucking my eyebrows into a thin take-all-the-expression-away line. My father caught me in the painful act, as I 'oo'd and ah'd'; and instead of repri-manding me, he enquired as only James Henry could, 'What are you doing?' 'Plucking my eyebrows,' I replied. 'It's the fashion.' '*Plucking* your eyebrows!' he echoed. There was a slight stage pause whilst he looked at me – it was a pathetic look – and then he said, 'And we bother to bloody well send missionaries abroad!'

I have already done the 'swank bit' about our side of Cheapside having three front steps to the front door, but there's more to those steps than that. There were the steps, the window sills and the large slab of Yorkshire stone at the bottom of the steps which was really a frame for the 'coal 'ole'.

And it really was a frame. There it lay, the slab, in all its scrubbed glory, with a circle cut out of the middle in which a disc of cast iron about a foot in diameter was set like a jewel, and if it was blackleaded successfully, it shone like a black pearl.

Now I want to stress something at this point – from about the age of six, I was taught to help in the house. Not forced. Not whipped. Just given little jobs.

For instance, like every other child in those days – and I only say 'in those days' because I am talking about a long time ago; things have altered so very much during my lifetime – like every other child, I had a little rolling pin and baking board, and when my mother was baking I was given a small piece of 'paste' as we called it, and I would make something like a jam tart, or with a few currants, it would become a teacake.

I loved doing this sort of thing. My pastry probably was a light shade of grey by the time I'd finished messing about with it – but at least it was always eaten by one of my parents and loving remarks were passed as they nearly broke their teeth on it.

I was taught housework in the same way and I hereby declare that whatever people may think of my acting endeavours, I'll take anyone on in the cleaning stakes. That's not boasting – it's a fact, and it brings me back to our front steps.

The scrubbing, rubbing-stoning and blackleading that was required came under the lovely northern heading of 'Doing the Front'.

I know that we use a lot of expressions that sound grammatically incorrect or clumsy, but at least these are expressive, and 'Doing the Front' is one of them.

I started 'Doing the Front' (when I come to think of it – it sounds a bit suggestive really) when I was about six and a half or seven. The full production was this: sweep the steps and the pavement in front of the house and then shoot indoors for two brushes and the blacklead.

We used Zebo. (If I'd been born a few years earlier I'd have had to mix a lump of blacklead with water in an old saucer or tin.)

Right, Zebo on and brush it well in until the dullness had gone and then a brisk polish with the polishing brush. I always did the round coal hole lid first, then moved on to the big grate under the (ahem!) bay window. This grate was a devil to do; it was iron and the pattern was like lattice work. Never mind, it got done and with the grates shining like black diamonds I'd shoot indoors for a bucket of hot water, floor cloth and scrubbing brush, the maula soap (which was brown and looked as though it was a piece of fudge with chopped nuts in it and smelt of lovely disinfectant) *and* the yellow rubbing-stone and its brush.

Now I must describe the rubbing-stone brush. It was really a circumcised scrubbing brush, or, in other words, a scrubbing brush whose bristles were so worn away that it was ready for the dustbin. Only then did it become a perfect rubbing-stone brush, the reason being that not only could you hold the wood, but the bristles were so short that after rubbing the yellow stone on the front of the steps you could smooth it over for a perfect finish.

I'll tell you this much – the front steps of the houses in Cheapside radiated the personalities of every householder. Ours were yellow stoned on the front face of the step as well as the sides; Number Eight had white stone along the edges of their steps, Number Ten had white at the sides, and so on. By jove, it was worth walking down Cheapside on a Friday or Saturday morning.

Of course one felt deeply distressed that our

neighbours on the opposite side of the street couldn't show off their artistic ability as much as we could, because, you'll recall, they only had one step each.

However, there I am one morning, doing the front, on my kness, my bottom on view to all 'The One Steppers' on the other side. Well, no – not my bottom; my knickers I should have said. Whether, in my imagination I was being 'Little Emmie, the poor Orphan Cleaner' or whether I was at school or dancing class, I always wore little white knickers with either pale pink or pale blue baby ribbons threaded through the embroidery round the minute legs.

I would wear a cleaning apron which in those days were of dark grey material. Mine came down to my ankles but my dress just covered the cheeks of my bottom, so you've got the picture – kneeling mat, cleaning apron and white 'knicks' with pink or blue ribbon.

A neighbour opposite came to her front door to look up and down the street – this was a habit most of them had, not out of noseyness, in fact, it was the only pleasure some of them had. She looked across and saw me – I didn't see her – but I heard her as she called laughingly, 'Thora! I can see your arse.'

Now on my word of honour, I had never heard that word before in my life. For one thing, although we were a great family for funny stories, and although I grew up to have a sense of humour as great, I hope, as my parents, my dad, who was not unknown to swear, had such a respect for women that he never used words like 'arse'. And, if he did, it was never in front of us. Hearing the neighbour call out this new word, I jumped up, ran indoors and asked my mother, 'What's my arse?'

Honest to God, she nearly jumped through the ceiling, '*What* did you say?' she asked.

'What's my arse?' I repeated in all innocence, '. . . because Mrs Mayton can see it – she's just told me so.'

It was my dear mother's expression in cases like this that I remember so well. I can see her now – she drew herself up to her full height (which was about 5 ft 1 in) and with flour all over her hands, a half-peeled apple in one hand and the peeling knife in the other, she said, 'Oh – *did* she! Well, I shall *have a word* with Mrs Mayton.'

This was an expression, this 'have a word', that was only used on occasions such as this; as we stood there, Mother with the apple and knife and me with the scrubbing brush and maula soap, she added quietly, 'Off you go, love, and finish the front and – it's your botty!'

I well remember another such occasion – I was down on my knees 'worshipping Allah' and scrubbing away when a man we knew very well – he had a business at the top of Cheapside – was coming along the pavement just as I plunged my hands into the bucket of water. 'Good morning, Thora!' he said. 'Oh, good morning Mr So and So,' I replied – you see, that was one great thing about 'doing the front', it was a kind of social reception centre. Quite a lot of people used Cheapside. Well, as I took the cloth out of the bucket to wring it out, he paused and looked down at me. He stood sort of posed – hands behind his back and I really thought he was admiring my craft as a step scrubber, but no, taking a deep breath – just like an actor about to deliver the big speech at the end of a play, he said, 'I take it your mother doesn't object to you putting your hands in a bucket of diluted dog shit!'

As I didn't know what he meant, I just laughed and said, 'Oh no, Mr So and So.' Really I laughed because he had used the word 'shit' – why do we always laugh at forbidden words when we are kids?

That's all he said and then walked off, but it was enough to make me laugh even more because he walked with a little tilt, like Jacques Tati in *Monsieur Hulot's Holiday*.

Up I got and shot into the house. 'Mam, what does diluted mean?' 'Diluted?' said my mother, who was hanging some sheets to air on the clothes rack. 'Well, love, diluted means to thin out, like – when we get the lime to do the yard we – what do you want to know for?' 'I only wondered,' I said, 'because Mr So and So just said he takes it you don't object to my putting my hands in a bucket of diluted dog shit!'

Now those readers who are *au fait* with a clothes rack know that it consists of long thin pieces of wood and is hoisted up and down with a rope anchored by a hook on the wall. The most popular place for a rack is obviously on the ceiling in front of the fire place.

Well, talk about perfect comedy timing! My mother, who was about to hoist the rack to its safe and warm harbour as I uttered Mr So and So's famous statement, pulled on the rope with such surprise, the rack nearly shot through into the back bedroom above. As she wound the rope, figure eight-wise, round the cleat hook, she once again drew herself to her full height and

18

said quietly, 'Oh – did he! Well, I shall *have a word* with Mr So and So!'

She never did, of course, but it was nice to think she was protecting my youthful ears. The amazing thing was that it never dawned on her I was only enquiring about the word 'diluted' – I knew what the other word meant.

I should hate you to get the impression that the adventures of doing the front were all on the dog excretions and botty lines – they weren't. I recall that on one occasion when I was about nine years old (and this was a madly romantic period of my life), the leading man from the visiting company at the Theatre that week was coming up Cheapside, maybe to call for his mail or, as it was a Friday perhaps 'The Ghost was Walking' which in theatrical jargon means that it was pay day.

Just as he passed our door my father came out, and after very civil salutations the handsome leading man put his hand into his inside pocket and brought out a really lovely gold cigarette case with diamond initials on it!

My first reaction was that he must be a millionaire. Oh, cripes! not only good looking, but the owner of a gold and diamond fag case as well.

He offered my father a cigarette, helped himself to one, snapped the case shut, accepted a light from my dad and they set off up Cheapside chatting.

Now you may think that story unworthy of recording, but I am here to tell you that at that very moment I made up my mind for the umpteenth time that not only would I be an actress when I grew up but that I would also be the proud owner of a gold cigarette case with diamond initials on it. It never entered my dreamlike mind that I might not smoke. It was the case, and the elegant way he flipped it open and snapped it shut, that was the bit that impressed me.

It's amazing how one can get through work if you imagine lovely, almost impossible things. I was always doing that, and I really enjoyed my day dreams. As I smoothed the yellow rubbing stone along the front of the steps I was practically opening 'my' gold case and the diamonds shone in the reflection of the highly blackleaded coal 'ole.

Little did I realize as I knelt there that one day I *would* own a gold cigarette case with my initials on it in diamonds. In reality, that cigarette case was to be a loving gift from my husband and daughter – one of the many dreams of mine that came true.

There always seems to be a spot of humour attached to the memorable moments of my life, and the day Scottie – my husband – and Janette, our daughter, presented me with the gold case can still bring a smile to our faces. I suppose every happy wife and mother feels the same way about an expensive present and even a sixpenny present is expensive if the donor has had to save up for it. Why do we nearly always say 'Oh, you shouldn't have' or 'Oh dear – spending all that money on me!' We don't really mean that 'they shouldn't have', we are wildly happy that they *did* – in fact, we are so damned happy we are crying as we embrace them.

Amongst my very important treasures are many little homemade gift cards that read 'To my Mummy with all my love, Jan – and it was very expensive.'

However, back to the presentation of the 'fag case'. After we had gone through the tears and running nose routine, I was informed that the present wasn't complete, and that if I went to the jewellers he would show me various designs and letters which I could choose and which he would then execute in diamonds and attach them to the case. In spite of the tears and nose blowing, I didn't need telling twice and off I went. Now although my stage name is Thora Hird – which is, of course, my maiden name – I'm really Thora Scott. So on arrival at the jewellers it was quite understandable that I should be asked 'Oh Miss Hird – do you wish for the initials T.H. or T.S.?'

The jeweller was a little love, but he didn't help much when he said, 'Well, pardon me suggesting "T.S.", but it *is* from your husband and daughter.'

He was right, so I made a quick decision and my gold cigarette case sports a beautiful bit of craftsmanship which reads T.H.S. The reason we smile about that day is that, after all the tears and nose blowing and ex-postulation of Oh, you shouldn't have etc., etc., I'd managed to get *three* diamond initials on my case instead of the intended *two*!

When I appear to 'go on a bit' about the kindness, warmth and loving gestures of the Lancastrians, I beg to be forgiven. I am quite sure the same sort of wonderful people are all over England, Ireland, Scotland and Wales – in fact, I know they are – but you will understand that as I spent the early years of my life in Lancashire, they are the people I knew the best and who impressed me the most.

Thinking quickly, I hope my husband forgives and understands too, because I have been married for 38 years to the best advert for Scotland imaginable. The early years, the tender years, the impressionable years are always the ones we remember best, tend to forget for a while, then suddenly, with the passage of years, remember more clearly than ever.

I know this is how both my husband and I are. Sometimes when we are sitting over a cup of tea or coffee, one of us will suddenly say, 'Do you remember gas mantles?' or 'Did your mother scrape the paper the butter or lard was wrapped in, so as not to waste any?' I adore these conversations we have because from a little remark stems a really interesting conversation that can last an hour. Nostalgia? Yes, but always loving and warm – *and* this is a great way of reminding oneself how much better off we are than those dear, wonderful women who cleaned, baked, washed and ironed; who went without things so that we could have 'em. And who *never complained*. O.K. – they didn't get the British Empire Medal, but they happily worked themselves nearly to death, content with a title given to them by us – Mother.

Before I finish about 'our front steps' and the kindness of our Lancastrian Lot, I would state here and now that sometimes it was carried a bit too far. At least, when you're six or seven or even eight or nine years old it can seem so.

What I mean when I say 'carried a bit too far' is this. One morning after I had finished doing the front, I was just emptying the dirty water out of my bucket down the grate in our back yard, when my mother said, 'Will you be a good girl and do the front next door? Mrs Houghton's in bed, poorly.'

Assuring my big-hearted mother I would, I put the big iron kettle on the fire for some more hot water. Meanwhile I went and swept next door's steps and front, and blackleaded the coal 'ole lid and lattice-designed grate under their bay window. The entire procedure was the same as I had already executed at the front of number six. (I was already preparing myself for twice nightly performances in the theatre in the years to come!) Knocking gently on their front door, I requested their white rubbing stone, which we didn't have, being 'yellow stoners'. Everything else I had provided – bucket of water, floor cloth, maula soap, etc., from my own personal equipment, rather like the adverts one sees in *The Stage* where it reads 'So and So unexpectedly free for Pantomime Season due to misunderstanding; cat or goose, own skin provided.' In my case it was 'Thora Hird, unexpectedly free for step scrubbing, bucket and necessary equipment provided!'

Right, so next door looked clean and cared for, and once again I was in our back yard emptying the bucket of diluted 'you know what' down the grate. I got as far as rinsing out the bucket when I *felt* my mother watching me; as I turned the bucket upside down to drain, she appealed – there's no other word for it – appealed to me thus.

'Would it be asking too much of you to do Mrs Baines at Number Ten? Her husband is off work ill and she has such a lot of extra work?'

Hecky plonk! What colour stone did *they* use? Right

23

you are then . . . as it was in the beginning! Kettle on, more hot water. But I didn't mind really because this was all part of life in Cheapside.

I *must* be honest though – as I finished Number Ten I can remember thinking, 'And if Mrs Rhodes is ill at Number Twelve her son Percy can scrub her blooming steps. I've washed and blackleaded half way down Cheapside as it is!'

Well – I *was* only eight years old!

I have already said that my mother's heart was too big for her body; she was always helping people, but I must add that this was the general attitude and way of going on of most folks in 'our street'. If anyone was ill, it was all hands to the pump – every neighbour would help in some way. One would do the shopping (so that the patient and family didn't starve) or one would do extra baking. All our mothers baked bread, fruit pies, meat pies, and teacakes – you only had 'shop stuff' at the last gasp! One would do the housework one day and another would do it the next – it was always done willingly without thought of reward. In fact, they were all so damned proud that you offered reward at the risk of offending.

I remember vividly that I would run errands for neighbours and my mother's last words as I left the house were always the same. 'And remember, love, *don't* take anything for going!' What a training – great! Oh, the times I have refused those pennies – don't think I didn't WANT to take them, I did, but it was a sort of 'on your honour' thing, so that was that.

Another lovable, neighbourly thing about being part of a street was new babies. Now that's another expression that we always used, new babies. I suppose it's silly really, because there aren't any old or second-hand babies. But that's what we called the latest arrivals – NEW babies.

Between the ages of six and sixteen, I think I saw every *new* baby in Cheapside. Oh, the pleasure I've had, just looking at *new* babies – only to be surpassed by those moments of indescribable joy when the mother would say, 'Would you like to hold it?'

Oh, mate! that lovely warm smell of baby and scented soap, that infinite trust the little soul has in you. (I mean, how do they know you are not going to drop them, or throw them up in the air and catch them, or *not* catch them – coming down.) Yet they seem just to lie there all crumpled and pink with their little fists clenched ready to knock their way through life fully aware of the character of the person whose arms enfold them.

I'm still barmy about *new* babies, but I suppose when I was holding the Cheapside ones I was too young to realize *how* barmy I would be when I held my own *new* baby – and that I would be barmier still when my own 'new baby-that-was held her own new baby-that-is'.

And if that isn't an original way of saying I'm a grandmother, I don't know what is!

We had tram lines in Cheapside, not those for electric trams but for horse trams. They started from the front of the Royalty Theatre in Market Street and trundled down Cheapside on the first part of their journey to Lancaster, four miles away.

The two horses were changed at the Tram Stables –

always an exciting incident in the journey – and changed again at Cross Hill on the return trip. I loved the trams and can remember how sorry I was when progress demanded they must finish.

I was sorry about something else, too. Now we had an orange box full of soil in our back yard and faithfully every year a green plant bloomed in profusion. The something else I was sorry about was that not only had the trams and horses gone, but so had most of the horse manure. Year by year, our plant had been fed on as much horse manure as would cover a two-acre field, but it never did as well after the trams finished. It seemed to 'cock a snoot' at milk-float horse manure or green-grocer cart horse manure, or fishman cart horse manure. Come to think of it, my parents were cocking a snoot at the amount of manure I used. I was a faithful believer in it, but I suppose it was overplaying a bit to put a whole bucketful on a window box when there was only a penny packet of Virginia stock seeds planted in it! Only one Virginia stock came up! I couldn't understand it – the poor little object had a very long thin pale stem – I think it was trying to get as far away from the smell of the manure as possible!

When our daughter Janette bought her first country house the grounds were delightful but a certain weed had taken such a hold that it was literally pushing the paths up – it was called *polygonum cuspidatum*, alias *reynoutria japonica*. It took two gardeners and a builder four months to stem its enthusiasm, and then the gardeners had to work for another year before it was finally ousted.

Have you guessed? Yes, it was the same as our green plant in the back yard at Morecambe, which my mother used to admire and say, 'Well, it's a lovely bit of green and it's not hurting anybody!'

When I was about five or six I went into business. When I say I went into business it was more a kind of barter, a sort of exchange and mart. I would take a bucket of peelings and exchange it for a cut apple or an over-ripe banana.

Right, now I'll explain. The drill was, first to persuade mother to put all the veg or fruit peelings into a clean enamel bucket. Then I would go up to Houghtons.

Houghtons was two shops, a butcher's and a greengrocer's, next to the front entrance of the Royalty Theatre – and the bucket of peelings was carried through the greengrocer's shop and emptied into a bin in their yard, to feed the pigs being reared for the butcher's shop. When the empty bucket was returned, you were given a cut apple.

A cut apple is an apple that has seen better days. Patchy brown bruise marks had been scooped out with a potato peeler and the remains, when presented to you along with thanks for the bucket of peelings, were rather like a piece of modern art. There wasn't much apple left, although, to be fair, we were offered the choice of either a cut apple or two very over-ripe black-as-night bananas.

In the middle of our living-room table there was always a bowl of fruit, oranges, apples, polished and shining, pears or whatever else was in season, and bananas – yellow, not black! So why in Heaven's name I should have gone to the trouble of trading the bucket of peelings is a mystery. I suppose it was because my friends in Cheapside took their offerings for a cut apple, and what was good enough for them was good enough for me.

Besides, I liked Billy Hadwen, who served in Houghton's. He wore a cap and a shirt with his brass collar stud showing, and was a very nice, kind young man.

Many years later, I was guest star at the Royalty Theatre – being invited there often. I certainly enjoyed going home, for the Royalty occupied a very special place in my heart. With a Royalty performance, I was obliging the Theatre management *and* myself! And, as I usually played there August Bank Holiday week, I was obliging the tax man too!

On this occasion I travelled to Morecambe to appear in one of the plays I had done in the West End. There was the usual press party held in the Dress Circle Bar, scheduled for the night of my arrival because I was going to rehearse for a week before opening night.

During the chit-chat I saw a man having a quiet drink on the far side of the bar, and I found myself unable to concentrate on what I was saying because I kept thinking – I know that man's face. Whenever I visited Morecambe there were lots of people and faces I knew and recognized by sight. I very rarely forget a face though I often forget the name that goes with it. On this occasion, my mind worked overtime trying to put a name to the face. Eventually, the man made his way to the side of the bar where I was standing and very

shyly said, 'Hullo, Thora, love – what are you having?'
I looked into the kind, good face – and – bingo! – I
remembered.

'A cut apple, please, Mr Hadwen!' I said.

4

There's no place like . . .

At the top of our three front steps was, of course, our front door. It was quite a solid job, opened by a large door knob about midway down on the right; to the left, on a level with the knob, was a letter box, horizontally placed and informing anyone who cared to look that it was there for the postman to push letters through. It had 'LETTERS' embossed quite clearly on its flap.

Of course, other things were pushed through – little envelopes inviting you to deposit a few copper coins inside for the Self Denial Week, bills announcing Great Jumble Sale, the daily and Sunday newspapers, *Comic Cuts*, *Chips*, *Rainbow*, *Children's Newspaper*, and so on.

It was quite a busy letter box. It was also used to pull the key through. By inserting the first and middle fingers of the right hand – left hand if you wished – the fingers could grope until they fastened on a piece of string that hung down for about two feet. The front door key was tied to the end of it.

Hung is the right word because our front door key was about five inches long and heavy; its appearance from the inside passage was rather like a body swinging on the gallows. I can literally *feel* the weight of that key, as I write this, and remember how embarrassed I used to be during my flapper days, when I was allowed to detach the key for late home-coming. The times I have had a Romeo escort me home after a dance and, as we said our good nights at our front door, I hoped he'd hop it before I opened my evening bag to expose the key. It was so large that it was about all I could get *into* my evening bag! Why couldn't we have a Yale key and lock? Something modern! I was going through a modern stage at that point – it didn't last long fortunately.

These days we spend hours at antique markets looking for things like our front door key. Why the heck I should have been ashamed of it I don't know – I *do* know I'm ashamed now of having been ashamed of it. Daft bitch!

Our front door opened on to a not-too-narrow passage that led to the middle door or living-kitchen door. This passage was covered with oilcloth (linoleum we called it), then with carpet, purposely narrow so as to leave a margin of oilcloth about ten inches wide at each side of the passage. Where the 'lino' and carpet started – at the top front step – there was a strip of brass which held the oilcloth together with the carpet, firmly in place. This strip of brass was polished, of course. The margins of oilcloth on each side of the passage were also polished and shone like glass. They were referred to as 'the sides'. The strip of brass, the boundary between outdoors and indoors, was referred to as 'the brass'. Hence, in cleaning jargon, one would be questioned thus: 'Have you done the brass and polished the sides?'

Along the passage, on the right, was the door to the

front room or sitting-room – it was referred to as both, depending on the mood you were in – and a little further along on the right were the stairs.

The first flight consisted of fourteen treads. These were carpeted with a bordered stair carpet which was held firmly in place by brass stair rods – which, each week, Nev or I faithfully unanchored from their harbour and polished. Again, the carpet was narrower in width than the stair treads – which meant that after brushing the carpet well with a stiff carpet brush (using a dust pan to receive the dust) there were still the sides to do! There were two sides to each tread, and the procedure was to wipe each side with a soft cloth wrung out in hot water, to which a drop of Izal had been added, wring the cloth out again, wipe as dry as possible, and then polish! The top of the stair sides were always conveniently dry by the time you'd wiped the bottom (excuse that remark) and one was able to start waxing. So it was continuous movement really.

What a performance! But, what a result! Smashing! But one can get just the same result today in about an eighth of the time.

At the top of the first flight of stairs was a small oblong landing with a door on the right leading into the front bedroom which was my mother's and father's room. On the left of the landing, facing the front bedroom door, was the door leading into the back bedroom. Making a rapid U-turn at the top of the first flight there was the second flight of fourteen stairs, at the top of which the landing was identical to the lower one, only the top front bedroom door was on the left and the top back bedroom door was on the right!

In retrospect, I realize now that my mother must have been a 'with-it' person, because she always had the bedrooms and staircase decorated in delicate shades of colour wash, which of course was the fore-runner of your modern distemper and synthetic paint. She used to say that the curtains and bedspreads and furniture made the rooms fussy enough and that plain walls always looked so fresh and clean! They always did! The only drawback was, it wasn't washable like today's miracle products, so consequently a bucket of colour wash was often to be seen in our house.

I wasn't expected to assist in the colourwashing until I was in my teens. Even then I was never any good at it! Mind you – I always fancied myself as a dab hand at the painting – I don't mean portraits or landscapes, but skirting boards and doors and window frames. So fair-do's, I always pulled my weight. If I had any paint left I would wander around the house looking for some-thing that needed the odd dab.

In my mind's eye I can still see the back of the door in my parents' bedroom. Whoever had lived in the house prior to us must have been very artistic – well, I suppose you'd call it artistic! The door was composed of four panels and in each panel an individual painting had been executed in oils. In the top left hand panel there were bullrushes in a pond and a bird hovering (a winged bird I mean); the top right panel had irises with leaves and buds; the two bottom panels sported flowers – I think they were geraniums and buttercups and poppies and cornflowers but I can't quite remember. What I *can* remember is that I thought they were *beautiful*!

Each time we decorated, I faithfully painted the woodwork white but left the panels untouched apart from a wash down. The end product gave the effect of a door with four narrow oblong oil paintings hanging on it! Every year when we started cleaning and decorating my mother would say, 'I think we'll paint over those this time, love!'

What? Sacrilege! I loved 'em! I can recall that I always used my little Orphan Annie or Ora Pro Nobis expression as I would plead, 'Let's leave them – just until next time we do the room – please?'

She would look at me ever so lovingly and say, 'All right then, love, leave them – some poor soul went to a lot of trouble.' Some poor soul! You see, there she was, my mother, conjuring up the idea of some poor soul on their knees for days, weeks or months painting away – never getting recognition for their talent. She saw my point – she always did – but I know why she agreed to leave the paintings on the panels. It was to give me pleasure.

When sitting in a theatre have you ever looked at a garden backcloth of a stage set and imagined what the rest of the garden round the corner would look like? I have, often. Neville and I knew every detail of the backcloths at the Royalty Theatre, knew them intimately and individually. They didn't stop at the edges for us – we imagined all sorts of extensions. The bullrushes and the irises, the geraniums and buttercups had the same effect on me – I made up a mental picture of the place where the bullrush pond was. As my mother would have said, 'Well – you're not hurting anybody!' Lovely expression that, isn't it? It condones so many things.

When we were little, the back bedroom was shared by Nev and me. He had a double bed and I had a single one.

I *loved* this room for three reasons. One, it had a small door on the left of the window. This door opened into a little room – about the same size as our back kitchen, which was below it – and it was the toy room.

This sounds as though we lived in a mansion where the governess would insist we put our toys neatly away in the special toy room each night. Oh, no! it was much more thrilling and exciting than that.

The toy room housed the greatest assortment of things imaginable. There were skips, or theatrical hampers, full of uniforms, dress swords, plumed hats. There was a leather hat box lined with cerise satin with a 'tall shiny' of Dad's in it. There were musical instruments we could have a go on, banjos, a harp, a euphonium, violins, a balalaika and a mandolin.

There was a tea gown of purple velvet with bishop's sleeves, satin slippers to match with little purple beads woven into a pattern all over the tiny pointed toes, and purple openwork stockings, an evening dress with an off the shoulder top all smothered in violets made of voile. There were various wigs – bald-headed ones, grey ones, a chinaman's pigtail. Oh, there was everything and it was all *to play with*! No holds barred! Can you imagine the glorious fun Nev and I had?

In our toy room, there was also my sister Olga's dolls' pram, which was a source of delight to me, though each time my mother looked at it her expression was heartbreaking, for Olga was knocked down by a motor bike on Morecambe Promenade and killed.

She was buried on her sixth birthday. I won't dwell on the heartbreak this caused.

My brother Neville was one of the funniest people I have ever met, and to have a brother older than oneself – and one you love dearly – is one of life's blessings. I have often wished I'd been clever enough to produce an older brother for our daughter Jan, but – what's the saying – it wasn't to be.

Our Nev could get some sort of a tune out of any musical instrument. I was always satisfied to dress up, especially in one of the tea gowns. I was never very mobile because most of the gown trailed on the floor, but what did it matter? I wish I could do full justice in words to our happiness in the toy room.

Reason number two for loving the back bedroom was what we called 'the corner'. It was nothing of the sort really, more like a miniature cave, an area about five feet wide and four feet deep that extended right back beneath the top flight of stairs – with only the opening on view. Great fun – there was an oil painting of Grandad Hird in there, still wrapped up with brown paper and string. It had been there since my father had come by it after my Grandmother Hird's funeral – it had been willed to him.

We were always about to hang it somewhere but never seemed to be able to find a suitable place, so there Grandad remained in the cave under the top stairs.

I write, with pride, that Grandad Hird – official title Captain Hird – owned his own schooner which was used for carrying cargo. He was a colourful, dashing character, with red curly hair and beard, and from the stories my father told us about him, we gathered he was a bit of a lad.

Sadly, there came a time when he *didn't* return from one of his voyages. Years later, a sailing ship took refuge from a storm in the mouth of a cave somewhere in the South Seas.

In that cave there was a wrecked schooner. They found the skeletons of the crew on board and locked in a chest, they found the log book of Captain Hird's ship. God Rest Grandad – the pirate!

The final attraction of the back bedroom was the toilet set. It was *lovely*. It had belonged to my Grandma Mayor. It was white with a two-inch band in the most wonderful, clear turquoise blue, all complete – bowl and jug, soap dish, tooth brush container and two 'gozunders' – and if anyone *hasn't* heard that old pantomime gag they've missed nothing. 'What's a gozunder? It *goes under* the bed!'

I was very fond of that toilet set. I don't know what happened to it but I do know that only a year or two ago I bought an old-fashioned toilet jug to hold flowers and bullrushes. Jan was visiting us from California. She went into raptures over it. It's in Beverly Hills now, gracing one of the loveliest homes in Coldwater Canyon. I hope it gives Jan as much pleasure as Grandma Mayor's gave me!

Perhaps it was the memory of Grandma Mayor's toilet set that inspired me to acquire a gozunder as a link with the past (also, a gozunder filled with sand makes a very useful large ashtray when you're having a party for friends on the lawn). But it's not as nice as those in our bottom back bedroom.

Right, Ladies and Gentlemen, if you will follow me down the twenty-eight stairs (and watch your step, they are rather steep and there is no light!) we will move into Happiness Hall – our living-room, I'd better explain that this room could go under the title of middle-room, living-room or living-kitchen, but that would be overplaying it a bit because it *was* the living-room and the back kitchen was, of course, a kitchen at the back! Well, it stands to reason it would be at the *back* if it was the *back* kitchen doesn't it?

As a child, I used to wonder why it was called the *back* kitchen, when we hadn't a *front* kitchen! Unless, of course, where we ate, laughed, entertained, played the piano and everything else, was called the *living*-kitchen. However, from now on I will refer to it as the living-room, which will be less confusing for anyone who intends to read on.

The floor of the living-room was of red and black tiles about nine inches square. I don't mean present day PVC adhesive ones, I mean quarry tiles, which were scrubbed with a hard scrubbing brush and plenty of maula soap. But this was only the first act of the domestic play – the second act opened with Thora on her knees with a saucer of sour milk (sounds as though I was doing a 'cat act' doesn't it?), which was rubbed over the tiles to leave a shine on them as the final curtain fell! Do you wonder I now use modern PVC adhesive ones on every possible occasion?

Mind you, our tiles looked jolly nice after they were done – that is, until they had been walked on. Half an hour later, I used to think – why did I bother to do those?

There's no place like . . .

The same feeling applies now as it did then with regard to housework – the effect doesn't last long, does it?

The living-room fireplace was, of course, the focal point of the room. It had a fairly high mantelpiece that was always skirted with a cornish frill made of the same material as the curtains and cushion covers. My mother was Champion of the Northern Union with a fourpenny Drummer Dye, and many a time I have gone to school leaving a mauve cornish frill, curtains and cushion covers and returned home to find them rose pink! The moment she had seen us out of the house the drill was – all down, all washed, all dyed, all dried, all ironed – all up! Fab!

The fireplace itself was a typical kitchen range of iron with an oven on the right-hand side. It was never used for roasting the meat or making the Yorkshire Pudding in my day because there was a crack in it somewhere, but it served honourably as a receptacle for our pyjamas and bed slippers which were popped in there about an hour before bedtime.

As kids, we undressed in front of the fire, opened the oven door, pyjamas out – quick, and there you were, in hot pyjamas, hotter bedroom slippers, drinking even hotter cocoa! All as a preliminary to going upstairs into the frozen north! Br-r-r-r, it was cold in those bedrooms. We rushed upstairs into bed, and moved the stone hot water bottles, which mother had placed just where our little bottoms would nestle, down to the bottom of the bed to warm our feet.

What a carry on! Of course we didn't think anything of it – our bedrooms were always cold, weren't they?

39

Unless we had measles or chicken pox, when the big firegrate in the bedroom would come to life with a blazing fire!

I never did like the cold, and I am sure a lot of elderly people don't like it either but have to suffer it. I think that Parliament should bring in a law that all old age pensioners on reaching retirement should be presented with a very safe electric blanket along with their pension book! Or – if they are nervous of electricity – a couple of bags of coal!

On the left of our living-room fireplace was a boiler with a brass tap on it, which never worked either, because of some deep internal crack. But, sitting on top of the boiler was a huge iron kettle and since this was next to the fire itself we claimed constant hot water.

Above the boiler, the fire, and the oven, was an iron rack with a polished steel edge, very useful for keeping toast or muffins or crumpets warm or for airing or warming pieces of underwear. We also used to air the handkerchiefs on it. As they were ironed and folded into what looked like square sandwiches, they were placed on a dinner plate on the rack. I wonder why we aired hankies?

The firegrate proper had bars in front of it, and the top three could be let down into a horizontal position for use as a hob. To the side of where the fire actually burned was another set of three bars. These could either be flush against the side or, like the hob piece, let down into a horizontal position which laid them actually over the burning fire. I don't know if there is another name for them and if there is I apologize to them because we always referred to them as bars – put the bar up, or put the bar down. Poor things, they had no separate identity because the same instructions applied either to the one over the fire or the hob piece in front of the fire.

Our fire! That's worth a couple of lines! My mother used to say, 'Come on, now, put some more coal on and let's have a royal standback!' That's just what it was. You *did* stand back, it was always such a beauty.

The fireplace I have described was blackleaded to high heaven, with the exception of the polished steel edge on the rack, which was rubbed frenziedly with emery paper. That and the top of the steel fender. The surround of the fender was blackleaded but that top! Oh mate! It shone like silver! Nev and I took it in turns to emery-paper the fender on alternate Fridays, because it really did need some elbow grease.

The hearth was of stone and that came under the scrubbing department. After cleaning with metal polish the brass tap (on the boiler that didn't work) one was only left with the pegged rug to shake.

How many of you have ever shaken one of these rugs? Some sort of mask would have been a help. The dust and dirt that would shake out of our rug was fantastic considering it was shaken vigorously twice a week! Talk about a foggy day in London Town! It was a foggy day in our back yard each time we shook ours.

In those days, people sat for hours during the winter months pegging small strips of material into a piece of sacking or canvas to make a rug. Any worn-out trousers or jackets were washed and cut into strips three inches by one and pegged into a pattern. They looked cosy and comfy – until someone put one foot on the thing and left a flat imprint. They were veritable dust catchers, and just about the most unhygienic piece of furnishing ever thought of.

(Phew! I'm tired out after describing all that cleaning of the fireplace! Or perhaps it was shaking the pegged rug that did it!)

A horsehair couch, not to be confused with a sofa, stood beneath the living-room window. Ours had two curled ends, very useful when Nev and I played cowboys – we each had a faithful steed.

We called ourselves Tom and Mary Whitfield – don't ask me why! There is no offence meant and none taken I hope, by any Tom or Mary Whitfield who may read this. We were very respectable cowhands and none came any better than Tom and Mary of Cheapside Ranch! By the time we were becoming too heavy for our horsehair horses, I had assumed the name of Pearl White – it was more exciting than being Mary Whitfield, the cowgirl.

The piano faced the horsehair sofa. There it stood, with its naked top. My father didn't approve of things being put on top of the piano, but with time a few artistic bits found their way there and stayed.

The piano was in the living-room because my mother felt Nev and I should do our piano practice, one hour a day each, where it was warm. I recall her saying that she thought it was inhuman to make children go into a cold front room, where most pianos were kept, to practise. We agreed. Unfortunately *we* thought it was inhuman to have to do one hour's practice a day each whether a room was warm or cold!

A lot of pleasure was derived from the piano being

on the spot. When my mother was ironing or sitting mending our clothes or socks, one of us would sit at the piano and accompany her while she sang. My favourite songs were 'Oh, where is my boy tonight?', 'Robin Adair', 'Sweet Violets', and 'Sweet and Low'. This was because they were in two sharps! Actually, I was passable in three flats, not too bad in four sharps, pathetic in four flats and damned awful in anything else. But in two sharps I was confident – I might even put a few twiddly bits in or a few runs. Oh yes, I was very fond of two sharps. Good old F and C! The sad end to this part is that I'm still only any good in two sharps, and not very good at that.

Nev had a violin, a guitar, a musical saw, a swannee whistle and, joy of joys, he bought a flexatone. It was great fun. My father had at one time forty pupils studying the banjo with him. He had learnt to play the banjo when he was with 'Moore and Burgesses Minstrels'. That was long before the church bells rang for me, but it will explain to you that he was a very good banjo player. My mother played a zither banjo.

Happy Days! Dad on the banjo, Nev on the violin, Mother singing and Thora obliging on the pianoforte, in two sharps! All the old Moore and Burgesses Minstrel numbers. Oh! I forgot to tell you that at fifteen years of age, my dad joined Moore and Burgesses as a boy soprano. I'm glad I remembered I'd forgotten to tell you that! So, we were able to provide our own entertainment! Many friends came to the house uninvited, and they were all made welcome. Mother preferred to know how many folks would call in, but nevertheless, a huge meat and potato pie would be sizzling in the oven, puffing out a mouth-watering smell, and the seven-pound jars of homemade pickled red cabbage and onions were always standing at the ready.

I don't wonder my generous parents never became rich, our house was like Dr Barnardo's. I once remarked to my mother in later years, 'Oh, love, you are always giving, you'll never be rich, will you?' 'But we *are* rich,' she said. 'We've got you and Neville, and your dad and I have got each other, and look at all the friends we have!' She was right, of course. She usually was!

One night, I was obliging by accompanying Neville on his violin. We were rendering 'Poet and Peasant' and Nev was proudly using a new bow he had just acquired for his birthday.

There is one passage where the pianist *can* add a few trills, but *shouldn't*, and when we arrived at it, I was really doing my lot. Nev stopped and informed me, 'If you are not going to play what's written, our kid, I'm not going to play any more; stop putting your own fancy bits in!' We started again and I faithfully played as per copy until we got to another passage where I again embroidered it a bit. The music stopped and he landed me one over the head with his new bow! What a shame! It looked so sad broken in two! I was sad, I was really, and sorry. Never mind, another lesson learnt, I didn't execute my own twiddly bits after that.

When I was invited years and years later to be a guest on 'Woman's Hour', they kindly asked me what music I would like to play me in – I requested 'Poet and Peasant' and then told the listeners why. It was the least I could do as a rather belated gesture to Neville for upsetting him so much, and for owning the head he smashed his birthday gift bow over!

Just a couple of words about the back yard. It was white-washed twice or three times a year, swilled and brushed every week, window sills scrubbed and yellow stoned. The toilet, which was in the covered wash house, sported what had been a varnished seat, wall to wall. This was scrubbed and scrubbed until only a memory of varnish remained at each end. The floor was scrubbed with disinfectant and then yellow stoned. The toilet paper was pieces of neatly cut news-papers, about eight inches by six, threaded on a piece of string. It hung on the wall to the left of the occupant and provided a little light reading if you were going to be in residence for long – a comfortable retreat to avoid washing up the dishes or for a secret smoke. Just the place to sit and meditate!

And that, Ladies and Gentlemen, concludes the tour of this ancient and historic building – will you kindly mind the three steps as you go out. I hope you have enjoyed your visit – your guide will be grateful for any little acknowledgement! Your charabanc will leave almost immediately!

Late note. Since writing the above I have acquired another rather artistic 'gozunder'. But here's the good bit! That is, if you are interested. Going through some boxes that had been untouched by human hand for many years, I found . . . yes . . . a 'gozunder' from Grandma Mayor's famous toilet set!! Thought you might like to know!

5

We never closed

'Are you there, Mrs Hird?'

This enquiry always followed a quick knock on our
front door, which was always open, that is from about
eight o'clock in a morning until eleven or later at night,
when my mother would say, very dramatically, 'Have
you locked the front door, Jim?'

I must admit there was no need to lock the front door
because we really had nothing of great value to pinch!
Well, no, that's not quite fair of me really. There were
things like the piano, my dad's various banjos, our
Nev's many musical instruments, my mother's very
tiny diamond earrings and silver coffee set, which an
aunt had left to her when she had passed away.

Apart from those, everything else was only of great
sentimental value, although, really, those *are* the most
valuable of all one's possessions I think! But, 'Have you
locked the front door, Jim?' was always said with such
dramatic feeling that after my mother had been
assured, we were able to go to our beds and sleep
peacefully and safely (even though the back kitchen
door was never locked because it couldn't be as there
was never a lock on it!)

So, our front door was open, eight to eleven. I'd like

to think the Windmill Theatre derived its slogan 'We Never Closed' from us. But it didn't.

Rat-tat!

'Are you there, Mrs Hird?' If I had a shilling for every time I had heard that, or, 'Can I come in for a minute, Mrs Hird?' or 'Are you in, Mrs Hird?', I'd be well off.

There's no doubt my mother was a Living Wonder – her great big heart seemed to beat solely for the purpose of helping people, and I sometimes try to comfort myself by thinking it was not surprising that she died when she was only sixty-two, of heart trouble, because she had used her loving heart so very much – it was tired out.

When she did die, there was a hush of respect and loss in the whole district and it is with the same feeling and great pride that I pen this next bit. 'Are you there, Mrs Hird?' As I say, there would be a quick 'Rat-tat' on the front door, the enquiry as to whether my mother was in (which in itself was a laugh as she hardly ever went out!) and then there would be one of the following various requests, 'Can you lend my mother an eggcupful of tea please?' or 'Please, Mrs Hird, can you lend me two candles?' or, offering the teacup they held in their hand 'Can you lend me a drop of vinegar?' or, a frequent request, 'Mrs Hird, me mother says have you please got a piece of brown paper and some string, she wants to send a parcel?'

My memories of these daily requests are very warm and loving ones and I can still remember my mother's soft smile as she would say, 'Yes, of course, love,' to the tea, candles or vinegar type of requests and 'Just a minute, love, I'll have a look,' to the brown paper and string appeal. (I still carefully fold a piece of good brown paper and I have a biscuit tin painted red that houses good pieces of string – not that it's likely anyone is going to knock on our door and request either, but I suppose old habits die hard, and even in this Sellotape age it's amazing how often one uses brown paper and string – and it would be great if one of my splendid neighbours were ever in need and I could oblige. I don't think they ever *will* be – because I'll bet *they* save nice big pieces of brown paper and good lengths of string. Who doesn't?)

I recall one afternoon when there was the usual rat-tat on the door and a voice called, 'Oh, can you come a minute, Mrs Hird, the baby's had a fit!'

Off went my mother. She wasn't a nurse or anything – the frightened mother of the baby knew this – but the fact that my mother was *there* until the Doctor arrived was all the young mother wanted.

Another type of 'non-paying customer' – and there were dozens of these, bless 'em – would knock on the door without calling out to see if my mother was 'There' or 'In' or anything else. This type would remain at the open front door until my mother answered the knock by joining them. 'Oh hello, So and So,' my mother would say and then after an answering, 'Hello, Mrs Hird' the dialogue would usually run something like this:

'Er – sorry to trouble you, Mrs Hird, but I'm going to a Fancy Dress Ball as a gypsy on Friday at the Ambulance Hall (or "The Albert Hall" – oh, yes, we had an Albert Hall in Morecambe – or "The Tower" – we'd one of those as well!) and will you make my face up please?'

There was never any hesitation on my mother's part. 'Of course I will, love, what time does it start?'

'Eight o'clock,' the would-be gypsy would reply.

'All right, you'd better come here about seven and – oh – have you got plenty of beads and some brass curtain rings for earrings?' 'Well, no,' would be the doleful reply. 'Oh well, don't worry. I'll get out the bead box and you can choose which you would like after I've made you up, love!'

I must add at this point that the 'Fancy Dress Ballers' who called weren't always going to the Ball as gypsies. Oh no, we were perruquiers and make-up artists to Grecians, Italians, Romans, Red Indians, clowns and . . . all for love! Never mind about 'We Never Closed!' We Never *Charged* either!

That was my mother's principle and, as she would say to my dad, 'Well, Jim, if it's giving them a bit of pleasure!' To which James Henry would reply, 'You'll kill yourself doing for other people. You never stop, you're so soft, you'll run when the dog won't!'

I never knew the meaning of that remark but one thing I *did* know, he wouldn't have had my mother any different!

The prizewinning request for help came one Sunday. There was the usual rat-tat and, 'Are you there, Mrs Hird?' followed by a tearful young neighbour coming along the passage into our living-kitchen.

'Now then,' said my mother, her own face looking as sad and troubled as the young neighbour's, 'whatever's the matter, love?'

The young woman wiped her eyes and blew her running nose and amidst sobs informed us that her young husband's father and mother had turned up unexpectedly. (I can vouch for the unexpected bit – if you live at the seaside you are expected to run a free boarding house for relatives and always have enough food in to feed 'em!) However, her in-laws had turned up for the day and she and her husband had had their dinner, two chops, half an hour ago, and as it was the in-laws' first visit since she'd married their loving son, she wanted to impress them.

Stopping to have another nose blow and wipe the tears away she said, 'I – er – feel awful asking you this, Mrs Hird – but have you done a roast?'

Isn't the Lancashire idiom lovely? 'Have you *done* a roast?' *not* 'Have you roasted a joint?' My mother looked at the young wife. 'Yes,' she said, 'as a matter of fact I was just going to carve – why?' 'Well – er,' and the tears flowed again. 'Could you lend it to me – I do want to create a good impression – I'll bring it back after!'

My mother's eyes did a quick side glance at my father – he was sitting by the fire reading the Sunday paper. He was no help – he didn't even look up, he knew what the result would be, and he wasn't reading either – I could see that – he was thinking!

'Now don't upset yourself like that,' my mother comforted as she darted into the back kitchen. She immediately produced a large black japanned tray from down by the side of the old fashioned kitchen dresser. Placing the tray on the top of the dresser, the part of the dresser she baked or cut bread on etc., the next move was to the gas stove against the opposite wall. Quick as a flash, the still-sizzling joint of sirloin beef on its meat plate was transferred to the tray.

Plonk! I can still hear that meat plate landing on the tray as I write this – and I can still remember my dad's expression as he very carefully and deliberately folded the *Sunday Chronicle* and put it down.

'You'd better take the vegetables as well,' my mother was saying, as vegetable dishes of steaming goodness were lifted off the plate rack on the stove where thay had been keeping warm. The next item was the gravy – which my mother always made in the meat roasting tin, using all the lovely succulent juices of the roasted meat as a base. By this time my dear father was in a state of trance or at least that's what he looked like. Next item on the menu? A large apple pie and a glass jug of custard waltzed their way onto the tray, as my mother was advising, 'And you'd better go out the back way, love, then nobody will see you!'

During that bit of the drama the dresser drawer was opened and a spotless white towel whisked out and laid over the large trayful of food. Amid sniffs of gratitude and thanks, the lucky winner was saying, 'Ooo, you are good, Mrs Hird. I don't know what we'd all do without you – ooo, you are that kind,' etc., etc. And out she went, the back way.

Now you know the sort of silence that hits you? We experience it at our little country place at night – one can almost 'hear the silence'. Right, that was the atmosphere in our house after the sizzling sirloin, roasted potatoes, cauliflower, peas, roasted parsnips, carrots and light-as-fluff Yorkshire puds, not to mention the apple pie and custard, had made their exit, the back way! Neville and I had never uttered a sound during the entire pantomime – we knew better. We also knew this was typical of our mother, and we also knew from experience the expression on Dad's face!

There was a deathly hush. In fact Nev and I were nearly at our tittering stage, because James Henry Hird was standing 'looking at nothing', chin in air; he looked as though he was contemplating the narrow border of wallpaper that divided the paper on the wall from the two foot frieze. He was what is known as 'containing himself'. After what seemed about two days, but was actually about half a minute, my mother, who was still in the back kitchen, started to sing a few bars of 'Oh, where is my boy tonight?' – very softly, of course, and then, just as though nothing unusual had happened or as though it was the normal routine to go to all that trouble to cook a big dinner for your loved ones and then give it away before they'd even sampled it, she called out, 'Can you eat *two* fried eggs with your bacon, Jim, love?'

By now, my father was viewing the table, almost as though he'd never seen it before – the white linen cloth, places set for four people, Victorian silver cruet (cleaned by yours truly every Friday!), linen serviettes in our individual rings.

'Can you eat two fried eggs with your bacon, Jim, love?'

'Yes, please,' replied James Henry, in the voice he used when playing kings or Roman emperors – while still contemplating the table. 'They'll be very nice with horseradish sauce!'

6

Salute to the Royalty

The Royalty Theatre – a lovely old building, a
wonderful theatre, acoustically perfect!

The few surviving records in existence report that it
was 'a compact comfortable and well-appointed place
of entertainment, a handsome stone structure,
designed by Frank Matcham in the classic style, first
opened April 4, 1898, with the W. Green production of
The Sign of the Cross. Capable of seating 1,400 people
with the stalls and pit on the ground floor, the dress
and upper circles on the first floor, and the balcony and
gallery above.' A contemporary chronicled, 'The
entrance is in Market Street with the pit and gallery
entrance in Cheapside. The Royalty Theatre and Opera
House is lavishly decorated throughout, and is one of
the most comfortable outside London.'

All the above (with the exception of *The Sign of the
Cross* bit!) was to be a great big happy and wonderful
portion of my life – some folks have all the luck! My dad
was Stage Manager – beg your pardon, Stage *Director*
cum-Front-of-House-Manager-cum-general-dogsbody!
Great! He would often put on a dress suit and deputize
for the Manager (on the nights when the manager
preferred playing snooker in the Conservative Club!).

The theatre was not only part of our lives, it was part of our home, too, because many was the time when most of our furniture was on the stage! It's a fact – my mother came in from shopping one day, walked into the living-room and thought she had walked into an empty house – the table we ate off, the chairs, cushions, curtains, hearthrug, fender and fire irons – all gone! She knew where they had disappeared to – the Royalty stage! Not so much a kitchen more a way of life!

Neville and I would be sent off to play on the stage if my mother wanted us from under her feet. This was wonderful because we let our histrionic ability rip to an imaginary audience.

At a very tender age Nev and I knew quite a bit about stage management – when I say we knew about stage management, I mean we knew what the words brace, weight, backcloth, wings, borders, cleating and iron sheet meant – it was all part of our education, part of life and growing up among these things.

Mind you, there were one or two occasions when we let it rip at the wrong time! The following episode occurred when I was about four and a half and Neville was six. There was a visiting drama company appearing at the time and we were standing on the 'Opposite Prompt' side of the stage – we should have been in bed, but we weren't – and we saw our mother on the opposite side, near the prompt corner. Being aware that if we tip-toed very quietly behind the back-cloth we could go over to mum, we set off. Nev was wearing a sailor suit in navy blue, complete with bell-bottomed trousers, lanyard, sailor collar and a sailor hat informing all who were interested that he was a member of the crew of HMS IRON DUKE. The hat, incidentally, showed his ears off to a disadvantage.

As for me, I was wearing a white needlework dress with what can only be described as a low waistline, very short, my hair in curls (of course! Cloth rags every night!!) and a crêpe-de-chine mob cap! We weren't dressed up *as* anything, these were our normal clothes, and forgive my mentioning this, we were always considered 'very well dressed'!

Anyway, as I said, we saw our mother on the other side of the stage, so Neville took my hand and we proceeded to tip-toe behind the backcloth. When we got half-way across we stopped dead – the backcloth had a centre opening, and there we were, *in full view of the audience!*

The drama was in full progress, the audience gripped in silence! Until it saw us! Cripes! A howl of laughter greeted our appearance and the poor actors and actresses who were acting their socks off wondered what they'd done!

I suppose the correct thing would have been for us to continue on our way, but, you see, we were pros' kids, and we thought that the audience might accept that we were part of the play if we performed. So we started to dance the military two-step.

There was a louder gale of laughter accompanied by a round of applause. Well, need I describe what a round does to an artist? There we were, me doing the curtsey and Admiral Hird doing the salute, and when we came to the end part of the military two-step we made our exit waltzing off!

I shall never forget my poor mother's face as we

more or less waltzed into her arms; she was trembling all over and hurriedly pleaded with one of the stage hands, 'Get them out of sight, Harold, before Mr Hird sees them!'

Harold did, and whisked us out of the stage door and into 6, Cheapside – pffpt! He was a wonderful man, was Harold, NCOIC of pulling the curtain up and down, right up to the time of my returning to the Royalty Theatre as guest star years later.

There was one person who had *not* laughed at our execution of the military two-step! James Henry! He was in the dress circle bar (just socially of course!) when the first howl of laughter broke the silence. He rushed out of the bar, wondering what the audience were laughing at – it was a gripping drama, don't forget – and as he arrived at the back of the Dress Circle, he was just in time to see Nev saluting and yours truly doing a curtsey! He rushed down the stairs, down by the side of the stalls and through the pass door on to the side of the stage, by which time Harold was sitting by the curtain rope as though nothing untoward had happened, and my mother had stopped trembling enough to follow us home. 'Where are they?' he hissed at Harold, but – and here's where the devil looks after his own – Harold heard the curtain cue and, hands above his head, he grabbed the rope of the curtain and got on with his job. End of Act I! I know it all upset my dad that much, he had to go back to the bar for another drink!

We were seriously reprimanded – and rightly so – and we behaved ourselves . . . well, for a fortnight anyway.

My mother used to provide accommodation for some of the pro's to 'help get the rates together'. Because my parents had been in so many 'digs' themselves, they understood how important it was to make a week's digs like home, and actors and actresses used to fall over backwards to return to my mother's wonderful cooking and kindness.

Needless to say, Nev and I would get to know our paying guests very well, and about two weeks after the last little 'cantata', we had the leading man from the visiting company staying with us. By the middle of the week we had become very pally with him – he was really a very nice person, and was to become quite a famous actor. There we were, standing on the O.P. side, quiet as mice.

It was the first time we had been allowed on the side of the stage since our military two-step episode – so we were relishing it; a drama again – drama was very popular and was played very successfully at the Royalty in those days. The scene was a churchyard and the 'grave drop' was in use that week with the property headstone pushed back flat on the prop grass. Standing at the side of the newly dug prop gravedrop was our friend, attired in seventeenth-century clothes and wig and performing a very heartbreaking soliloquy. It was all very, very sad.

Suddenly, Nev nudged me gently, and putting his mouth to my ear he whispered, 'That's so and so who's staying at our house!'

'No, it's not,' I whispered back.

'Yes, it is,' whispered Nev.

You know what brothers and sisters are like – the

'No, it's not,' 'Yes, it is,' went on for a bit. I couldn't recognize our friend who played 'Snakes and Ladders' and 'Ludo' with us, in his old-fashioned get-up. 'Yes – it – is!' stated the Admiral and without more ado, walked onto the stage, tugged at the grief-stricken actor's long jacket and enquired,

'*I* know *you* – don't I?'

That did it! Big howls of laughter! I only stood in the wings, weakly pleading, 'Hey, come off, our Nev!'

When I grew old enough to understand what a terrible experience we had put the leading man through, the part that struck me as funniest was the actor *ignoring* Nev and carrying on with the very, very sad soliloquy, while trying to brush Nev's tugging hand off his coat!

Poor Harold was standing by to do his whisking!

The Iron Sheet (the name for the asbestos curtain) is the fire curtain that must be lowered once during every performance, to prove that the stage can be cut off from the audience in case of fire. The curtain at the Royalty was covered with advertisements. Not everyone bothered to read then, but the tradespeople who had paid to advertise on the curtain hoped the audience would! The adverts were very instructional and enlightening – you were *informed* that Dr Williamson manufactured 'Pink pills for Pale People'; you were *instructed* 'Don't wear a Truss – see us!' and the name of the firm who were 'Us' was there in its glory; you were *told* that you needn't suffer a cough if you tried 'Veno's Lightning Cough Cure'; and you were *shown* the figure you could achieve by wearing 'Spirella Corsets for Ladies'. (If you weren't a lady it was no use trying them, I suppose!) You were *advised* to use 'Ven-yusa Vanishing Cream'. Oh, it was an education in itself was that curtain! It was always lowered and raised very slowly because of its weight, being guided into position by a series of rings attached to its sides, which moved with the curtain up and down a strong wire. It's amazing the feeling of anticipation one could get when, after the interval, it started to go up! The noise of chattering would subside and by the time the iron sheet had slowly disappeared, the auditorium was usually quiet.

After the *I*-know-*You* episode, Nev and I were forbidden the stage during a performance, though we were allowed on the side of it during the interval. The iron sheet was down and the coffee and biscuits were being served. It was a play with the same set all night – so there wasn't even the excitement of a scenery change. I can only think that Jolly Jack Tar got a bit bored – whatever the reason, he suddenly thought he would have a 'look through' at the audience. Why not? – there might have been someone in front we knew!

Pushing his head, with the sailor cap on, between the guide wire and the iron sheet, he surveyed the house. This was great! He faithfully reported anything of interest to me, and then the first bar bell rang at the side of the stage – the signal to start to raise the iron sheet!

Immediately the first bell rang Nev started to withdraw his head, complete with cap; as he did so, the guide wire of the iron sheet put a brake on the proceedings – it wedged behind his ear!

It's all right saying that if he had gone forward again he could have backed out sideways, but you don't think of such technicalities when you are six! The more he backed the more the guide wire stuck in the back of his ear where it was attached to his head. He gave a piercing howl – the chatter stopped, the coffee cups rattled – and the entire audience looked round about them in wonderment trying to discover where the howls were coming from. Suddenly, someone spotted the sailor cap anchored in between the side of the curtain and the wire and shouted, 'Eee, it's little Neville Hird!'

By now, the brave sailor was not only in pain but frightened to death! The audience laughed, of course, it must have looked rather comic. James Henry was in the bar, but like a flash, same route as usual, he reached the stage and released his son in time to prevent any serious damage. That little episode made us behave ourselves for a long time afterwards.

And, of course, it didn't do our Neville's ears much good!

As far as I can remember, we were never allowed to stand at the side again, but we were allowed under the stage or in the 'prop' room and for the benefit of those who have never been in a prop room, I hereby declare they have missed a lot! Magic! Pure magic! Gold painted goblets, cushions, curtains, photographs in 'solid gold' painted frames, artificial flowers, thrones, suits of armour, swords, lances, Roman soldiers' helmets. You name it – it's in the 'prop' room.

We could even play 'house' there, for there were always stacks of pots and pans, cups and saucers; and we could be a Chinese Mandarin and his wife if we wanted – the prop headdresses were there; or a Zulu warrior and his wife, if we felt in that mood, since the horsehair, feathered headdresses and spears were there for the picking up.

Our vivid imaginations carried us into a world of make believe in this veritable Aladdin's Cave. Fantastic! Who wanted to stand at the side of the stage and watch the acting when there was this wonderland?

And talk about being lucky, it wasn't the only 'prop' room of which we were to be given the free run, because when my father left the Royalty to work on the Central Pier, we discovered to our indescribable joy that the Pier Pavilion and Concert Hall boasted a smashing prop room as well. But that will have to wait until I get to the 'Pier Period', later on!

7

'All that glitters'

It has always been the little seemingly unimportant things in life that have been important and given me the most pleasure. Take for instance, the stage door or doors of the Royalty, they were double doors but were always referred to as the stage door. If you wanted to get in you put your index finger into a hole at the joining of the two doors, a hole that had grown bigger with wear over the years because of the thousands of index fingers that had attacked it. If you were coming out, you pushed the crush bar up and made a hell of a noise by doing so, which you were warned, could be heard on the stage. The notice on the back of the door read, 'Please use care when using the stage door during a performance,' and another one read, 'Please close door quietly whilst the play is in progress.'

The doors of the dress circle were magnificent (I thought) and when I was very small I used to pretend that they were the doors to my Mansion, with solid gold handles! Solid gold, they weren't really of course, they were brass, but the cleaners would clean and polish them until they looked like solid gold, well, they did to me anyway, and when you are a very little girl with a vivid imagination, who would want a Mansion with brass handles? And once again, to quote my mother, 'I wasn't hurting anybody.' Little did I think that years afterwards I would be asked if there was any small piece of the Royalty I would like as a keepsake. I don't need to tell you what I requested, do I? That's it! Of course I chose the dress circle door handles.

Psychiatrists say that events in one's childhood affect life later on. Well I'm not clever enough to spout about that, but I do know that in our Mews House in London, we pull open the inner door with one of the brass handles from the late lamented St James's Theatre dress circle doors and another one opens the house door that gives access to the garage. The door to the stairs pulls too beautifully with the brass handle from the Pass Door from the late Exeter Theatre Royal. *I* clean all these – I love 'em! And although it may sound unbelievable and boring when I say that my husband and I have never had what you would describe as 'a real row', I hereby declare that I nearly hit him with the tin of metal polish when he suggested having the handles lacquered.

8

Walloping

It was a great advantage having a dad who, entertainmentwise, was as professional as mine. Everything, but everything, had to be rehearsed and rehearsed, timed and timed again, until the end product appeared to be done with complete ease. At the tender age of three I was taught my first 'break', or step, towards becoming a 'walloper'. Walloping was like clog-dancing, which later became step dancing, which later became tap dancing. I was very lucky in that respect, too. I had five cousins – Madge, Nellie, Queenie, Gwen and Alys (that was short for Alice), of whom Nellie and Alys were 'wonderful wallopers'. They were all in the theatrical business, with the exception of Gwen.

Alys taught me my first steps in walloping. Our living-kitchen floor's being red and black tiles was most accommodating (not because the tiles were red and black but because I could hear the taps of each break I made: 123, 123, 1234567). As we entered our living-kitchen from the passage from the front door there was a grained and varnished wooden partition from floor to ceiling, I suppose it was there to keep the draught out, but to me and our Nev it was always, 'the wings'. It was great, one could stand behind it and then make an entrance 'on cue' or make an equally convincing exit behind it!

I can remember as clearly as though it was yesterday, and I couldn't have been more than three and a half or four at the time, how I requested my audience (Mum, Dad and Neville) to 'Please watch me do this break!' Off I went behind the partition, made an entrance, did my break and made an exit! Don't think I got a lot of hand-clapping and praise, because I didn't. As I remember it, my mother said something loving and encouraging, but James Henry's contribution was constructive criticism and remarks such as, 'Smile!' and 'Don't stick your tongue out!' (This is a habit of mine while concentrating – in fact, I am doing it as I type this.)

Little did I know then that he would always criticize my work – but never destructively – and that I would only be able to repay his patience and teaching by trying my best to become a professional . . . and by loving and admiring him as much as any daughter possibly could.

During a visit to London, Neville told me how very well measured the tongue and grooved wood of the partition in our living-room was. He explained to me that there was not a nail or a spot of glue in its entire construction and that it stood perfectly between the living-room floor and ceiling, like the Trojan Wall! We had a very small wall built in our London home quite recently, and it was six inches out of plumb from floor to ceiling. You can't help laughing, can you?

9

The little urchin

As a little girl I attended a dancing class at Miss Nelson's School. Well, the school would often receive requests for children to entertain at church garden fêtes or bazaars or suchlike. The following little 'cantata' in my life happened when I was about eight years old.

One morning a gentleman called at the school and, after the usual amount of flattery, asked Miss Nelson if twelve of her 'very clever little girls' could appear at 'George Hall's Benefit'. Now George Hall was a very popular figure in Morecambe. He was a good-looking man and a splendid entertainer. He presented a concert party each summer season in a wooden structure on the promenade, and they revelled under the name of 'The Merry Japs'. I have no intention of underestimating anyone's intelligence by explaining that the artists were dressed in Japanese costume, but this was only for the first half of the programme. After the interval, it was concert party tradition for the gentlemen to wear tail suits and the ladies evening gowns. But I mustn't allow myself to get carried away about concert parties at this juncture because I shall endeavour to do full justice to them later on, because concert parties were responsible for a very happy portion of my life.

So now, where was I? Oh, I know. As I said, this gentleman came to the school and requested the artistry, talents, free services or whatever else you like to call it, of twelve little girls. I was one of the chosen few and off we went accompanied by Miss Merci Nelson, on a horsetram along the promenade.

When we arrived at the 'Merry Japs' we were received as though we were late, which of course we weren't, but isn't it strange that, quite often, if you are giving your services free of charge, you are treated like some amateur who is 'dying to go on the stage'? And the culprit is always someone who is being paid!

We were ushered into the empty auditorium – empty, that is, apart from the lone cleaner and 'The Not-so-Merry Japs'. Miss Merci instructed us to take off our coats and fold them and place them neatly over the backs of the empty stalls and then to change into our dancing pumps, 'as quickly as you can, girls, please.' We were then called on stage and asked to stand in a semicircle around the light comedian. We did this and then we were given a few moves and actions by the nice stage director, who I shall refer to from now on as the NSD.

The light comedian, who appeared to me to be 'so very good looking' (and was a bit bored as I remember it), started to sing a song, a little number that went something like this:

> When Rastas Brown goes to town
> You bet a dollar he's down
> Every night soon after dark
> He wends his way to the park

Children all run off to bed
They've seen a bogey 'tis said
Can't you hear him shuffling along
The bo-oh-gee man.

Now during these lines we talented little girls had to do what can only be described as, and was indeed called, the bobbing step, which was executed thus: step to the right with the right foot (of course), bend both knees and 'bob', step to the left with the left foot (of course), bend both knees and 'bob'. Now if you sing the first four lines – although you are not familiar with the tune – and you 'bob' on 'Rastas', 'Town', 'bet a', 'down', 'night', 'dark', 'wends', and 'park', you'll find that it fits. When he sang 'children all run off to bed', we got a greater opportunity to show our ability, for on this line we ran 'Pluto fashion' down right of stage. Then, on 'They've seen a bogey 'tis said', we ran back to our original semicircle, but at the same time we had to raise our hands in horror and fear and call out '*Ohhh!*' Now then, hold on a minute, because here comes the clever stuff. On the next line we had to really act and speak!!! As the light comedian sang, 'can't you hear him shuffling along?' we had to put our right hand cupwise at the side of our mouth and call out 'Whose dat?' and 'his nibs' very obligingly answered our question in song with, 'The BO-OH-GEE Man.' I should add that on 'the night' the very good-looking light comedian was blacked up with burnt cork for this memorable production number.

The lone cleaner and the 'Not-so-Merry Japs' all seemed extremely satisfied with our rehearsal efforts and whilst we were sitting resting in the newly dusted stalls the NSD came down from the stage, by the three little steps that were painted the same colour as the proscenium and imparted the news that the following week they were holding a 'Go-as-You-Please Talent Competition'. Now for the sake of any reader who doesn't know what a GAYPC is, may I explain that it is really a '*Do*-as-you-please competition', meaning that the contestants may sing, dance, recite, juggle, play spoons, do acrobatics, play the piano or any other musical instrument, yodel or anything – well, er, nearly anything. Talent and entertainment value are judged by the volume of applause afforded each entrant. At the end of the competition all the contestants stand on the stage in a row and then the master of ceremonies or the compere holds his hand over each hopeful's head and either the audience applaud, or, in unfortunate cases, they don't.

Right, the NSD went on to say that 'it would be a very good idea if you extremely clever and talented little girls were to come along and enter the contest.' I laugh now when I think of the NSD's performance . . . 'extremely clever and talented little girls', aged eight and nine!! What he really meant was, that he was making sure of plenty of contestants. Bless him, it's the same whole world over – a bit of flattery from the opposite sex goes a long way, even if you are only eight years old.

Well, anyway, we were quite excited and the NSD was very nice and kind really. The moment he gathered we were very enthusiastic, he struck whilst the iron was hot and asked us all what we each had in mind as a competition piece. My form mate Phyllis said she would do a bit from *The Merchant of Venice* (which wasn't surprising, as her brother was a very good amateur Shakespearean actor). Maudie was going to sing 'Men of Harlech' (which was only natural when you come to think of it, her parents being Welsh). I can't remember what Vera was going to do, and I can't remember what Madge or Mabel were going to do, but I vaguely remember that Ada, well I think it was Ada, when asked what she would be doing replied without hesitation, 'The Valeta'. 'Oh yes,' said the NSD 'who with?' 'By myself!' replied Ada. Well, as I say, I think it was Ada. But whoever it was or wasn't I can clearly remember thinking 'By herself! – I wonder how that's going to look!' The above named were all my *best friends*, so whatever they chose to attempt I knew it would be all right.

'And what are you going to do?' the NSD asked me. 'Does the pianist know, "Ours Is a Nice House, Ours Is"?' I enquired. 'Does the . . . yes, I'm sure he does,' he replied, slightly surprised at my unexpectedly forthright request. 'Look, dear, go up those three little steps at the side of the stage and ask him!' So I did! The pianist was sitting at an upright piano having a cigarette after his patient efforts in the 'Rastus Brown' number. I stepped on to the stage and approached the piano. 'Excuse me,' I said, 'can you play "Ours Is a Nice House, Ours Is"?' His reply was to do so immediately, whereupon I politely stopped him carrying on by saying, 'Excuse me but will you give me four bars in please?' Honestly, he nearly fell off the piano stool. 'Will I give you four bars in . . . and how do you know about four bars in?' he asked, laughing (although I couldn't see anything very funny in what I'd said).

'Well,' I explained, 'I need four bars to make an entrance . . . please.' 'Certainly,' he replied, still laughing, and into the four bars he went. Bless him!

Now I must explain, four bars in, an orchestra tuning up, curtain music or anything in that line has the same effect on me as the 'Stripper' music had on the stripper who always started to strip when she heard it – wherever she might be! I don't mean I started to strip off . . . I was only eight . . . but remembering my dad's tuition, 'You must always make a polished entrance and exit,' and hearing the music, like a flash I was in the wings and then 'Making an entrance!' I sang one chorus of 'Ours Is a Nice House', and, as I was getting near the end of it I called out, 'One more chorus please!' On went the pianist, this time an octave higher, and into my 'wallop routine' I went. It's a great tune to wallop to and luckily I knew enough 'breaks' to last a chorus – well, just about. When the music arrived at the last line of the chorus I did what was to be my first 'big finish', the shoe wipe! Eeee, hecky plonk! The shoe wipe! Right heel forward, left heel forward, step back with right foot, step back with left foot, bend down and pretend to wipe toes of shoes from left to right and from right to left. The whole thing is so elementary it's difficult to describe, but it looks rather effective when you are only eight! I thanked the pianist (rather like a variety artist thanks the orchestra in the band pit) and tripping down the three little steps I returned to my seat in the stalls to as much applause as about twenty people can muster.

The NSD and some of the now 'Very Merry Japs' clustered round me bombarding me with questions such as 'Where did you learn to do that?' and 'Who

taught you all about making an entrance and an exit?'
and 'How old are you?' (What a question to ask an
actress!) and 'What's your name?' I only answered the
last question. 'Thora Hird,' I said. 'Hird?' said the NSD.
'You're not Jimmy Hird's little girl are you?' 'Yes, I am!'
I replied. 'Aw, well then,' added the NSD, 'I don't
bloody wonder!'

As we sat in the horse tram going back to school, I
didn't bother to think what it was that he didn't bloody
well wonder at, because I was too busy bloody
wondering how I could enter that 'Go-as-you-please
competition' without my parents knowing. Should I
ask their permission and risk being refused? Or should
I confide in my hero, our Nev? Yes, that would be the
best thing, tell our Nev, he would advise me, he always
did, and in any case he was the only person I could
think of who would lend me the penny to pay my fare
on the horse tram that was to carry me to George Hall's.
I could pay my own fare back.

Well, and I say this modestly, I won, but first things
first.

We all appeared at the benefit as arranged, Rastus
Brown strode to town, we did the bobbing step magnif-
icently, and that was that. Oh, and I think and really
hope that George Hall really benefited from his benefit.

When the day of the GAYPC arrived, the following
week, I went to school as usual. I'm going to describe
what I was wearing, as it is quite important to the story.
I had on a white knitted jumper with a pale blue
crocheted edge round the neck through which was
slotted a chainstitch cord with a little pom-pom on each
end. When the neck was drawn up the woollen cord

tied in a bow, leaving the pom-poms at chest level. Right? Now with this I wore a pale blue pleated skirt (mini length) made of silk morocaine, very short white socks and white buckskin strap shoes. Add to this rather innocent and charming sight . . . my curls! These were the result of my sitting each night before I went to bed, having my curl rags put in. Any reader who has suffered this form of torture will be aware of the procedure but for the benefit of all those lucky people who have been blessed with naturally curly hair and know not of what I speak, allow me to explain.

Curl rags are to encourage ringlets. The straight-haired victim such as I was (and still am) assumes a sitting position, whilst her loving mother, who is standing (and therefore at an advantage to lop you one with the hair brush if you don't keep still), with gentle care brushes out a strand of hair; one end of a curl rag, which varies in length according to the length of the victim's hair, is then passed over the head of the would be curly top and that same end is held tightly in the childish fist, whilst the other end of the rag is held equally tightly by the loving mother who then proceeds to wrap the strand of hair round her half of the rag. The victim's half of the rag is folded over the wrapped round hair and tied in a bow at the bottom of the now prepared ringlet. This process is repeated as many times as the thickness of hair allows, and the result is that the victim is reminiscent of the wonderful invention that landed on the moon! I will admit that when my curl rags were taken out in the morning, and the corkscrews of hair brushed round my mother's finger, it was worth all the agony – well, for a couple of hours, anyway. My being blessed with the straightest hair conceivable, and our living at the seaside, where the air is always a bit damp, meant that by lunchtime my curls were rather pathetic. Anyway, you've got the picture of me on the day of the GAYPC.

I'm sure you must be wondering why all the secrecy and the 'not telling my parents' bit. Well, you see, as I have already told you, my dad was a perfectionist and very professional, and even at that tender age I knew that he would not let me enter the competition until my simple little effort had been rehearsed and rehearsed – even if he had allowed me to enter at all, which was doubtful. Neither he nor my mother wanted Nev or me to be bitten by the acting bug: 'It's too precarious a business,' they would insist, hence the big secret with Nev. I can honestly say that it was the first time I had ever deceived my parents. Mind you, at eight years old I should hope it was!

I'm not making excuses, but everything fitted in perfectly, and that alone encouraged me. My dad was on the pier and my mother was 'doing the make-up' for the Amateur Shakespearean Company who were playing next door at the Royalty and having a go at *The Tempest*, so each of my parents would be leaving the house around five-thirty or six. I can't remember what time Nev and I set off for George Hall's and 'The Merry Japs', but I know Nev put me safely on the horsetram and I paid my fare with a penny of my own, saving the penny Nev had lent me to return home, which I did flushed with success and the proud recipient of a gold bracelet. It wasn't late when I returned home, and my parents were still out, so after a cup of cocoa (which didn't seem to go with winning a gold bracelet!) Nev and I went to bed where I kept looking at the little gold bracelet round my wrist. Surely my parents would be delighted? Or would they? Anyway, I didn't risk anything. I carefully took my prize off my wrist and tucked it under the pillow (for secrecy or safety, I can't remember which).

The following morning we got up for school as usual. I had to have my hair well brushed and plaited because, my mother having been at the theatre the night before, hadn't been able to put my famous curl rags in, and my hair looked like weary golden seaweed. Whilst my mother was plaiting my hair, I kept looking at Nev who really couldn't have cared less about my guilty secret.

I would like to mention something at this point. I suppose we have all had little daft habits when we were children – well, if we didn't we were very peculiar children, weren't we? If Nev and I had a secret or a bit of information that was very private to us alone, I would only have to look at him and I would start to titter. He would look at me with a Groucho Marx expression, and I would titter more than ever. After a while he would start tittering at me tittering – well, you know how it is with kids? Sometimes, when we were having a meal Nev would do things like nudging me ever so gently, and I would turn to look at him to find he was pointing his finger at the side of my head, and so his finger end would go in my ear 'ole. It would make me jump, and then I would explode with laughing and 'have to leave the table' – to return only when I could 'behave properly'. When I come to think of it, it was worth it because nobody has ever made me laugh more than my brother Nev. So who better than he to write some of my funniest and most successful stage comedies, many, many years after we'd tittered at the table? And although all this sounds as though we were the Barretts of Wimpole Street, with James Henry as Mr Barrett, please scrub that idea immediately, my parents were only making sure that we were obedient and observed our table manners. This they achieved. Hey, listen, I know this may sound rather old fashioned, and I don't care if it does, but I can honestly say that I get quite a lot of pleasure out of watching a child who has good table manners. I can say, just as honestly, that I get equal pleasure out of watching a scruffy, uncared-for child (who doesn't know any better) wolfing a large bread and jam sandwich!

What I'm not too fond of is the 'couldn't care less' middle attitude. But, of course, that's only my opinion.

However, back to the morning after my first act of deceit. Nev and I finished our breakfasts and I felt that that could have been the moment to confess all. But I didn't and after a quick nip upstairs and another admiring look at my gold bracelet, I wrapped it in my clean hanky and tucked it in the small pocket on the right hand leg of my knickers. I came downstairs, kissed my mother 'goodbye' (which I always did when I left the house, as though I were off on a world tour instead of only going to school), and Nev and I tittered our way out of the door and into Cheapside.

During that morning my mother was at the front door, sweeping the steps, when a lady we knew very well happened to pass our house. As she approached my mother she cheerfully said, 'Good morning, Mrs Hird, how are you?' 'Very well, thank you, Mrs Richardson . . . are you all right?' my mother replied. 'Yes thank you,' said Mrs R. 'Eeee, I say, your Thora at George Hall's last night . . . wasn't she grand?' There was a slight pause while my mother assured herself that she had heard right. Then she said, 'I think you have made a mistake Mrs Richardson, it was the last week she was at George Hall's, with some other pupils from Miss Nelson's. They were helping at the benefit you know.' And my mother continued with the job she was doing. 'I've made no mistake, love', stressed our friend. 'I was there myself last night and *saw* her. She sang "Ours Is a Nice House, Ours Is" and did a little step dance and won the Go-as-you-please competition. She didn't half get some applause and she won a gold bracelet!'

It's writing about moments like the ones that followed Mrs R's declaration that prove to me, more than ever, what a wonderfully faithful and loving mother I had. You see, there was no point in arguing with Mrs R because she had *seen* me with her own eyes and she knew me very well, so it required some rather nifty thinking on the part of my mother . . . Marie Mayor, Actress! 'Oh yes, of course,' said Marie, 'what am I thinking about! Jim was on the pier and I was making the amateurs up last night, so we couldn't go!' I think she said this because she was such a good mother that she wouldn't let me down, or show me up, and I'm sure she couldn't have borne anyone thinking that we, her children, didn't confide in her. I realize now, that she must have been wondering why I hadn't told her I was going. 'Oh, what a shame you couldn't go . . .' – Mrs Richardson was off again – '. . .what a little artist! and what a good idea to dress her up as a little urchin . . . hee, hee, that dirty face, mucky white shoes, one sock up and one down, and her hair . . . eeeeeeee, no curl in it . . . ooo, the detail, I'll bet all that was her dad's idea, wasn't it?' *Her dad's idea!!!* It was nobody's idea! It was the result of a day at school, dressed in pale blue and white, and due to the fact that Miss Trilby Hird and her personal manager Mr Svengali Hird had stayed out after school was over, getting increasingly dirtier, the curls dropping straighter, the white socks and buckskin shoes attaining a somewhat 'french-grey' appearance and the white woollen jumper losing what had been that clean, crisp, fresh look! In fact, I must have resembled a somewhat shop-soiled, eight-year-old edition of one of those grubby looking with-it pop singers we see today. (The only defence I can put up is, that *they* are old enough to know that cleanliness is next to godliness. I wasn't!)

As my mother turned back into the house (she told me all this afterwards), her first reaction was, how dare anyone accuse one of her children of looking like an urchin! That was overshadowed, however, by her sense of humour as she saw the funny side of the remark, 'I'll bet that was her dad's idea!' For she knew full well that Dad would go mad when he heard I had entered the competition, especially as I had done so on the sly, though at the same time he would be secretly proud I had won it!

When I came in from school at dinner-time, I sensed a doom-laden atmosphere as my mother said quietly, 'Sit down a moment please.' I did as I was told. 'Now, what's all this I hear about you being at George Hall's last night?' That gentle, loving face, those grey eyes so full of humour, looked straight at me. Now I can honestly say that I was never afraid of my mother, nor did she ever frighten me in any way, but when she added, 'Well, I don't know what your father's going to say I'm sure.' I can remember the ache that gripped my throat as I tried not to cry. I knew I had no cause to cry, my understanding mother was not scolding me, but even at eight years old you can feel guilty and wonder why you bothered to have a secret you needn't have.

It was at that moment we heard firm footsteps approaching along the passage from the front door. 'Here's your father,' my mother breathed . . . as if I didn't know! It's funny how my dad was always referred to as 'father' when the incident was serious enough to warrant it. Otherwise he was always 'dad'.

I put my hand in my knicker-leg pocket and clutched the bracelet as if it were a charm to ward off evil spirits! As my dad entered the living-room we both looked at his face. There was no need for Mum to explain anything, it was obvious he had already heard!

He looked at me then went straight into the back kitchen to wash his hands (I don't mean he went to wash his hands because he'd looked at me, I mean, I'm just explaining what he did). I heard the tap water running, then I heard the piece of carbolic soap thud gently back into the enamel soap tray and the little tinkle as the loose top of the soap tray settled back comfortably into position. My hand was like a clutching claw over the bracelet. Dad came back into the living-room drying his hands with great precision

. . . he often did this when he had an important announcement to make, then he looked straight at me. When I was old enough to understand 'that look', I realized it was the same look of determination that the fifteen-year-old boy who had run away from Todmorden (the Lancashire side) had had when he joined Moore and Burgesses Nigger Minstrels. But of course I wasn't realizing anything that day other than that I was going to cop it in a minute!

'And what's all this I hear about you entering a "Go-as-you-please competition" at George Hall's last night?' This was asked as he carefully folded up the towel he had been using, which was unnecessary, really, as it always hung behind the back kitchen door. I looked up at *my* dad – the man who was to teach me so very much in the ensuing years – and the pain in my throat burst into sound as the tears flowed. 'But I won, Dad! I'll won a gold bracelet!' I sobbed as I fumbled in my knicker pocket to prove it. As I did so my mother said to James Henry. 'Did you meet Mrs Richa . . .?' He decided that it was the moment to present her with the folded towel. He did this without taking his eyes off me. 'All right,' he said sternly, but not too sternly. 'All right. I'll forgive you *this* time, but don't ever dare . . . are you listening? . . . don't ever *dare* to enter a competition or anything else without first asking either your mother or me if you may and until whatever it is you are going to do is properly rehearsed and presented . . . (pause) . . . understand?' I nodded, with a sob. He offered me the clean hanky from his breast pocket (which was a beautiful gesture, really, because that particular handkerchief was the one 'for show and not for blow'). He did this because I was fumbling for my clean hanky, which as you know was in my knicker pocket, wrapped around my prizewinning gold bracelet, and not too easy to free. As he approached his chair at the dinner table he turned and said, 'And if there ever is a next time, for God's sake remember to have a *wash*! Little Urchin! . . . Bloody cheek!' The last part of the remark was obviously directed at someone who wasn't with us at that particular moment, so it seemed pretty certain that Mrs R had nobbled him as well as Mum. Pulling his chair out with great dignity he sat down. It was all beautifully done and the timing was perfect!

I wiped my eyes and blew my nose (on his handkerchief). I can't quite remember if I promised anything, but if I did I shouldn't have, because the following week Nev and I were on the sands and we heard the comedian in the pierrot show shouting, 'Now are there any little boys or girls in the audience who can dance, sing or recite? Come along and win a solid gold clock (this was said with a wink) or a cash prize!'

I'd like to think I weakened because I owed Nev a penny – not that he had asked me for it outright, but I had had a few brotherly reminders. However, whatever the reason, I found myself on that little wooden platform which was erected on wooden trestles about a foot above the sand, politely asking the pianist, 'Excuse me please, but can you play "Ours Is a Nice House, Ours Is"? And will you give me four bars in, please? Thank you!'

He could. He did. I did. And I won the cash prize . . . one shilling!!!

10

The monied lot

The prize – one shilling. When I think of the pleasure Nev and I had out of that shilling it seems unbelievable. Just wait whilst I describe what we did.

On the foreshore of the Central Pier were all sorts of automatic machines; so first of all we decided to be weighed, not on an automatic machine, though, on the jockey scales.

How lovely these particular scales always looked, all the brass shining like pure gold, the red plush upholstered hanging chair and the excitement of going up and down as weights were put on or taken off the brass plate that formed the other end of the scale. I used to love that. We each got a little paper ticket with our weight written on it in pencil, and all that only cost us one penny each, so we still had tenpence left between us.

Our next move was to put a penny each into an automatic machine. I got a little pink cardboard box of cough pastilles and Nev got a little green box which contained one Richmond Gem cigarette and a match. (He was nearly eleven and was already experimenting with a sly drag in the lavatory in our back yard.)

Now we had eightpence so we each had a go on another automatic machine.

This machine was very interesting. The top of it was like a big clock face but, instead of numerals only, it sported the letters of the alphabet as well. You inserted a penny and then proceeded to move the large iron pointer, which was similar to the big finger on a clock, round to the letter of the alphabet you required, pulling a lever after each letter had been duly pointed to. Then – this was the wonderful moment – you pressed a button and the end result was that out shot a strip of metal with your name pressed or impressed on it! On each end of the strip a hole was conveniently punched, so of course if you so desired you could nail it on a door, a box or anything you fancied.

On mine I had recorded the words THORA HIRD – ACTRESS, well, I had just won another competition, hadn't I? I think Nev only recorded his name on his strip, although I suppose he would have been eligible to have added, MONEYLENDER!

So we had sixpence now. Talk about blow the expense! We went to Anthony's Ice Cream Stall and each of us bought a halfpenny cornet. These were miniatures of the present day cones, but even so, Mr Anthony, a big, kind-hearted Italian, who knew us through Dad, to whom he paid his rent, gave us a lovely big top on our little cones.

We took our time over the ices because, well, we were getting a bit low on funds after our mad spending spree. Our method of ice cream cone eating enabled us to make them last longer: it was, lick the ice cream until it was a smooth point and then nibble a bit of the biscuit cone all round, repeat this procedure until you had a perfect miniature cone about half an inch long containing ice cream.

Right, what did the plutocrats do next? We went to Mr Bradley's pitch and had our photographs taken. This always fascinated me. I don't mean having my photograph taken, I've never enjoyed that – I mean the particular way it was done at this particular stall.

The subject sat on a wooden stool, was requested to 'smile please' and then, click, the photographer (pardon the expression) seemed to snatch something from the back of the camera, dip it furtively into an adjacent biscuit tin that held some mysterious fluid and then, the quickness of the hand deceiving the eye, plunged his hand into a bucket of water that was conveniently placed on the ground next to the legs of the camera, swish his hand about, one, two, three, four, and hey presto! the customer or subject – yes, I think 'subject' would be the better word – was presented with a tin disc about the size of a shilling, all wet! A little pin was attached to the back of the disc and on the front – hecky plonk – there was a picture of yourself, with a very wet grin, all for a penny!

One small copper coin! I confess that during my childhood I had dozens of these executed, but here's the sad bit. By the time one got home, however near one lived to the photographer's pitch, the recorded image had always grown so faint that it could have been a photograph of anybody – or anything! But who cared? Talk about your modern high speed Polaroid cameras – it will have to be damned quick to beat Mr Bradley!

We suddenly realized we only had three pence left! It

was at this juncture that my loving brother reminded me that, if I would excuse him mentioning it, I did still owe him a penny. It's amazing, the extraordinary shareholders' meeting that can take place when the final item on the agenda is what to spend the remaining capital of twopence on, something that can be shared equally between the only two shareholders in the company. Quite a lot of thought went into that, as Nev pinned my very wet photograph onto my cotton dress.

It was unanimously agreed that a penny bar of Cadbury's Nut Milk Chocolate each would be quite satisfactory. What a wonderful afternoon! I have often wondered how much I would need to win today, to do and to enjoy all the things that the shilling prize afforded us. And, please bear in mind, I was out of debt as well!

On my dressing table at the moment, I have a favourite picture of Jan as a little girl. It was taken by a visiting school photographer and had the school's brick wall as a backing. It cost ninepence. I mention this because, although it is in a Victorian silver frame, at the bottom of the photograph, wedged behind the glass, is a precious gift from our nine-year-old daughter that was. It's a strip of metal and pressed or impressed on it are the words, 'To my Mummy from Janette.'

When I was playing at the Palladium in 1966 Lawrie Kingsley and Michael Craig, the scriptwriters, called to see me and saw the above framed photograph on my dressing table – a week later I received their offering, a metal strip which read THORA HIRD – ACTRESS. They'd discovered an automatic machine in the north, still working! Aren't we all barmy? And isn't it lovely?

11

The Central Pier

There is no doubt at all that the Central Pier was responsible for a very long and happy portion of my life, in fact, during the period that my father was Manager there, I will go as far as to say it *was* our life.

Marvellous, indescribable! The hours Nev and I spent on the Pier were enjoyed to the fullest. The antics we got up to, the excitement we experienced, the jobs we had – all these things were handed to us on a plate during the period in which we grew from very small children to teenagers.

Central Pier! According to Research: 'In November 1867, public notice was given by local businessmen of their intention to form a company with the aim of providing the increasingly popular little resort with a pier. By March, 1868, the Central Pier Company had been formed, and in 1869, the Central Pier opened, apparently using some of the basic structure of a pier which had been bought for £2,500 from, apparently, Liverpool.

'The Central Pier cost £10,000 to erect altogether and was enlarged in the 1870s at a cost of a further £5,000. Architecturally, it resembled the Taj Mahal and its appearance in Morecambe Bay was certainly striking.

Left: My lovely mother on her wedding day.

Right: My professional dad.

Me (*notice the low waistline*), my cousin Glad
(*who wasn't my cousin, really*) and Neville (*the Admiral*).

Here I am with our Nev. This is just how we were dressed when we executed the military two-step.

Left: This is me when I was three. (*It looks as if I've only got one leg!*)

Right: Ladies and gentlemen, Thora Hird will now oblige you with that well-known song - 'My Sweet Little Alice Blue Gown'!

Left: This is the first charwoman I ever attempted, in the school concert.

Right: Morecambe's May Queen - I was ten. A leg broke on the homemade throne and I toppled from grace...

Above: Here it is! The Central Pier
(*the northern Taj Mahal - please note the domes*).

Below: George Hall's 'Merry Japs'.

This is the result of them 'glamouring-me-up' for my first film test, complete with cupid-bow lips.

Happy, happy wedding day. Notice my clutching fingers holding his arm so he couldn't get away...the lilies seem to be wilting a bit!

It featured an aquarium, baths, saloons, catering and refreshment rooms, and an observatory with a large telescope, in addition to sun decks and promenades. Later, accommodation was provided for dancing and roller-skating.

'The Pier was also used as an anchorage for ships in the late nineteenth and early twentieth century; these vessels were primarily pleasure steamers.'

Little did that English Taj Mahal know that during its chequered career it was to be invaded, cared for, enjoyed and loved by the Hird Family!

Where shall I start? That's the difficulty. I think I had better tell you about the Skating Rink first.

For those of you who roller skate, don't bother to read the next few lines – but for those of you who don't and never have – oh mates, you've missed a lot! The uninhibited freedom, the speed, the turning round and going backwards, you couldn't see where you were going but you could see where you'd been! Great!

Right, then (new readers start here), my dad had a pair of 'King of the Rink' skates made specially for me – size O. In those days the roller skates were slightly different from present-day ones. There was a leather strap attached to the back of the skate, which came round the front of the foot, just above the instep, and buckled at the side; but the front part of the skate held a sort of vice-like clip each side, which the skating rink attendant screwed tightly and savagely to the shoe sole, with a special key.

After the 'skating fiend' had collected a pair of skates (sixpence), the next bit of the procedure was to sit down, taking your turn in a row of anxious would-be champions, and when it was your turn, one foot was placed on a wooden rest – similar to the ones that are used in shoe shops these days – and then the other foot, while the attendant tightened the clips with his special key.

However, there was a bit of a drawback to this method, because, if you were a keen attender of the rink, eventually your shoe soles began to part company from your uppers! Hence the reason for most 'regulars' leaving a pair of old boots in the 'skates department'. Ooo, that room did smell awful! As the wheels of the skates had ball bearings in them, that meant they required oiling, so what with the smell of oil mixed with the smell of feet and old boots (because no regular skated in shoes) – blimey! I don't know how the attendant stood it without a gas mask!

I *loved* it all, especially the little stage at the far end of the rink. There was usually an orchestra there on a Wednesday and Saturday, not that anyone could hear the music, but you could hear the skates! It was during the 'Hird Dynasty' that a new, modern, breathtaking composition floor was laid. It was wonderful for us, we were able to skate at twice the speed we had managed on its predecessor, the wooden one. The only drawback was the *noise* – it was deafening! But we didn't care. Nev and I would waltz! Yes, *waltz*! We'd skate side by side and execute the 'Two-Step' with our arms round each other's waist, then Nev would skate backwards and I would skate forwards – we held hands for this bit – then a quick turn – whoops – and yours truly would go backwards and Nev forwards. Oh, all good stuff – no rubbish!

There was one regular called Rosie. Hecky plonk! What a wonderful skater! I used to admire her so much! *Not* her skating, her skating *boots*. She had painted them *gold* and instead of ordinary laces she used red ribbon! To my childish eyes they were smashing! I know I asked my mother if she would gild my skating boots if I brought them home, and her reply was quick and to the point, with a definite finality which informed me that I hadn't a hope of red ribbon laces either!

It was great fun for about ten skaters to form a chain, similar to a conga chain, and pretend to be a train. Unfortunately it was considered dangerous, as the speed attained by the back end of 'the train' as it whipped round corners, was terrific, and rightly, it was forbidden. So, while we might get once round the rink in that formation, we were always halted by the referee's whistle the attendant used to blow! The attendant rather enjoyed blowing his whistle. It gave him an authoritative feeling of power, and it made him feel superior. One couldn't begrudge him it really, as he didn't get much chance of feeling superior in the Skate Department, amongst the smell of sweaty boots and oil! I often wondered if he came out and blew his whistle just to exhale and get away from the smell!

Actually, blowing his whistle was not to be compared with his performance at closing time, because for the ceremony he used a big brass handbell which he used like a fiendish Town Crier. He must have been fairly strong because that bell was a helluva weight. I once tried to pick it up and nearly fell on my face. Of course, I was only a child and never massive at that, but his handling of it, as he rang it, seemed to be child's play. What a row – I'll bet they could hear it across the Bay at Grange-over-Sands.

Sometimes he would 'build his part up' by hollering 'All off! Clear the Rink! Closing Time!' and with a final 'two-step' or 'waltz' we would make our way to the grained and varnished forms that ran along the wall of the rink, and sit in line while he performed the task of unscrewing our skates. If nobody was looking we would undo the ankle strap and kick the two back wheels of our skates against the six inch high surround of the rink, thereby releasing the skate from the boot sole. We never did that if my Dad was there, but one thing we always did was to put our own skates away, instead of passing them through the pigeonhole to the attendant.

We suffered the smell only long enough to put our skates in their own 'hole', and why not? In half a tick, we would be out on the Pier deck inhaling the healthy and invigorating sea breeze which on dozens of occasions when it was behind our backs nearly blew us down the pier!

It's funny that I have just referred to coming off the Pier, as *down* the Pier. I'll tell you why. I do know that grammatically I should say 'on the pier and off the pier', but when I was little we always used to say, 'I'm going *up* the pier' or 'I'm going *down* the pier'. The dozens of times Miss Elizabeth Nelson, my headmistress at school, corrected me about my grammatical error. She used to correct me by putting her arm straight up above her head, pointing heavenwards and saying,

'Does the pier stand on end and go upwards, Thora?' and I would reply 'No, Miss Nelson, I'm sorry, I meant to say "*on* the pier".' She was a wonderful person – God rest her – well, she must have been, because I loved school so much.

I left school when I was fourteen, prior to the Whitsuntide holidays and I didn't *want* to leave a bit. The 'Whit' holiday was always a short one, a week or ten days, and although I loved school holidays like any other normal schoolgirl, that particular holiday was rather marred by the fact that I wouldn't be returning to school after it.

The day arrived when school started again – I was miserable. Quite a few of my friends used Cheapside en route for Union Street, where the 'Preparatory School, Morecambe' was situated, so I went and stood at our front room window, to watch them enviously on their journey back.

When I got up on that particular morning, I had dressed in my gym slip, clean white blouse and school tie. Wishful thinking I suppose.

I heard my mother call out, 'Where are you, love?' when she couldn't see me in the living-kitchen.

'In here,' I replied on a dull note. That was all. In a couple of minutes I heard my mother coming along the passage and then entering the front room (or sitting-room), I didn't turn round, well, not immediately, but I did a couple of seconds later as I heard her say, 'Here you are!' With these words she handed me my leather school bag.

'Go on,' she said smiling, 'and see if Miss Nelson will let you start another term.' The hug I gave my understanding mother nearly broke her neck. Pffft! Grabbing my school hat, I was out of the house and had caught my pals up before they'd reached the top of 'our street'.

As we all filed into school Miss Nelson was performing her usual ritual of Good morning, Madge – Good morning, Una, Good morning, Ada, Good morning Mabel – between each of these greetings there was a 'Good morning, Miss Nelson' from each pupil. On she went, 'Good morning, Maud – Good morning, Lilian, Good morning, Thora – Good morn —' By then I had walked past with the rest. However, she caught up with me, and very kindly asked, 'What are you doing here, Thora? You're supposed to have left school, aren't you?'

I looked into her face, and started to say, 'Yes, I have left school *really*, Miss Nelson, but I saw the girls coming back this morning and I wondered if . . .'

I didn't get any further, I didn't need to; she looked at me steadily – d'you know, she was quite moved? It was with a very soft and gentle voice she assured me, 'Of course – I'm proud to have you back – now, come along, girls!'

This last bit was in her normal Headmistress's voice, and, clapping her hands, she instructed us all to get in line. Quite honestly, I don't think I have ever sung 'Holy, holy, holy' better, or with more gusto!

So, I was back at school – good egg! Back with Ada Lob, Mabel Bagshaw, Una Yates, Kathy Mortimer, Lilian Cross, Maudie Poles, Vera Muff, Madge Peel and Uncle Tom Cobley and all – *my lot! My friends!*

Now, you've just read that last sentence and you are thinking I've made up those wonderful names, aren't you? Oh yes you are! Well, I haven't! And I'll tell you this, when our register was called at school and the surname of the pupil was called out first, it was like a funny story because it sounded like this: Lob Ada, Muff Vera, Cross Lilian, Hird Thora, Stretch Billy, Peel Madge, etc. etc., Cross Lilian heard Thora stretch Billy peel Madge!

It is with the greatest affection and respect I tell you these names, and it is with happy remembrances that I mention them whenever I play a summer season anywhere. I'm not taking the mickey out of them, it's because I don't want to forget them. They were all part of the time when we were all preparing to become decent citizens of the future. God bless 'em!

I must think of some way to get my train of thought back to the Central Pier – I *do* go off the subject a bit – don't I?

Actually, it was only shortly after I had made my 'return visit' to school that I got a job – on the Pier. But all that I will tell you later on.

The Central Pier Pavilion was a really magnificent structure. The wooden steps that were the approach to its front doors were very wide. I can't recall how many there were but I do remember that just ascending them gave you the feeling that you were going to be entertained to a really first-class evening of enjoyment. You weren't disappointed either. It *was* first class entertainment. No doubt about that!

The theatre part had a most imposing stage, splendid electrical equipment, gantries, the flies – oh, everything. The boxes in the auditorium were each supported by three nude women, my 'Vestal Virgins'.

Well, I say they were nude, they were nude to the

part just below their navels, beyond which they were swathed in plaster ninon drapes. Their arms were behind their heads and their beautiful faces with blank eyes were crowned with wavy plaster hair, parted in the middle and kept in place by a soft-looking plaster turban.

They each sported a beautiful pair of wonderfully moulded breasts. I was very fond of these shameless ladies and I really cannot understand why we are supposed to 'tut, tut' at a permissive society when we have always been allowed to gaze freely at statues. Even undraped statues!

As young as I was then, I thought my 'Ladies of the Boxes' were really beautiful, and they didn't shock me in any way. I had my own 'Temple of the Vestal Virgins' right there.

As a point of interest, although I adore Greece and have visited it several times, I cannot honestly say that standing in front of the remains of the authentic 'Temple of the Vestal Virgins' gave me as much pleasure as my plaster friends who appeared to support the Central Pier Pavilion boxes did!

There was a great advantage to the structure of the Northern Taj Mahal – in front of each of the two smaller domes gracing the roof was a small balcony. Yes, very advantageous were those two balconies. Nev and I grew mustard and cress on one, and kept doves on the other! I'll tell you about the Market Gardening first.

Having acquired four shallow wooden boxes, we pestered my mother until she gave us small pieces of a woollen blanket. These were wrung out in cold water and placed in the boxes, and then we diligently sprinkled mustard seed in two of the boxes and cress seed in the remaining two. You see, the idea was, to present my mother with not only 'mustard and cress' but mustard *or* cress. How about that, then?

It grew like mad and we looked after it with loving care. As soon as one crop had been gathered in we planted another lot. The balconies were real suntraps – we had access to them through two doors high up in the balcony of the Pavilion (we were only allowed through either of these doors and on to the balcony outside when Dad was with us!). The aforementioned doves were really Neville's concern and in the winter, when the weather was not really suitable for human beings to be out in, never mind gentle doves, he kept them indoors in Dad's room at the side of the stage.

During the summer season on the Central Pier, there would be various Concert Parties in the Pavilion. These were really first-class productions, with excellent artistes who were always beautifully dressed. 'The Superbs', 'The Emeralds', 'Frills and Flounces', 'The Ideals', 'The Seven Nobody's', 'The Mountebanks' and 'The Pelicans'.

They always opened the first half of the show in the traditional pierrot costumes, wearing ruffles and pierrot hats, and clothes as well of course. How I used to admire the ladies' short, full and frilly skirts, and the net and sequin ruffles.

You see, each Concert Party had a different colour scheme for costumes and the drapes on the stage, and I could get quite excited with the anticipation of wondering what 'Next week will be like!'

Nev and I 'lived' in the Prompt Corner. We were now a bit older and more aware of behaving ourselves than we had been during the Royalty Theatre days. Something else was great fun, too. On 'thin' matinee days, when the weather was fine Nev and I would sit in front and help to swell the laughs and applause, or, stand in the Prompt Corner and hope to be taken on stage during one of the sketches! This was what we really preferred.

The first half of the show always finished with a sketch. When I say we took part in some of the sketches, I don't mean we ever had speaking parts – oh no, we would oblige by being part of a funeral procession, or members of a jury, that kind of thing. We were, you will gather, very versatile! I mean, we were only young children. And I might quickly add, we only ever appeared on 'thin' matinee days! It was 'just a bit of fun!'

Many of you will know what I mean, when I say, we only appeared on the occasions when the artistes would remark, before the curtains went up, 'Mr and Mrs Wood and family are in front' or 'I see Rosa is in front!' Both sarcastic remarks mean, 'rows of empty seats!'

There was 'your bit of culture' on the pier as well, you know. Herr Von Beck, the 'cellist, and his orchestra were employed by the Pier Company and often performed for the Sunday Night Concerts in the Pavilion.

But before I forget to tell you about the Iron Sheet or

Safety Curtain in the Pavilion, I'll do it now. It was lovely! John Birkett, a Morecambe chemist, and a gentleman if ever I met one, distilled his own perfume; it was called 'AMO-DEL' and it was very fragrant and pleasant. He hired the entire safety curtain and advertised 'AMO-DEL' on it. It was very artistically and attractively done. The picture was of an Indian canoe full of flowers floating down a wide river with an Indian, complete with feathers, 'paddling his own canoe' as you might say. The background was mountains in hazy mauves and blues, and the only lettering on the curtain was 'AMO-DEL', in a half hoop in the sky portion of the picture, and underneath it stated 'THE GATHERED FRAGRANCE OF INDIAN DALES'.

Now I've no doubt a lot of people will feel like laughing at that! I hope they don't, because compared to some of the present day advertising and some of the words that are used, the AMO-DEL idea is very ahead!

The programmes of the performances which took place in the Pavilion were all dipped at one end in 'AMO-DEL', so you don't wonder that I used to love selling programmes! I can see that line of print now, as I think of it: 'THIS PROGRAMME HAS BEEN PERFUMED WITH AMO-DEL'. The programmes were threepence each, and on the occasions I was employed as 'a seller of same' my salary was threepence for every dozen I sold. Not bad money, was it? Apart from that, one went home 'smelling gorgeous!'

By the way, next to handbags and shoes I'm mad about perfume, and I am wearing a perfume at the moment that is really – Ooooo, smashing! When I first acquired this particular perfume I remarked to Scottie

'Oh, that's nice, isn't it? – go on – have a smell!' He agreed it was eligible to go on the list of 'driving him up the wall' or 'attacking the first female he saw' (I don't mean *me*, we've been married 38 years!) and so on. All that day I kept on saying, 'Oh, it *does* remind me of something and somewhere!' In fact, during the first week I used it I nearly drove myself barmy trying to think what it reminded me of and where I'd smelt it before. Ladies, *please*, if anything 'dawns on you suddenly' don't do what I did. One morning, after my bath, I was in my room dabbing half a pint of the 'madly expensive elixir' here and there, when it dawned on me what it reminded me of – I flew into the bathroom, flung my arms round Scottie exploding as I did so, 'It's *Amo-del*, darling, *Amo-del*!' As he withdrew his shaving brush from his mouth and started to spit the lather out, he blubbered, 'What is?'

Sorry, Scottie!

We all know that most theatres sell 'goodies' during the interval – ices, soft drinks, chocolates and so forth – but the Pier had a very original little offering: jellies! They were made in 'little tiny pudding basins'. Just like my mother's white basins in the kitchen at home but in miniature! It was the basins that first attracted me to the jellies. Each jelly – various flavours, strawberry, raspberry, orange or lemon – was turned out on to a small saucer and then surrounded with ice cream. Threepence!

On the left-hand side of the stalls next to the orchestra pit was the 'Pass Door' (No Admittance) and on the right-hand side was a corresponding door, with a small hatch in the top half of it. Through this hatch were passed the trays of jellies! If trade was brisk, the drill was: the attendant, with empty tray, approached the 'jelly door' rapped briskly on it twice and demanded, 'More jellies please!' Or perhaps she might be even more explicit and say, '*Two* more jellies please' or '*Five* more jellies please!' or, and the next request was a more descriptive one, 'Two more jellies please, a red and a yellow!'

Right then. The occasion arose when – and I can't think why it was – Nev and I were asked whether we would 'Assist with the jelly sales'. Certainly, we were very happy to oblige – same contract as before – threepence for every dozen sold – *and* – a bonus. The bonus was, if there were less than four left over we could eat them! I mean to say, what about that! Mind you, I had never known when there *were* any left over – but the sporting chance appealed to us.

So round the auditorium we went 'plying our trembling jellies' and we did very well. I was in my element when I was able to go to the hatch and knock twice and ask for 'More jellies please!' It had a sound of authority!

As the safety curtain and the advert for 'AMO-DEL' slowly began to disappear upwards towards the Indian Dales, it was accompanied by the sound of spoons being rested in saucers and smacking of lips. Of course, there were none of your plastic spoons in those days – oh no, every piece was genuine 'hotel ware'. Nev and I made an exit through the door with the hatch, to discover that the charge hand who had been pushing the jellies through had gone – well, at least she wasn't there. On the bench that ran along the side of the wall was a tray, and sitting on it, dithering away – two jellies! One red, one yellow – I've already told you – some folks have all the luck! Right, get stuck in, one each!

Bear in mind, if you will please, they were only small jellies and by the time I had scooped a good teaspoonful out of mine, you could say it was half gone.

Oh yes, this is the life, very nice I must say, I thought as I next helped myself to a spoonful of Anthony's Italian Ice Cream. Nev had progressed about as far as I had when, knock, knock, 'One more jelly please!' sounded through the hatch! We stopped dead just as though we were playing 'statues!' We each had our mouths full and as soon as we'd swallowed the contents we looked at each other and the 'great idea' seemed to dawn on us both at the same moment.

'We'll have to stick both halves together on one saucer, won't we?'

'But they're different colours!'

We decided that couldn't be helped, and stick 'em together we did! Thank the Lord we hadn't eaten more than we had. Gently, putting the remaining half of my jelly on Nev's saucer, I sort of stuck the two halves together with my fingers, with gentle pressure – no sculptor used more care – then, putting my remaining ice cream into his saucer we arranged it rather neatly over the join of the jellies.

'One more jelly, *please*!' the urgent request came from the other side of the hatch.

'They are bound to notice it's two colours,' I said.

'No they won't,' comforted Nev, 'the house lights have just gone down!'

And the multi-coloured jelly trembled its way through the hatch!

'When I appeared in Opera!' I throw that line away. No, wait a minute, I won't throw it away. I'll tell you about it! If you insist!

'John Riddings Opera Company'. Oh yes, they used to arrive for a six weeks' season on the Pier. What an education! Fabulous! Year after year they came. *Maritane, Il Trovatore, Faust, Martha, The Bohemian Girl, Rigoletto, La Traviata, Daughter of the Regiment,* and *Lily of Killarney.*

All these, for the pleasure and delight of the public, and Thora and Neville Hird. I reckon, considering we were only children, Nev and I knew as many opera and operetta scores backwards as the next one.

It was in *The Bohemian Girl* that I made my 'debut'. As is well known, the young daughter of wealthy parents is stolen during the first act by Devilshoof, the gipsy king. The dramatic bit, or so I thought, was where the gipsy king carries the child over the property rocks at the back of the stage set, whilst the child's parents and their faithful retainers are kneeling at prayer down at the front of the stage. Actually, they are praying on behalf of their stolen chee-ild! I played the stolen child! On my left forearm was a birthmark, which had been put there by applying a stick of carmine No. 3 greasepaint and running it along my forearm for about four or five inches. The size and length of the fake birthmark had to be large enough for the audience to see from the back of the auditorium!

If you are not familiar with the story of *The Bohemian*

Girl I'd better explain that the birthmark is put on the arm of whoever plays the child because in Act II the leading lady takes over, indicating that the child has, by then, grown up into a beautiful gipsy maiden! So, of course, she has the carmine birthmark, too, otherwise you wouldn't know who she is, would you? I mean it wouldn't matter how much she waved her arms about when she sang 'I Dreamt That I Dwelt in Marble Halls' if she hadn't the carmine on her arm, would it?

Well, as I say, there I was, appearing in Opera. I had no script to learn because I had nothing to say, so it was just pure acting! When we got to the part where the gipsy king carried me across the rocks – I *did* put on a frightened look, as a matter of fact, because 'Devilshoof' looked enough to frighten anybody – he'd gone a bit mad with his make-up!

There knelt my heartbroken father (John Riddings himself – no less) and my stage mother, and all the servants – eyes closed (but of course, otherwise they would have seen Devilshoof carrying me across the prop rocks!), hands together in prayer and singing really beautifully, very softly. As the gipsy king and I approached our exit, I can vividly remember thinking, 'Well, I haven't done much!' so, before we disappeared out of sight, I assumed a heartbroken voice, and stretching my arms towards the praying family I wailed, 'Daddy! Daddy!'

I must have 'moved' Devilshoof with my perform-ance because he nearly dropped me on the prop rocks! Oh dear, I thought everyone would be pleased, but I didn't realize of course that I'd shouted 'Daddy' so loudly that even allowing for stage licence Daddy and

Mummy must have appeared stone deaf not to have heard me! Of course they *did* hear me, which made John Riddings do a startled twitch, but they went on praying as though they hadn't. Good job, too, otherwise there would have been no reason to continue with the rest of the Opera!

My salary for that piece of histrionic ability was a bottle of Lime Juice and Soda per performance, it was one of those exciting bottles with a glass alley in the neck. They are collector's pieces now. I am lucky enough to own three.

Faust was one of my favourite operas – I loved the music and still do. However, it's not the music that I wish to tell you about. I don't know whether you will believe it, but I assure you, it did happen. The leading lady in the John Riddings Opera Company was called Miss June.

She was 'a really fine looking young woman' – well, I say 'young', I reckon she would be thirty something or other, and that's young enough, isn't it? Well, I think it is, at my age, but of course when one is only round about the tender age of eight or nine or ten, anyone who is over twenty-one seems rather old, don't they?

Back to the subject. Miss June was 'a fine figure of a woman', and she was also a very fine singer, which of course came in useful as she was in an Opera Company!

It was on a matinee day that the following happened. I saw Miss June coming 'up' the pier looking very smart. She was wearing a navy blue serge costume; you'll notice I say 'costume' – that's because when I was young I can't remember anyone referring to that type of feminine wear as a 'suit'. Ladies always wore 'costumes' and only men wore 'suits'. Even on the beach the feminine gender wore 'a bathing costume'.

However, as I say, she was coming 'up' the pier in this smart navy blue costume. The skirt reached just below her calves – rather like today's fashion, really – the jacket was well in at the waist, and the entire cut displayed her figure to advantage. Her hat was a white panama, rather on the Breton sailor lines, with a broad black ribbon round the crown of it. She presented me with a dazzling smile and accompanied the smile with a rich-voiced, 'Hello, my dear.'

When 'half an hour please' was called at each dressing room door the well mannered artistes all acknowledged it with musical voiced 'Thank you's'. I give full marks to opera artistes, they are all very professional, serious with it – and by and large a happy and laughing lot. There wasn't much to laugh at on that particular matinee afternoon. The audience numbered seventeen! After the 'quarter of an hour, please', had been called, Miss June came down from her star dressing room and on to the stage. 'How's the house?' she enquired in her rich musical voice. Without waiting for an answer she proceeded to have a look for herself. This was going to be quite an achievement, really, because at this juncture of the proceedings the iron sheet or safety curtain was down, informing the seventeen avid opera fans sitting in front that AMO-DEL was the gathered fragrance of Indian dales, and the velvet swish curtain was down hanging behind it. The usual procedure was for the Safety Curtain to start to rise as the orchestra took their positions in the pit prior to the overture.

Actually, it's considered 'not done' to go peeping at the audience before 'curtain up', but everybody does it. I know I do, providing there is the 'wherewithal' to do so.

Miss June approached the swish curtain and, inserting both her thumbs in the centre part, where they swished together, opened them minutely and gazed with one eye through the little hole that someone had conveniently made in the Indian's canoe on the Safety Curtain. It was only a tiny hole, so there was no fear of the canoe sinking into the Indian River! She peered through, and (it's amazing how much one can see with one eye through a little hole, isn't it?) she then stepped back, drew a deep breath through her nose, which raised her ample bosom, exhaled through her nose, which lowered her ample bosom, and declared to the empty stage, as she made her exit, 'I shan't bother to change!' And she didn't!

Have you ever seen Marguerite in *Faust* played wearing a navy blue serge costume and a white panama hat? I have! I saw it at that matinee. I don't think it mattered so much until she got to the Jewel Song. There she was, kneeling on the stage, golden-handled mirror in one hand, the other hand taking ropes of 'prop' pearls and glass diamonds out of the jewel box and putting them round her neck (which is no mean feat when you're wearing a panama hat) and singing, 'Oh, no, this is not I! Oh, no, this – is – not I!' I'd gone 'in front' to swell the audience to eighteen, and I felt like calling out 'No, you're right, it isn't you,

Marguerite – it's Miss June in her navy blue costume and panama hat!'

The incredible thing was that, although it had nearly reduced me to 'my tittering habit', the remaining seventeen opera lovers didn't seem to notice or mind! They'd only come for the singing or a rest! Dear Miss June, perhaps you were the instigator of playing Shakespeare in modern dress!

12

Firm as a rock

Neville didn't get the chance to display his histrionic ability by 'appearing' in any of the Operas, but he did get a chance to 'save the sinking ship' as you might put it, and who better than Admiral Hird to do so?

I can't remember which Opera it was but I remember that there was a 'rock' made of scenery that was involved in the story, behind which one of the players had to hide.

During the setting of the scene, the stagehands couldn't find a short enough 'brace' to hold the 'rock' in position. Bear in mind, it was really only a flat piece of scenery, but the scenic artist had painted it so realistically that it would have fooled anyone, even if they were sitting on the front row of the stalls!

When the 'quarter of an hour' was called the stage hands still hadn't found a short enough 'brace' *and* they still hadn't told my dad that they couldn't find one. At the 'Five minutes please!' my dad was informed and 'a bit of quick thinking' took place. The 'rock' had to be held as firm as the Rock of Gibraltar – Dad wouldn't endure any 'trembling or waving' rocks, I can tell you! So he said to Neville, 'Will you lie down behind that rock and hold it still and firm?' Would he?

You bet he would – and he did – for a whole Act!

Poor little blighter. In the first place, it's not easy to hold a piece of scenery by the wooden frame even if there is a cross-piece, and in the second place, he took his life in his hands each time the actor darted behind the rock! However, cramped but victorious he crept from the back of the rock as the curtain dropped on Act I.

Nev was kept on to assist with the properties (or in case the rock was needed again) and on the Saturday when my dad made up the wages for the stage staff, an additional wage packet was prepared, marked 'N. HIRD, ASSISTANT PROPERTY MASTER', and it contained half a crown. You see however you looked at it I suppose Neville was 'indispensable' – especially if the 'rock' was needed on the set, and that was more than I was, because any little girl could have played the stolen child in *The Bohemian Girl* but *anybody* couldn't hold a 'prop rock' still and firm for a whole ACT! My brother could – I was at his feet in admiration. Neville presented his wages to my mother with as much aplomb as Clive Jenkins orders twenty-five hand made shirts!

The halfcrown was quite yellow, even though it was still in the packet, when we found it in my mother's Jewel Box after she died. There was something else in the Jewel Box as well – but I haven't told you about that yet.

I was rather partial to the Ladies' Lavatory that was situated on the left-hand side of the Pavilion and was for the 'convenience' of outdoor patrons. What I mean is, it was not a Pavilion toilet, the Pavilion had its own, indoors. It wasn't the Skating Rink Ladies' Toilet either, the Rink also boasted its own 'Ladies' and its own 'Gents'. No, it was a Ladies' Toilet that went entirely under its own title – it wasn't in partnership with any other part of the pier. A 'Ladies' Toilet' was all it was and all it intended to be.

The charm of it was the decor, the furnishings, and the equipment therein. It had obviously been there since 1869, and if it hadn't, it had certainly taken up residence no later than 1870 when the Pier Company had splashed out and spent another Five Thousand Pounds. The joy was, during the winter months it was hardly ever used, and ten to one if it was it was only by the woman who cleaned it, and I didn't begrudge her!

The washbasins were of pale grey marble, quite large really, and there were two large brass taps gracing each bowl. Even the plug was brass on a brass chain.

Under each basin was a wooden cupboard with a brass knob on it. The cupboards weren't there merely to hide the plumbing, because each contained a small shelf. Even the panels on the cupboards were graceful and feminine. But the thing that impressed me so greatly was – it was all spotless!

The taps and plugs and knobs gleamed, the marble was washed regularly, as was the white paintwork. It was really due to my dad. I don't mean he cleaned it, I mean he was very particular about the entire pier being kept clean. The toilets themselves were more on the 'throne lines' than mere pedestals, and even the brass chain and handle that brought forth 'The Handle Water Music' (sorry, Mr Handel!) were cleaned with metal polish, and to prove it there was quite a deposit of dried polish left in the links of the chain.

Yet much as I loved all the above, the one thing beyond price in all that luxury, as far as I was concerned, was a small round mirror about the size of a pudding plate. Printed on it, the letters going round like numerals on a clock face, were the words, MENE TOWELS FOR LADIES, and I loved it. Never mind the large mirrors above the marble basins, they were very nice but not to be compared with my little round one that declared there were 'many towels for ladies'. Of course, I didn't know what the mirror was advertising until I was of an age when I might need to know. I made so many computations of those letters it isn't true. Let's remember I was only young, and not a child genius. One of my favourite arrangements of the letters was 'MEN ET OWELS' which to me sounded like 'Men ate owls'.

Of course, 'The Ladies' was also a great place in which to play house, with all its little cupboards and running water, and often I would share my 'private residence' with a few of my friends when we had gone on to the pier to play after school, when it was too cold to play on the sands.

Summing things up, I realize the big advantage was – and I speak about during the winter months – it was private! The Boys weren't allowed in there! And that was another rule of my dad's!!

13

Madame Rosa Vere

At the far end of the pier, over the steamer landing stage but constructed on the deck of the pier itself, was a high diving board. Now there's nothing exciting about that, I know, but if you add Madame Rosa Vere, in bright red satin bathing costume, trimmed with sequins, and legs encased in red tights, the entire ensemble hidden tantalizingly under a red cape, you must admit it's not a sight you will see every day. Yes, that sight was something else the pier offered.

Madame Rosa's long black hair flowed down to her waist, and she would execute the high dive mornings and afternoons according to when the tide was high. To avoid disappointment, there was a board nailed on to the diving structure which displayed not only a photograph of Madame Rosa Vere in tights and sequins but also the times at which she would 'take the plunge'.

I loved the entire performance and stood holding my breath hundreds of times. She would mount the diving platform and stand there with her hair blowing about and the sequins on her cape sparkling, and announce, 'Ladies and gentlemen, I crave your indulgence . . . I shall do a high dive from this board into the open sea.'

At this point she discarded her long cape and revealed all. A gasp of admiration would escape from the crowd of holiday makers, who all thought they were about to witness not only a breathtaking spectacle but a free one. They were soon enlightened, however, as Madame continued, 'I receive no salary from the Pier Company, so if you will kindly show your appreciation in the usual way, my assistant will pass amongst you. Thank you!'

Her assistant was her mother, and who better to do the bottling? If you don't know what bottling means, it's going round with a small black bag on a little wooden handle as a rule, like the Punch and Judy man does. So round her mother would go whilst Rosa stood poised on view, keeping an eye on the amount of coppers flopping into the little bag. When the bottling was over, Madame prepared to take off. Hands and arms high in the air, she would hesitate long enough for all the crowd to get the full effect and then, whoops, off she went. As she entered the sea to a round of applause, I used to think to myself, 'Oooo, how brave!' She would then swim to the pier iron steamer landing, pull herself out of the mighty sea and then disappear into the rope hut, out of sight. And that was the end of the performance. Not bad for a copper coin, eh?

If ever I said to Dad, 'I'm going to watch Madame Rosa Vere' he always gave me a few coppers to drop in the little bag. In fact, I was often the first of the amazed audience to show my appreciation in the usual way!

When the decision had been arrived at to change the Pavilion from a concert hall into a ballroom – and here I must add that my father not only suggested it, but worked every hour God sent to achieve it – the first job was to remove the rows and rows of seats. This was quite a mammoth job and during the achievement of it I kept thinking, 'I see "Rosa" is in front!' or 'Mr and Mrs Wood are in front!' as piles and piles of seats were transported down the pier. I was remembering the remarks made by the performing artistes when it was a small audience. Some of the seats were saved and put round the sides of the ballroom – but they weren't 'The Wood Family' or 'Rosa' because in their new positions they were always full.

My father lived in a pair of overalls at work and helped manually all that winter. He worked like a slave which, happily, encouraged the workmen employed to do the same thing.

Nev and I would go on the pier after school, out of sheer interest in 'the great change' but before long we went there for sheer fun and took our school friends with us! I'll tell you why.

When, eventually, the maple floor was finally laid, we borrowed about a dozen 'kneeling mats' from the pier char-women (Cleaning Ladies would be a better title). I haven't seen a 'kneeling mat' for donkey's years so I wonder if you know what I'm talking about? A kneeling mat is made of coarse coconut fibre, half moon shaped, with about a six-inch-high gallery round the semi-circular part of it, leaving the front entrance without a gallery, for the knees to go in!

They are marvellous really, because if you are in a kneeling position to scrub or wash or polish, you don't need to get up to move your mat – you simply push your knees against the gallery bit and 'Shuffle off to Buffalo!' Anyway . . . that is a kneeling mat, and as I've already said, I haven't seen one for years! I suppose there's no call for them in these days of long mops, vacuum cleaners and so on.

Well, we borrowed the kneeling mats and fastened a long piece of rope to the front of each one. The idea was for the girls to assume a charwoman kneeling position on the mats, and the boys (after removing their boots or shoes) to pull us round the shiny and highly polished floor! Chariot races took place, we would have heats and then the grand final. It was great! Some kind of powdered polish, French chalk and wax I think, had been scattered over the new floor and we were helping to polish the wood! Get the idea?

My dad willingly allowed this, providing we didn't scratch or harm the floor, because we really were helping to achieve a mirrorlike finish. We also achieved a few holes in our socks or stockings because the girls had to take their shoes off as well. We had more school friends during that period than 'soft mick' (and I don't know what *that* saying means either!).

The 'Big Night' arrived. Grand Opening of the Central Pier Ballroom! Dad had arranged for two dance bands so there would be non-stop dancing – this was quite an innovation, I can tell you.

The stage with its commanding proscenium had been left in its original form apart from the fact that the stage area had 'boxed in' to make a more appropriate size to accommodate a dance band. At the opposite end of the ballroom a new band stand had been erected, so that as the music finished at one end, the opposing band struck up at the other! Fab! A large fountain, surrounded with fresh flowers and ferns, played non-stop in the centre of the floor. Different coloured lights were directed on to the fountain by using lime lights (today they would be called spot lights) from the lime perches, which were rigged up in the stage boxes and manipulated expertly by Neville Hird Esq in one box and Jack Carr Esq in the opposite box. My 'Vestal Virgins' displayed their figures with pride as they held the boxes up and I was very content that they played their parts in the exciting and successful evening!

The new ballroom had a full capacity opening night! There were even a lot of people there who had paid!

I must just digress for a moment, having written that last line. My dad had a sensible, clear idea about 'Free Pier Passes' or 'complimentary tickets'. A lot of Morecambe business men – councillors and suchlike – used the bars on the pier as a kind of rendezvous. They spent a lot of money as well, so my dad felt it was unfair to ask them to pay pier toll (3d). To be quite honest, the free pass holders thought it would be unfair as well – hence, as Dad put it: 'It pays to give them yearly free passes because of what they spend in the bars – summer *and* winter!' And it did!

It sounds a bit silly when I say I had every intention of being 'the first on the new dance floor' – but bear in mind that it was my dad's brainchild – and I *had* helped to polish it! So that was excuse enough.

The usual hubbub of laughing and chattering and excitement filled the atmosphere when Benny Bolton and his band took their positions on the band stand.

Miss Mercy Nelson – better known as 'Merce' – and I stood at the side of the floor, at the ready. So did dozens of other couples, but I record with pride that without cheating or 'jumping the gun' – *we made it!* And we did a nifty foxtrot to 'Oh, Horsey! Keep Your Tail Up!' with victorious abandon!

I was so enthusiastic that, even though 'being first on the new dance floor' had been achieved, when the opposition band struck up for the first time I was 'first on' again.

14

My bosom friends

'Open air dancing at the Pier Head, mornings and afternoons.' That's what it said on the bills.

And that was good fun if you like! It was quite a large dance floor and there was a solid, well constructed band stand – none of your rickety make-shift things – well built to stand there for ever, so one hoped! In fairness, I should say that it had a proper stage and proscenium, wings, backcloth and a couple of dressing rooms.

When my father first went to work on the pier, the pierrots used to perform on there, but when dancing became so popular they were promoted – or demoted – to the big stage in the Pavilion, where they performed until it was decided to change even that into a ballroom.

On the left-hand side of the dance floor was quite a big cafe where you could get ices, mineral waters, afternoon teas – at popular prices – and on the right-hand side was the deck chair house where all the deck chairs slept at night and therefore were kept clean, with no fear of soiling your summer frock! This was another of my Dad's ideas. He said, 'People don't want to pay 3d for a dirty deck chair!'

If the weather was warm and sunny, there would be an evening dancing session, and I used to love that. Coloured lights would be festooned round the dance floor and although it sounds so simple, it really was quite romantic. When my friends and I were about fifteen, we would often 'click' or 'get off' (they were popular expressions in those days) with boys who were on holiday in Morecambe, and a spot of dancing under the coloured lights never did hurt anybody, did it? I think probably the sexiest thing we ever did was to look into each other's eyes over a cup of hot Horlicks – but it was living!

My pals and I rarely let on we were locals – we'd decide beforehand where we were supposed to have come from, but we never told our dancing partners until they told us where *they* came from, just in case we'd decided on their hometown. It was a bit difficult if they asked us to go out during the day-time, but we usually got over that by saying we had made arrangements for the day (indeed we had – we were at work!) and we would meet them on the pier the following night.

My friends were well in, anyway, because I took them on the pier for nothing and we were usually entertained to a Horlicks or a cream soda! Sophistication! Yes sir! That was us – flat chests and the lot!

I could go on for ever about incidents that involved the pier, but I won't although Carnival Week is worth a mention, I think. All right, perhaps we couldn't compete with a continental 'Mardi Gras' but all the same it used to be a great week in our lives, and of course the pier entered into the spirit of carnival one hundred per cent!

When I recall that people walked about in carnival costumes throwing streamers and confetti at each other and blowing 'tommy talkers' it seems as though I have imagined it! But it's a fact!

We always had a sack of confetti at 6, Cheapside, so that we could fill and refill a large bag to take with us as we went out! None of your small twopenny packets – a sack! One year everybody sported the 'Morecambe Carnival Colours' – rock pink and pale blue – lovely ordinary people walked about in an original costume they had enthusiastically 'run up' in pink and blue sateen, which was about 9½d a yard! A carnival song was composed and published and the happy carnival-minded population and visitors sang it lustily. It was a little number that went something like this:

> It's carnival time once more, it's carnival time once
> more.
> Young and old come from near and from far
> To join in the fun and say 'Well, here we are –
> Hey Willie, why, lad it's you – I thought I had seen
> you before!'
> Cheerio! Toodle-oo! It's a right champion do
> It's carnival time once more!

The above may not be word perfect and I apologize if the song-writer is still alive – but I can vouch for all the lyrics except 'Cheerio and Toodle-oo!'

A year or so later, another carnival anthem was born, incorporating an advert for the town, and that one went as follows:

Dear old Morecambe – more come to Morecambe
  by the sea,
There's good fresh air – from Heysham up to Bare,
Jollity everywhere. So, throw away your care
And come to dear old Morecambe
Here's to its prosperity
Folks don't die and that's the reason why
More come to Morecambe by the sea!

What about that, then? Rows of revellers would walk along the promenade, arm in arm, singing away, the illuminations would sparkle from lamp post to lamp post, while the flower beds in the promenade gardens were a mass of twinkling lights! This effect was achieved by placing thousands of night lights in little coloured glass containers. They were replaced and lighted each evening by hordes of volunteers armed with tapers and matches! How they used to pray for a calm evening! It's amazing how people always state the obvious – as you walked along the prom, you would hear this remark dozens of times: 'Oh, look – there's one there gone out!' or 'Oh look! There's one there not in!' Never mind all the others that were twinkling away – it was the ones that had given up the ghost that were noticed the most!

Oh, yes, they were wonderful times, the carnival procession; the ox roasting (and the excitement of watching the brick enclosure, which housed the revolving spit, being built on the previous night, to the ox's cremation); the firework display on the Friday night; the prayer of all the locals, 'I *do* hope it doesn't rain for the firework display!' (It nearly always did!) It was all marvellous, I thought, and I am sincerely grateful for having experienced those times.

Isn't it sad that in this modern age things have become so sophisticated and commercial that the 'Carnival Spirit' and the 'Hail Fellow well met' seems so old fashioned and out of place. May the Lord preserve me from ever trying to 'spout' or appearing to be a 'do-gooder', but when one reads about, or sees on television, the evil vandalization that takes place at a football match and the way the 'rotten sports' of supporters slash the railway carriages for the 'fun' of it, I think I shall stick to my opinion that the hosts of un-sophisticated ordinary people who enjoyed More-cambe Carnival were to be admired! All right – so perhaps they did knock back a few beers but they didn't knock the railway carriage to hell on their way home! And as my mother would have said, 'they weren't hurting anybody!'

15

Watch it!

It was bang in the middle of James Hargreaves', Jewellers, shop window! It was unbelievable! I'd never seen anything like it before! It was so small, yet perfect! It hypnotised me! Just imagine being the proud owner of it! It was only as big as a plum stone! I knew it would be dear.

It was a watch! No, not *a* watch, *the* watch! All this was years ago, I had just entered my 'teens'.

Without any hesitation, I darted into the shop. We knew Mr Hargreaves very well, he was 'our' jeweller. When I say 'our' I don't mean he was a jeweller exclusively on our behalf – I mean he was in the same category as 'our' grocer, 'our' fishmonger, 'our' coalman and 'our' insurance man!

It was a good job he knew me, otherwise he might have taken offence at my first remark.

'That little watch in the middle of the window, Mr Hargreaves, does it go?'

He assured me it did, and enquired with a smile, 'Do you want it?'

Did-I-want-it? At that moment I wanted it more than anything else in the world!

'Oh, *no*!' I answered quickly, thinking he meant did

I wish to buy it. 'No, it's just that, isn't it lovely?'

He was a very nice man and, as I say, he knew our family well.

'Would you like to look at it?' he enquired in a very understanding way. I said, 'Yes, *please*!' before he'd finished his enquiry.

He took it out of the window, and the moment he laid it with reverence on the piece of black velvet on the top of the glass counter, I can remember thinking, 'Fancy anyone *owning* that!'

I'd like to explain something at this point, if I may, and I find it a bit difficult to put into words. I stood there, full of admiration for the watch and although, as I have just told you, I wanted it more than anything in the world, never, for one moment, did I think 'I must have that!' and I wasn't in any way envious of the person who would eventually own it. I know this sounds a bit argumentative, but do you understand what I mean?

In the first place, I *knew* I couldn't have it and in the second place I was getting so much pleasure out of just looking at it that I was quite satisfied to stand there and admire it! Does that all sound a bit daft? If it does, I'm sorry, but that is how I am. It's amazing the pleasure one can derive from just looking at something beautiful, isn't it?

I thanked Mr Hargreaves for having gone to the trouble of disrupting his window, and came out of the shop in a very happy mood and feeling better off for having looked at something which in my opinion was very lovely. I was only thirteen, and, don't forget, a tiny oval watch was a bit unusual in those days.

When I arrived home, I related the incident to my mother, with a few embellishments of course!

From that day forward, part of my daily routine was to go and have a look at that watch in the centre of Hargreaves' window. The shop was on Market Street, one minute from Number Six, Cheapside, and therefore conveniently situated for viewing purposes. The 'peak viewing time' was usually after tea. I'd nip up our street, stand looking in the window, with all its bright lights making everything glitter, and pay homage to *the* watch! It deserved it! The bonny little thing!

There it reclined, centre stage, holding the fort, as you might say. As a matter of fact, I went to pay homage so often that I had almost reached the stage of saying 'Hello' to it, as I arrived faithfully each late afternoon to pay my respects.

I was having my tea one day, and bear in mind, tea in the North is a knife and fork affair, usually something a 'bit tasty', and not cucumber sandwiches and sponge cake. The weather was dreadful, it was blowing a gale and the rain was pelting down. (And that remark was unnecessary, because nobody ever saw the rain pelt UP! Did they?)

I had to go to the post office for some stamps or something, I can't remember, so as soon as I had finished whatever it was I was eating, I put my oilskins and sou'wester on (oh yes, I wore this type of sexy and smart rainwear) and left the house looking like an advert for Skipper Sardines!

As I came out of the post office, which was in Market Street at the top of Cheapside, I thought, I'll just go and have a look at my friend, the watch. I walked along Market Street – correction – I was *blown* along Market Street, but it didn't worry me, we were used to this kind of weather and thought nothing of it. The rain lashed down and by the time I had taken my position at Hargreaves' window I was sopping wet – well, no, *I* wasn't but my oilskins were. The rain was streaming down the plate glass window making it practically opaque, but that didn't matter because as a 'constant viewer' I knew the exact position of the watch. I peered through the rivulets of rain that were racing down the window and – *Tragedy! Panic Stations!* The watch had gone! Without even waiting to think that probably the window had been redressed, I flew into the shop like a rocket!

Mr Hargreaves came out of his little office.

'Hello, Thora,' he said as he moved to behind the counter. 'What a dreadful night, isn't it?'

He could say that again! It certainly *was* a dreadful night for me if *the* watch had disappeared from sight forever!

'Excuse me, Mr Hargreaves, but – er – have you sold that little watch?' I enquired painfully.

I stood there whilst the rain ran off my oilskins and proceeded to make a pool on his very clean shop floor!

'Yes, as a matter of fact, I have – why, did *you* want it?' he replied quite brightly.

By now, the rain that covered my glasses (I've worn specs since I was eleven) was plopping on to my face and dripping off my nose end.

'Oh, no!' I informed him. 'No, it's – er – just that I enjoyed looking at it, that's all!' I added rather lamely.

As I had used the word 'no' twice, and accompanied it with a shake of my head, the rain on my sou'wester had shaken free and added its contribution to the steadily increasing pool round my feet.

'Oh well, that's all right them,' he assured me. 'As a matter of fact, I sold it this morning.'

I stood there, in my own personal pool of rain! So that was that! It had gone!

I was grateful for the remaining rain on my glasses. Even with all those bright lights it was impossible to distinguish tears from raindrops, and with a much too brittle brightness I said, 'Oh well, thank you, Mr Hargreaves – good night!'

Leaving my personal pool of rain on his clean floor to prove I had been there, I retraced my steps and forlornly left the shop, without even a passing glance at the brilliantly lit window.

16

A pinch of cinnamon

The fashionable colour that autumn was cinnamon, and the 'with-it' material was velour cloth embossed with endless curly lines running all over it. Like the wavy lines of a jigsaw puzzle. It sounds awful, doesn't it? But I can assure you, it was very smart, the wavy lines weren't really noticeable until you handled the cloth. One of my best friends had acquired a coat in cinnamon complete with beaver rolled collar. Although by today's standards we were unsophisticated at that age, we were all a little bit fashion conscious and all of us managed to be quite smart. It was usually in the autumn we got our new winter coats (for best!) and the comparing and admiring of each friend's new outfit afforded us quite a lot of pleasure. Here again I go quoting my mother, 'And we weren't hurting anybody!'

At the beginning of October, I had voiced 'my desire' for a cinnamon-coloured coat, with a rolled squirrel fur collar. The coat was to be my Christmas present. We duly ordered it through a shop that we dealt with, therefore the shop came under the heading of *our* Drapers and Outfitters'. Miss Jowett, who was responsible for the ordering was 'as nice a person as you would meet on a day's march'. (And it took years to work out what *that* Northern expression meant!) She assured us that it would arrive in about a month's time.

Owing to the fact that it was 'a special order' we felt that was quite a reasonable period to wait, and in any case, as I had no intention of wearing it before Christmas Day, I was grateful for 'the waiting period' of the delivery, because it meant by the time it arrived at the beginning of November, we should be so much nearer Christmas Day and 'the wearing o' the cinnamon!'

By the end of October I was excited at the thought of the coat with its squirrel collar, and why not? I revelled in the anticipation of folding the wrapover front about me and snuggling into the soft fur as it embraced my throat and neck on Christmas Day. You are probably thinking, 'Why wait until Christmas Day?' Well, you see, it was to be a *Christmas present*, so, of course, I couldn't dream of wearing it until – the day! Yes, I would quite enjoy waiting to put it on, I'd be able to *look* at it, wouldn't I? The lovely warm cinnamon colour on a dull day, the pale grey of the squirrel collar – I'd be able to blow gently on the soft fur and it would be reminiscent of a miniature field of grain in the wind. There's no doubt, it would all be worth waiting for! Oh, to be thirteen! Wonderful! Events impress you so deeply when you are thirteen!

The coat hadn't arrived by the end of the first week in November, but who was worrying? Plenty of time yet before Christmas!

By the end of the second week, I was calling at Miss Jowett's daily – no coat! From then on I almost lived at

Miss Jowett's. It was no fault of hers that it hadn't arrived, in fact, by the first week in December, she had written so many letters to the firm who were supplying the coat that she nearly had writer's cramp!

Second week in December – no coat. One evening I even went down to Euston Road Station (now defunct) and enquired at the Parcels Office if a large parcel had got pushed behind something and been forgotten – still no coat.

On December 23rd, Miss Jowett received a very apologetic letter from the firm in Manchester, informing her that due to the extensive orders for cinnamon-coloured velour cloth with wiggly lines on, they regretted they would be unable to execute the order until early March. They also assured her of their *prompt* attention at all times!

Early March! Early Blooming March! That was next year! Early March, well they could stick it, that's what they could do, and their prompt attention with it! Oh God! Was life always going to be full of tragedies? It was just one disaster after another. Mr Hargreaves had sold the watch, and Miss Jowett couldn't get the coat!

17

The velvet hand in the bright red glove

'Never mind, love, don't be too disappointed, we'll go up to the West End (in Morecambe, not London) tomorrow, and see if there's a coat like you want in one of the shops!' My loving mother tried to comfort me with these words. It was Christmas Eve.

Now just hang on a minute, will you? Before I go any further, I am going to admit, here and now, that I am ashamed to write the next few paragraphs. What I mean is – I am ashamed of my attitude and behaviour on that never-to-be-forgotten Christmas Eve. My dear patient mother should either have 'given me a fourpenny one' or taken my pants down and tanned my behind in the middle of Regent Road. She *didn't* – but she should have done!

Get the picture, if you will, please. It was pouring down in bucketfuls – the wind was howling and blowing from the sea, it was cold and ready to snow any minute. Well, that's a good backing for a drama anyway. We pushed our way along the promenade, leaning against the wind, we couldn't talk much because the wind almost took our breath. After we had been in about four shops we practically gave up hope of my appearing on Christmas Day in a cinnamon velour cloth coat!

All the assistants knew us and assured us they could order a coat for me for the New Year, but that's not the point, is it? If for weeks you have dreamed of wearing said coat on Christmas Day?

During our entering and leaving shops, my mother was in full sympathy with me and although, as I have admitted, I was ashamed of my behaviour, I don't mean I was cheeky or rude to anyone, I mean that I kept on 'moaning'. Moan, moan, moan, 'Oh, I did want it for Christmas Day!' 'Oh, I wish Miss Jowett could have got one!' 'Why couldn't the firm in Manchester have let us know earlier' – all that sort of thing. 'Niggling', non-stop! Never once did my patient mother reprimand me. We exhausted all the shops in Regent Road and after catching a bus to the Central we got off at Euston Road and made our wet and weary way to Queen's Street.

Even the brightly dressed Christmas display windows failed to cheer me up.

Edgar Bell, Gents' Outfitters, was situated a little way down on the right. The window was dressed in a Christmassy way, quietly, because it was what we call in Lancashire 'a classy shop'. The gents' ties bore small, holly-decorated tickets informing the world at large that they were 'A Suitable Gift!' The tickets on the shirts were 'Wishing you a Merry Christmas!' and the tickets on the pyjamas were appropriately decorated with mistletoe and proclaimed that they were 'A Seasonable Gift!' which struck me, because of the mood I was in, as though Christmas was the only time men wore pyjamas!

One side of the window displayed ladies' gloves.

131

They draped themselves in a ladylike way, one hand placed delicately over the other and instructing you in the fact that they were 'Real Nappa'. I was standing there in the rain and wind thinking that when gloves are displayed in that way it looks as though there should be a pair of legs underneath them, one leg crossed over the other and the hands of the gloves crossed and resting on the knee, when my mother asked, 'Do you like those?' As she asked me this she was pointing to a pair of ladies' *red* gloves! *Red!* Are you listening? Quite honestly, I had never seen a pair of coloured leather gloves before. I'd seen coloured leather gloves in Costume plays in the theatre and I'd seen them in the Opera Company on the pier, but never had I seen coloured leather gloves for ordinary outdoor wear.

The gloves in the window were a lovely holly berry red, beautifully made. One glove had the wrist part turned back to prove to all and sundry that they were lined in wool knitted in a Fair Isle pattern! I couldn't believe it! They must have been the first pair of coloured leather gloves in Morecambe.

'Those are unusual, aren't they? Would you like them?' I heard my mother ask. 'They would help to take away a bit of the disappointment over your coat!' she added.

Would I? I would! We went into the shop, Mr Bell took them out of the window and I tried them on. *They fitted!* I felt like Cinderella at the end of the pantomime when she tries on the glass slipper and the entire company shouts, 'It fits – it fits!'

How marvellous! Oh, how lovely they were! Oh, what

a wonderful mother mine was! Oh, how happy a time Christmas is! Oh, how lovely all the world is! (You'll gather I was rather pleased!) Wishing Mr Bell a Merry Christmas we came out of the shop – my mother walked, I floated. Did I say it was pouring down and blowing a gale? *I* didn't notice it! *Red gloves!* Bluddy 'ell!

Christmas Eve was always magic at 6 Cheapside. The door was open for anyone to pop in and be wished a Merry Christmas whilst they drank a glass of you-name-it-we-had-it!

Jobs were done during the evening before to lighten the burdens of Christmas Day. The vegetables for dinner were washed and prepared, sage and onion stuffing and apple sauce was made, six dozen mince pies were baked, fresh fruit was arranged artistically in a rustic basket and decorated with sprigs of holly, dishes of nuts and raisins and boxes of dates and figs, Turkish delight and crystallized fruits were allowed on top of the piano, and a large fruit dish was ready to receive the contents of the box of tangerines and the fresh pineapple that Dad used to bring home along with twelve new gramophone records every Christmas Eve, without fail!

The 'Royal Standback' fire would be blazing brightly and the emery-papered and blackleaded grate reflected the flames as its contribution to the warm welcome extended at Number 6. The aroma of mince-meat, pastry, apple sauce, etc., from the back kitchen was mouthwatering. Add to all this the smell of ever-greens arranged behind each picture above the big old clock on the wall and along the mantelpiece, and the slight whiffs of alcohol and cigars as different friends popped in and lifted their elbows to wish you 'all you wished yourselves' and the only word you have to describe our living-kitchen on these occasions is *Magic!*

18

'Hail, Smiling Morn'

Well, back to the 'Cinnamon coat replaced by the Red Gloves Christmas!' I was telling you about.

On Christmas morn, we were awakened as usual by the Salvation Army Band, who were standing in the middle of the road in Cheapside and musically demanding that 'Christians Awake! Salute this Happy Morn!'

Whether we were Christians or not we awoke, and as Cheapside was such a happy street, we saluted the happy morn without any trouble. The band always arrived fairly early, invariably catching the Christians *out* by catching them *in* – bed! The Salvationist who carried the wooden collecting box would knock on each door. Bedroom windows would be pushed up and offerings were thrown down.

Mind you, lots of the Cheapsiders were up and about, in which case they would come and stand at their front doors and enjoy the seasonable carols and hymns. When your own personal knock sounded on your front door, it was really the beginning of your Christmas Day! I was NCOIC of carrying coins to box and wishing the Salvation Soldier a Merry Christmas! About half an hour after the Salvation Army had gone the Morecambe Borough Band arrived to play. Their opening number was usually 'While Shepherds Watched Their Flocks By Night', and then there was the same ritual as previously, only there weren't as many bedroom windows opened because most of the people in the street were up and about by the time 'The Boro' started to perform.

On the particular Christmas morning I am telling you about, by the time the Sally Army had gone I had begun to open my presents.

It was a lovely old-fashioned custom of ours always to hang up a stocking – we usually borrowed one each from my mother. Small-sized gifts were put in the stocking and larger-sized gifts were laid at the foot of our beds. In the stocking, without fail, there was always an apple, an orange, some nuts and a new penny, which all helped to fill the foot part. In my case there was always a tablet or tablets of scented soap – glycerine and cucumber for preference! The annual Christmas joke and always a 'sure laugh' was when our father unpacked his stocking and feigned surprise when, after pretending to expect an apple and an orange etc., he discovered an onion, a potato and a carrot! Big laugh that! Poor old Dad!

I started to empty my stocking – handkerchiefs, a little manicure set – I say a *manicure* set, it comprised a small piece of sandpaper stuck on cardboard, a piece of red wax nail polish the shape of a lipstick and a small buffer, all of these being in a miniature red oilcloth envelope-type case that fastened with a red-domed press stud. I thought it was lovely! And it *was*! It was from one of my best friends and it had cost her tenpence.

There was a little bottle of 'Sweet Pea' scent (just what I wanted – honestly), a box of miniature Christmas Crackers made of gold paper, and the little label on the box they were in assured me that each cracker contained a gift, a paper hat and a motto – smashing!

Next out of the bran tub was a packet of sugared almonds, after which came the orange, the apple, the nuts and the new penny.

In the toe of the stocking and extending about a third of the foot was an oblong packet the size of a glycerine and cucumber tablet of soap. But as I drew the box out into view I saw it was a little white jeweller's box. I was quite excited wondering what could be in it, and pressed the little catch on the front of the box and opened it.

I gasped – I couldn't believe it – it was lying on a white velvet pad – it was looking up at me! It was the watch! I was holding it in its bed of velvet – in my hand! THE WATCH!

I literally flew into my parents' bedroom and flung myself on my mother, who was still in bed. I was trying to say, and not doing it very coherently, because I was crying with joy – and *shame* – I was trying to say, 'Thank you and I couldn't believe it was mine and I was sorry I had moaned last night about the coat and she shouldn't have because she'd bought me the red gloves and –' . . . once again I was nearly breaking her neck as I smothered her with kisses and tears.

She kissed me in return and then gave me her handkerchief from under her pillow. As I wiped my eyes and blew my nose she said, 'I nearly told you about the watch a dozen times last night, when we weren't able to get you the coat, but I didn't want to spoil my own pleasure of seeing your face this morning!'

I put the watch on to convince myself it was mine and after 'showing it everybody' (my mother, my father and Nev) I took the little box back into my room. In my excitement I had not noticed a visiting card of my mother's that must have fluttered down on to my bed. I picked it up, saw what it was and turned it over. On the back was written: 'Just to fulfil one desire, I wish I could fulfil them all! Mother.'

Out in Cheapside the Boro' Band were playing 'How Beautiful Upon the Mountain', double forte.

It's understandable that as soon as the shops opened again after their Christmas holidays, I went in to see Mr Hargreaves. He told me that on the morning of the day I had stood in a pool of rain in his shop and he had broken the news to me that the watch was sold, my mother had gone in to ask him to put the watch 'on one side' and had left a deposit on it. Apparently, when my mother had 'made someone up' for a Fancy Dress Ball for which she would never charge, quite often out of gratitude, people would insist she should 'have a drink or some chocolates' and had left two shillings or half-a-crown. Every time, she had put the money away, and then taken it to the jewellers towards the watch. She added the balance when Christmas came.

I shall always remember Jim Hargreaves' face as he told me how my mother had saved for it, just as I shall always remember something he said, 'So treasure that watch, Thora, your mother denied herself a lot of things so that you could have it!'

I *have* treasured it, Mr Hargreaves, I promise you. A few years ago I did a television show called 'The Magic Box'. The idea of the programme was, if you had a magic box, what would you keep in it and why? I told Margery Baker, the Director, about the little watch and said I would like to keep it in my magic box and bring it out and look at it if ever I felt like 'moaning' or 'niggling' because it had really taught me a lesson when I was young. She's a very imaginative director and an understanding one, and agreed immediately that I should use the 'watch story'. I did. As I held it up (it was given a 'full frame to itself') I said to Kenneth Robinson who was interviewing me: 'Of course, it doesn't look very small compared with today's little watches', and I showed him the watch I was wearing, which has a dial no bigger than a piece of confetti. We laughed because I have to take my glasses off to see the time by it! Scottie gave me the tiny watch on my opening night at the London Palladium. I also told Kenneth, 'Of course, this treasure my mother saved up to buy me doesn't "go" any more, but I wouldn't part with it for anything.'

The following week I received a most charming letter from a jeweller in Dumfries. He said he had seen the 'Magic Box' programme and would I trust him with the watch because he felt sure he could do something with it. He did, too, bless him. He returned it to me, all clean and bright, in full working order, and apologized that he had been unable to replace the black moire silk strap and would I suffer a black nylon one. This was all done with his compliments.

Aren't there some nice people in the world? And aren't I lucky, because I'm always coming across them? I wore the watch for my BBC television series *The First Lady* – I felt the title of the series fitted my mother.

19

Now being played

You will recall I returned to school after I was supposed to have left. Right! Well my return visit only lasted two and a half weeks because, one morning, much to my surprise, my father called at the school and after a short conversation at the school door with Miss Nelson, I was brought out of the class to join them.

Apparently, Arthur Hickman-Smith who ran the music shop on the Central Pier required an assistant for the season and had asked my father if I would be interested. I was *very* interested! Miss Nelson agreed this would be 'a very nice kind of occupation' and when my dad asked her if it would be convenient for me to go along with him then, she said 'certainly' and added her blessing!

I went to the cloakroom to collect my coat and it dawned on me that I was leaving school for the second time in a few weeks, but this time I didn't mind.

'Hicky' Smith was a friend of my father's of many years' standing. I could not have wished to work for a kinder or more thoughtful employer – he was a dear man.

My duties were simple, when I say I worked at 'The Music Shop' that is precisely what it was – a shop that sold music. You'll appreciate that when I was fourteen, people on holiday always bought copies of popular songs, they were sixpence! It was quite an advantage having a jazz band playing on the outdoor bandstand on the pier too, because they would play all the up-to-the-minute numbers and in turn we would sell the music in the shop, which was situated on the side of the Pavilion that was about twenty or thirty yards from the Open-Air Dance Floor! Couldn't be better, you see!

During the band interval we made hay while the sun shone. There was an upright piano practically in the shop doorway and on the top of the piano was a little easel, just big enough to display a copy of music. I would play the popular number on the piano and as I did so Hicky Smith, in his splendid voice would announce to the crowd of holiday makers, 'This week's popular number now being played! Sixpence a copy!'

After I had played a couple of choruses, I would get off the piano stool like lightning and help 'to wrap'. It was great fun, really, and I loved it.

There is only one thing about that period I didn't love. I was developing a bust! Now just hold on a minute, before you say 'And what's wrong with that?'

I agree there is nothing wrong with that and indeed I would hate to be without half an inch of my present day thirty eight inches! *BUT*, when I was on my way to fifteen years old we were going through the flat-chested period! The dress fashion was on the tubular lines, the length was above the knee and as I was fashion conscious, I was wondering what the heck I could do with my bust. I'm laughing whilst I'm writing this because I've made it sound as though I was the owner of a forty-two inch bust! Not at all – it was only about thirty inches, but it was big enough to *show* I had one! Or two!

One morning, I had put on a favourite dress; it was pale mushroom coloured fine woollen stockinette. Well, every woman reading this knows how stockinette *clings*! I looked at myself in the mirror and thought, 'Oh crumbs it's all sticking out worse than ever!' Not to be beaten, I slipped the dress off and tied a piece of ribbon round my womanly assets, pulling the points of my feminine trademark flat! 'Good, that would do it,' I thought. I nipped back into my dress and set off for the Music Shop, flat chested and full of confidence.

Perhaps it was playing the piano, perhaps it was rolling the copies of music up, perhaps it was the heat, I don't know, and I never will know. It wasn't until I saw a customer giving me a rather quizzical look that I took a quick look at myself in the shop mirror. The ribbon must have rolled in to the width of a piece of string because to my horror and embarassment the reflection revealed that I had not only two breasts, but four! I looked like that advert for Michelin Tyres!

Bust or not, I enjoyed every second of that musical, double breasted summer season!

When 'The Music Shop' closed at the end of the season and I was 'at liberty' as you might say, I didn't waste my time.

I attended night school four nights a week during the winter. The subjects I decided on were Monday, French and cookery – Tuesday, book keeping and accounts and English Grammar – Wednesday, shorthand and

Thursday, typing. You'll gather I had decided to accumulate a little knowledge that might assist me to get a job if I didn't enter the precarious business called 'The Theatrical Profession!'

But wait . . . during that period between finishing in the Music Shop and going to work in my dad's office the following season, I entered into a very precarious bit of business. And all because of a pair of shoes. I must have wanted my brains washing!

20

A life on the instantaneous wave, or, It's enough to make your hair curl!

> I grumbled when I had no shoes
> Until I met a man who had no feet

Isn't that a wonderful saying to read daily? We have it framed and cannot avoid seeing it as we approach our front door. I wouldn't *want* to avoid it – I think it's a great mind jogger!

This episode is about shoes. They were in the middle of 'Tyler's' window, real patent leather in black – no toe caps – tie-ups – a little heel – *and* – (this was the detail that took my eye) narrow black ribbon instead of laces.

Fourteen shillings and elevenpence they were. Oh, there was no doubt about it, they lived up to Tyler's slogan – *North, South, East or West – Tyler's Boots Are The Best!* Suddenly I knew, they were the only pair of shoes in the world for me! Bear in mind I wasn't yet fifteen!

I've always had a lot of imagination and I've always got a lot of pleasure out of life by imagining and anticipating things. There I stood and, as I looked at the shoes, I was imagining them on my feet the following Sunday. I was also anticipating how, each time I took them off, I would faithfully stuff newspaper into the toes and rub them with Vaseline so that they wouldn't crack across the instep – yes, I would certainly have to put Vaseline on them, especially as they had no toe caps. Thinking back, this Vaseline procedure was a lot of old codswallop, because patent shoes *always* crack where your foot finishes and your toes start! But never mind that – they were lovely, fourteen and eleven-pence! Dirt cheap really! Well, no, they were quite expensive to tell the truth and the sad thing was, I didn't really need them.

I debated with myself whether to tell my mother about the shoes, but bearing in mind that I'd left school (for the second time!) and I wasn't earning anything at that moment, I didn't! It was no great shakes to forget them – it didn't bother me! Much!

Anyway, in a few months the summer would be with us, so I would be wearing sandshoes a lot of the time. Sandshoes or ropesoles, which, of course, are referred to as Espadrilles nowadays, were our usual footwear during the summer. They were in natural, or, to be more precise, oatmeal coloured canvas, with a good thick plaited ropesole. They tied on with a piece of white tape which threaded through the front and then through two holes in the sides. They cost the large amount of fourpence! We would wear them until the soles looked like Grandad's Whiskers and then throw them away and get another four pennyworth!

It's a joke when one thinks of the price of a pair these days, isn't it? Of course, nowadays they are made in every colour under the sun and perhaps dye is expensive.

However, 'the real patent leather jokers' were to

remind me of their existence within a week of the day I had knelt in worship 'at their feet'. It was thus.

On the following Wednesday I saw an advert in our local paper, which goes under the splendid title of *The Visitor* (good name for a holiday resort paper, isn't it?). The advert informed me: 'Girl required to assist at stall at Trades Exhibition, Winter Gardens, *must have long hair*. Apply – stall 47, Wednesday, twelve noon.'

Very interesting! I had a plait of auburn hair to my waist – I was 'at liberty' at the moment, and the real patent shoes were in Tyler's window! I might just stroll along there about twelve o'clock – no harm done. And as my mother would have said, 'I wasn't hurting anybody!' Well, it would be more to the point if I said, 'I didn't *intend* to hurt anybody!'

When I arrived at the Winter Gardens I thought there was a fire or an accident, there were so many women round the stall, but I soon discovered they were all applicants for the job! I stood at the back of the crowd. I couldn't *see* anything because everybody was taller than me.

Have you ever noticed that if you 'stand still' in a crowd and you don't push or 'shuv' you automatically and magically move? I did – I suddenly discovered I was in a position to peep through a four inch slit between two bodies! I listened and discovered the stall was for demonstrating and selling 'haircurlers' – the stall wasn't 'in business' at that moment, of course, but would be later in the day.

The gentleman who had requested us to be at the Winter Gardens complete with our long hair, at twelve noon, was explaining why we had been invited. He wore a white overall, but a white overall with a difference – well, I'd never seen one like it before. It had a polo neck and buttoned down the side, I remember thinking as I looked at 'our host's' overall, 'Oh, yes, very smart.' It impressed me very much.

The would-be employer was talking in a cockney voice explaining what the job involved. Suddenly he pointed and called out,

'Hey! You – you, the young lady with the glasses on!'

Well, I'm only five feet one inch tall *now* so you'll appreciate I wasn't very tall then! I didn't think for one moment that he was pointing to me, so I just stood there. When nobody moved, I turned round to see who it was he was pointing to – and found I had been pushed to the back row again and there was nobody behind me!

'You – you at the back there! Come along, come forward please!' I realized it *was* me he was referring to, so with a few 'excuse me please-es' I joined him.

He invited me to sit on a stool – which I did. He asked me to undo my plait – which I did. Although I had left school (for the second time, you'll remember), I still wore my panama school hat, minus the school badge, because, to tell you the truth I rather felt it suited me! I often wore my gymslip with a white crêpe-de-chine blouse as well, for the same reason. When I had removed my panama school hat, 'my auburn tresses covered my shoulders like a cape' (writers always used that description about the heroine's hair, in magazines), but he broke the spell by starting to look through my hair with a comb! How dare he! The indignity of it!

I whipped round on the stool – as a matter of fact, I whipped round so quickly I nearly fell on to the floor (this got a laugh of course). Anyway, firmly back on the stool, I demanded 'Excuse me, but what are you doing? I've nothing in MY head!'

This expression was one we used at school when referring to our unfortunate play mates whose mothers didn't use a 'small tooth comb' as often as they should, and we would remark in the 'charitable' way kids have, 'oo-heck . . she's got things in her head!' I was furious! He ignored my remark and like lightning enquired, 'Can you go 'ome, wash your 'air and be back here by 2.30?' Like lightning I replied, 'I can be back here at 1.30 if I've got the job!' There was no impudence in the way I said this, it was just a statement of fact, and I was a bit on the defensive because he'd dared to look through my hair.

'You've got it!' he stated. 'Fifteen shillings for the four days, afternoons and evenings!'

Fifteen bob! FIFTEEN BOB! And the real patent leather shoes were fourteen and elevenpence!

I quickly plaited my hair, banged my panama hat on and shot out of the Winter Gardens like a dose of salts!

I ran all the way along Northumberland Street – whizzed round De Lacy's Corner and along Victoria Street, crossed Market Street and pelted down Cheapside at the rate of knots!

I was home, putting the kettle on for some hot water to wash my hair, when it suddenly dawned on me – my mother and father would 'go mad' if they knew what I had taken on!

Try to understand, there wasn't an atom of snobbery

in either of my parents (thank God!) but what they lacked in snobbery they made up for in pride! I *knew* – and I freely admit this – I knew that they would not approve of my taking on a job of this sort, and quite honestly, I didn't know myself why I had! Just as I didn't know why I didn't tell them about it – perhaps the real patent leather shoes had something to do with it, perhaps I wanted to show my independence. Anyway, I didn't tell them.

After all, they had 'made me' between them so I suppose each of them had inbred a chunk of pride in me! I vividly remember thinking that I would be able to buy and pay for the shoes myself, without bothering them. At least, I comforted myself with that thought and it eased my conscience a bit!

By the time the water in the kettle was boiling I had decided to 'go it alone!' (That's what Pearl White would have done!) I was running some cold water into the enamel bowl in the kitchen sink when my mother came into the kitchen.

'What are you doing, love?' she asked

'I thought I would just wash my hair,' I replied in a nonchalant manner. I was grateful for the steam that rose from the boiling water as I added it to the cold water in the enamel bowl, it covered the guilty expression on my face a bit! 'Wash your hair – at dinnertime – on a Wednesday?' my mother said, as though she couldn't believe it.

May I explain why washing my hair at dinner-time on a Wednesday seemed such an unusual occurrence? It was because I always washed my hair on a Friday night with carbolic soap and a pinch of borax in the final rinsing water to make it shine – so why the heck was I washing it on a Wednesday, at dinner-time? Cripes! What would Pearl have done?

'Well, I thought as it is such a lovely day I would dry it in the sun, in the back yard!' I explained feebly.

Isn't it amazing how the romance goes out of anything if you use the word 'back yard', 'back street' or 'wash house'? However, my explanation appeared to be accepted (which made me feel more guilty than ever!), and a very worried 'Thora the Cheapside Mermaid' sat in the back yard in the sun amid the aroma of carbolic soap – 'codgertating! (And they can't touch you for it!)', as Ken Dodd would say!

When my 'cape of hair' was passably dry, I went indoors and started to plait it. There's an advantage about a single plait – it's difficult to see whether the hair is perfectly dry or not.

I guzzled my lunch, pretending I wasn't doing so at all – and gazing at the big kitchen clock, I saw it was by now 2 o'clock. Great, I had time to have some apple pie and custard, which I did. Well done – if I ran I could easily be at the Winter Gardens with ten minutes to spare. I did and I was.

His nibs was there, preparing the stall and arranging pyramids of little oblong pink boxes, which, I discovered later, housed three curlers each. On the demonstration table was a small appliance, the sort of thing hairdressers used to push curling tongs into to heat them, and a couple of tortoiseshell combs. However, it was none of the aforementioned that my eyes had riveted themselves on – it was a wig block and wig.

I say wig, for want of a better word. It was pathetic –

there's really no other way of describing it. There were a few tufts of hair, dead straight, gallantly holding on to the wig lace, and, as wig blocks in those days were usually made of wood and not at all like the polystyrene five-bob jobs one can buy today complete with a face, you can imagine the picture. I'm glad really that it hadn't a face because if it had had one I would have imagined it saying, 'Don't blame me – *you* try having your hair curled day after day, year after year, with those damned curlers!'

There was another small surprise for me. A young lady was there who had also been engaged by 'his nibs'. She was much older than fourteen and informed me that she was receiving the princely wage of thirty bob! Oh, so that was the way things went, was it? All right then, a bit of competition never hurt anyone (said Pearl White in an undertone).

We were both given an overall to wear, and don't think for one moment that 'Pearl slipped the overall on and it fitted her perfectly.' Honest to God, I think the one 'his nibs' handed to me had been made for a woman six feet tall and sixteen stone in weight. Never mind the wig and block looking pathetic – I looked tragic or barmy – both, I should think.

However, as there wasn't another overall available and the other woman looked as though hers had been made for her, there was nothing for me to do but roll up my sleeves, which I did. Then I took off my gym slip girdle, which was navy blue plaited cotton, put it outside the overall and took the overall in to my own waist size. The overall result (that's not meant as a pun) was disastrous! I looked rather as though I was entering a carnival competition with the massive rolls of sleeves round my little biceps, my little waist and then a sort of white starched crinoline effect. Never mind, in for a penny, in for fifteen bob! My instructions were to loosen my plait and sit on the stool. His nibs would do the 'spiel' and demonstration, using my 'auburn cape of hair' instead of the wig block.

All right then, and why not? The shoes in Tyler's *were* 'real patent leather'.

The doors of the Hall opened and in came the public. Quite a few people approached the stall – well, they had no choice really – because we were in the middle of a long row of stalls running down right of the Hall, opposite the entrance.

Quick as a flash his nibs started the spiel.

'Now just a moment, ladies, this instrument is known (he was holding a curler in the air with great pride) as the Ideal Instantaneous Hairwaver, and with it I guarantee to give you as good a wave in two minutes as any hairdresser will give you all day.' He took a breath here.

'All you have to do is take a piece of hair' – at this point he took a strand of my hair, running his comb point along the crown of my bonce – 'as you will observe, the Ideal Instantaneous Hairwaver is comprised of a small hollow tube, a small double-ended pin and a clip which embraces the tube and holds the waver firmly in place.' Another breath. 'All you have to do is to place the tube as near the head as you can reasonably get it and wind the hair round in the same manner as I am doing, and I ask you to notice there is no trickery in the winding!'

152

No trickery! Perhaps not, but blimey, he had wound my hair so tightly round the little tube that I thought it was coming out by the roots!

'Now, here we have the small double-ended iron or pin which I shall place in this heating contraption on the table – kindly lent to me by the Morecambe Gas Company who are exhibiting at Stall 93 on the balcony. Place the pin in the heater and when you think it is sufficiently heated place the pin into the tube – you cannot injure or harm the hair in any way.' Another breath.

'Leave the curler to do its work for two minutes only.' (Dramatic look).

Now at this point, he really started to act and informed the interested onlookers, 'With a Hine's waver or curler, what do you do? You sleep in them or you walk about in them all day – but with an Ideal Instantaneous Hairwaver you can be invited to a Ball or Banquet . . .'

This made me laugh – Ball or Banquet in Morecambe! – and he caught me a quick flick on my head with his hand, without even looking my way!

'Yes, ladies – invited to a Ball or Banquet and within ten minutes your hair can look as I am about to show you in a few minutes.'

In a few minutes? He'd just told them *two* minutes and anyway the tube was burning my scalp! I put my hand up to my head, to sort of ease what felt like a red hot metal tube from my scalp – and, quick as a flash, another quick flick of his hand, this time on my fingers and a hissed, 'keep your 'ands down.' Just for a second, but only a second, I felt the tears sting my eyes and I remember thinking, all in the same second, 'Oh I wish I was at home – my mother doesn't flick me across the head like that!' He then repeated the waver procedure and put two more curlers or wavers in. By now he was explaining to the crowd that 'I shall now take out the waver and show you the breathtaking result – release the clasp – remove the tube – and allow the hair to be free.'

He took out the Instantaneous Hairwaver then carelessly cast it on to the table and it just caught the side of the wig block where its face would have been had it had one, and I suddenly felt so sorry for it – it really looked sad with its awful bits of hair. In fact I became devoted to it there and then. We had something in common – His Nibs had flicked me twice, and had thrown a curler at 'poor old wiggy!' Never mind, the shoes were real patent leather. Oh God, off he was going again, 'I shall now run my comb through this piece of waved hair' (he did) with great experience and then with a sort of sigh of incredulity, he breathed, 'A more symmetrical or more even wave – is it possible? Now, if you go to your hairdresser's for a Marcel wave he will charge you at least 1s 6d, but the Ideal Instantaneous Hairwaver is *not* 1s 6d, ladies. This week, as a special Exhibition Concession, we are offering you not *one* waver, not *two* wavers *but three* in the small pink box for – 1/-! Now, who will be the first – we have only a limited supply.'

Talk about a rush! Purses were being opened at express speed, and pockets were being fumbled around for shillings. His nibs and the young lady in an overall that fitted her were passing the pink boxes across the front of the stall like hot soup to the starving. Success – for his nibs. Meanwhile I sat there on my little stool looking like God-knows-what in my comic overall, my hair hanging limp over my shoulders, with the exception of one thin strand that was waved and the two remaining curlers. I was too disheartened to think of 'the auburn tresses like a cape' bit. I looked at my friend – 'old wiggy' and I'm damned sure it said, 'See what I mean?'

Closing time – thank heavens – and after what seemed thousands of demonstrations, it was time to go home. Actually his nibs was quite grateful for the way we had assisted him to have a very good day financially, and as I got to know him better he turned out to be quite a decent sort. The fact that he had flicked me was, I suppose, because I had rather let him down as regards the 'cannot injure or harm the hair in any way' bit by putting my hand up to the hot curler precisely as he said that. All the same I had a little blister on my scalp to prove that the blooming Instantaneous Hairwaver had instantaneously burnt me!

Now, if I was a clever writer, I would be able to give a credible description as to how I looked when I left the Trades Exhibition. *Please* try to visualize the picture. His nibs had given demonstration after demonstration and as each demonstration required a strand of my 'auburn cape' to be wrapped round the tube of the waver – you can imagine by knocking-off time I looked like a Fiji Islander or a modern 'frizzed out' hippie. I couldn't plait my hair and I couldn't get my hat on!

As I left the Winter Gardens, I really felt guilty, not only guilty but embarrassed, and I knew if I walked into our house, looking as I did, it might frighten my mother to death.

I ambled home with my hands behind my head, rather as though I was lounging on the beach – only standing up to do it instead of lying down. I had a lot of school friends who lived quite near, and it dawned on me that I might pay one of them a social call. I did. Talk about 'the devil looks after his own' – my friend herself answered the door and, after nearly jumping through the ceiling of their vestibule at the sight of me, she burst out laughing and couldn't stop!

I endured that – I deserved it! As she wiped her eyes with the back of her hand, she tittered, 'Aye, Hirdie, what have you done to your hair?'

'Can I come in a minute?' I asked.

As we walked into their kitchen she was still laughing as she said, 'Me mother's gone out – ee, I wish she could have seen you!'

Well *I* didn't wish her mother could have seen me! I then gave birth to an idea – I would take my friend into my confidence. I told all.

'Oo, heck, what will your mother and father say?' she asked.

'They won't say anything if they *don't know, will they*?' I said with firmness. 'And they won't know if *you don't tell them – will they*?' I added.

She thought it was great fun, the two of us 'having a secret', so she showed no surprise when I said, 'Can I wash my hair to take this frizz out and dry it in front of your fire?' She said I could . . . so for the second time that day I washed my hair, half dried it, plaited it, pulled my panama hat on. I thanked her profusely and set off home.

'Is that you, Thora?' my mother called out as I

entered our open front door. 'Yes, it's me, Mam!' I answered.

'Wherever have you been 'til now – I was getting quite worried,' she said as I entered the kitchen.

Now I would have defied anyone – *anyone* – to lie to my mother if they were looking into her eyes. I could never lie to her – in any case, I never wanted to or needed to – but I didn't want to tell her about my fifteen bob job – yet!

Quite truthfully, I answered, 'I've just *come from* Dolly's!' This was true, and although I hadn't answered her as to where I'd been I had told her where I'd come from.

'Oh, well that's all right then, love – would you like a cup of cocoa?'

Would I like a cup of cocoa? And I hadn't really told her where I'd been – I could have cried. I was rotten, that's what I was, *rotten*! I'd been sitting on that stool, in a stall, at a Trades Exhibition. I'd called at a friend's and washed the frizz out of my hair and she, my lovely wonderful mother, knew none of this and was mixing a teaspoonful of Bournville Cocoa with some sugar and a drop of milk (so it would form a paste) to which she would add the hot milk – for *me*! *Rotten*, secretive old Thora!

As I went up the 'fourteen treads' to bed, I really was very unhappy. I had my own room by now and as I undressed and put on my (get this bit) crêpe-de-chine nightdress, I thought, 'How am I going to be able to go to the Trades Exhibition tomorrow without telling them?'

When I was in bed, my mother came in the room to

'kiss me good night and God Bless' – she always did this – until she was bedridden, and then we always kissed her good night and God Bless.

As she bent down to kiss me, I threw my arms round her neck and nearly strangeld her. 'Oooo, I *do* love you!' I said.

'Yes – I know you do,' she said, 'and I love *you!*'

When she had gone downstairs, I lay there thinking for a time – but I was so tired I could hardly keep my eyes open. I remember, though, I wasn't too tired to decide that the deceitful life I was living wasn't worth a pair of real patent leather shoes! It's funny how out of proportion things could look when you are young.

When I was having my lunch the following day, my mother asked me, 'And what are you going to do this afternoon?' It was asked very pleasantly.

'Can I go to the Trades Exhibition?' I asked, and added, 'If you don't mind.'

'Yes – if you want to, love,' and that was that. 'Don't worry, I'll have a cup of tea there,' I said, and went.

When I arrived at the stall I immediately felt there was 'something up'. His nibs was building the pyramids of pink boxes and the 30/- assistant was putting her well fitting overall on.

'Good afternoon,' I said.

'Oh, good afternoon, Thora,' he replied. Well I say he *replied* – he *croaked*!

'Am I in a mess?' he went on. 'That this should happen to me and such marvellous business – my bladdy (he pronounced bloody, "bladdy") voice has gone!'

'Oh, what a shame!' I said, well, I couldn't think of anything else to say that sounded comforting.

'I don't know *what* I'm going to do!' he said, in a croaking whisper – he paused, contemplated the pyramids – he looked so sad – I really did feel sorry for him and I suddenly heard myself saying, 'Don't worry, Mr P. *I* know the patter!' He spun round and looked at me as though I had told him he'd won the pools, 'Do you? – d'you think you could manage it with the block?' he croaked.

'Well – er – I could try!' I said shakily.

Work – with – the – block! What was wrong with Miss Well-fitting-overall sitting on the stool and me demonstrating on *her*?

However, that was *out* because she was required to pass the merchanise over for the shillings – so poor old 'wiggy' and I had to attempt to 'go it' alone. What a double act! Me in my comedy overall outfit and poor 'old wiggy' looking as though he had 'the mange'.

Now, if you're not born beautiful, I am convinced God gives you other assets as compensation. One of the assets he kindly bestowed on me is a photographic memory in conjunction with an ear memory. What I mean is, if I hear something often enough, I can repeat it – well, nearly always – and this was one of the instances when it worked. I had heard his nibs doing the spiel so often the previous day that I really did know it DLP (for the uninitiated – dead letter perfect). In any case – and this was the biggest blessing – I wouldn't need to sit and have my hair waved and have to go home looking like a Fiji Islander!

Great! Poor 'old wiggy' would have to suffer – and

159

look like a 'mangy Fiji Islander'. I ran through the spiel
to assure his nibs I knew it and he was so relieved I was
glad I had offered my services.

The doors opened and we were ready for business. I
felt a bit nervous, especially as the first two might-be
customers who approached the stall knew me.

'He-he-he-heee. Hello, Thora!' one of them said.

Please don't get the idea that the 'He-he-he-heee'
bit was because they were laughing at my overall
or anything – it wasn't. It's something that many
Northern people do when they meet to prefix an
opening sentence with 'He-he-he-heee!' such as 'He-
he-he-heee, what are you doing here?' or 'He-he-he-
heee how are you?' and it's meant as a sound of
pleasure when meeting anyone and meant very kindly.

After they greeted me, one of them said, 'Are you
working on here?' (meaning the stall).

'Yes,' I replied very timidly.

'Are they any good?' she asked (meaning the
curlers). Immediately the business part of me took
over. 'Any good? They're marvellous!' I stated – with
authority.

Overture and beginners, please! by now the people
were in clusters in front of the stall. 'Go on then!'
croaked Mr P. 'Raise the curler in your right hand!'

If I hadn't been so nervous, I'd have seen the funny
side of that and proclaimed, 'I swear by Almighty God
that the evidence I shall give', etc., etc., but I didn't –
off I started.

'Good afternoon – now this instrument is known as
the Ideal Instantaneous Hairwaver – and with it I
guarantee to give you as good a wave in two minutes

as any hairdresser will give you all day!'

On the demonstration table in front of me sat old wiggy, daring me to continue.

'All you have to do is take a piece of hair' – this bit was rather difficult because wiggy's mangy tufts were not to be compared with my 'auburn cape of hair' and I had slight difficulty in getting hold of a piece of hair to run my tortoiseshell comb through. However, on I went. (The real patent leather shoes in the window at Tyler's would be *mine*, paid for with my hard-earned money, within a few days!)

We did excellent business and by my third demonstration I felt as though I'd never done anything else in my life but demonstrated haircurlers. Never mind my 'crinoline' overall, I was quite enjoying myself – and so was Mr P. About half an hour before closing time, I started on a demonstration – by now it was somewhat of an achievement to find a piece of hair on Wiggy's head that wasn't waved! I got to the bit of spiel where I had to say, 'We are offering you not *one* waver – not *two* wavers – but *three* in the small pink box for – 1/-! Now, who will be first? We have only – '

I *was* going to say 'a limited supply', but before I'd got that bit out, a very quiet but familiar voice said, '*I* will.'

It was my mother! I handed her the little pink box and she gave me her shilling – we looked straight into each other's eyes and I suddenly saw two little tears begin to spill out of hers.

'Thank you, Madam,' I said (nearly crying myself), and then continued passing the little pink boxes over for more shillings as fast as I could, *because*, just behind

my mother's black and gold lace toque I had seen a
bowler hat. I had seen the expression on the *face* under
the bowler as well! Only one man could look at anyone
as that man was looking at me – my dad!

Bloody 'ell! Caught in the act!

As the customers moved away, I kind of frantically
combed Wiggy's waves. When the stall was deserted,
I heard the 'voice that breathed o'er Eden' say very
firmly – but quietly – 'Come *here*.'

'Yes, Dad,' I replied like a bullet from a gun and came
round to the front of the stall and stood in front of him.

I've already explained that one of the wonderful
things about my parents was that they would never let
you down or show you up in front of a third party and
my dad didn't fail me in this instance. As I stood in
front of him, I could see he was furious. Nevertheless,
without raising his voice, he looked me straight in the
face and said, 'And what, in the name of *hell*, do you
think *you* are doing?'

My mother (the peacemaker) was wiping her nose
with a lace edged handkerchief as she said placatingly,
'Yes – well, Jim – don't carry on. We can talk when we
get home!'

Being a mother myself, I honestly think the sight of
the white, starched crinoline overall had upset her – to
her I looked pathetic, not comic.

'Never mind about when we get *home*,' said James
Henry, emphatically, 'I want to know what she's doing
here! Who's employing you?' he darted the last bit at me.

'Er – Mr P. – but I only did it so that I could buy
those patent leather shoes in Tyler's and he is paying
me fifteen shillings and the shoes are only fourteen and

elevenpence and he's ever so nice and he's lost his voice so I did the patter and he never asked me to, I offered, would you like to meet him but don't be mad at him, Dad, *please!*'

'Yes, I would *very much like to meet him*,' my Dad said, punctuating each word as though he was playing 'Hamlet'.

By now my mother had fully realized why I had taken on the job – the shoes! As she gave me her handkerchief to wipe my eyes and nose she looked at me so understandingly and lovingly. I introduced my parents to his nibs and after the usual salutations, my dad said, full of authority, 'I suppose you realize how young this child is?'

Mr P. said he did, and that it was remarkable how I had deputized for him, and that he would have been unable to open the stall without me – and so on and so on.

He was most flattering (as he scooped up the shillings and deposited them in his overall pocket). On the other hand, I could see he was well aware that in speaking to my Dad, he was *not* dealing with a 'gormless Northerner' *and*, give the man his due, *he* didn't know my parents were unaware I was working for him.

I know he looked most relieved when my father announced, 'Well – she took on the job and she must fulfil her obligations.'

I took my crinoline off and put on my coat and panama hat.

'Good night, Mr P. – see you tomorrow,' I said – very quietly.

'Good night, Thora, and thank you – thank you very

much, dear! Good night, Mr and Mrs Hird,' croaked
Mr P.

We were all rather quiet as we walked home. My
father hung his coat and bowler hat up on one of the
hooks in the passage and then came into the living-
room.

Nobody spoke.

My mother went into the back kitchen to prepare
some supper. My Dad took the fireguard from round
the fire, which had been left banked up with slack (fine
coal). I got the table-cloth out of the table drawer and
spread it on the table.

Still nobody spoke.

As my dad inserted the poker underneath the well
packed fire and wiggled it about, there was the lovely
little explosion of flames that was usually the result of
this. There was another explosion as well when my dad
spoke – 'I wouldn't *mind*!' he said, 'I wouldn't *mind* –
but – BLOODY – HAIRCURLERS! And on a *stall* at the
Trades Exhibition! *You* standing there – what the *hell*
are people going to *think*? That your mother and I
couldn't *wait* to send you out to *work*?' With each word
in italics he jabbed the poker into the coal of the fire and
beat it into life. The poor slack suffered.

'I'm sorry, Dad,' I said. 'But I'd seen those shoes in
Tyler's and . . .'

'You could have *had* the damned shoes – have you
ever been *denied anything*?' (jab – jab).

'No, Dad,' I replied – the flood gates were beginning
to open by now, 'and I only did it because, well, I
thought – I –' (Pause.)

'Have you no pride?' he expostulated.

By now, the cups and saucers and plates were rattling in the back kitchen much more than was necessary and it was obvious that my mother was killing time until my dad had had his say.

'Well, I'm sorry, Dad, but I thought if – ' I was crying now, and that brought my mother out of the back kitchen.

'Now, Jim,' she said gently, 'she's said she's sorry – let's have our supper.'

You know – when I got a bit older, I was able to understand my dad so very well – and *appreciate* him, and I wish that during this little cantata I had had sufficient sense to realize that he wasn't cross with me really – he was *hurt* – his pride had been hurt because I hadn't told them about the job. And yet, I know he was really *proud* of me for doing what I had done!

As we ate our supper, Nev arrived home from the scouts or somewhere, and as he was always good for a laugh, things returned to normal.

When it was time for bed, I kissed my mother 'Good night and God Bless' and then went up to my dad who was sitting in his chair by the fire, smoking a 'Gold Flake' cigarette.

'Good night and God Bless, Dad,' I said, as I bent down to kiss him.

Now, I must explain something. When James Henry felt emotional he always showed it because his nostrils dilated. It was his way of suppressing tears, strange as this may seem. I saw it happen hundreds of times. Well, as I kissed him, he looked at me, and I saw his nostrils dilating.

'Good night, love,' he said, and then looked straight

into my face and added quietly, 'Bloody haircurlers!'

The following morning there was a knock on our front door. My dad was just going on the pier to work, so he answered the door on his way out.

A well-dressed man was standing there and after the usual 'Good mornings' had been exchanged, he asked father whether this was where the young lady who demonstrated hairwavers at the Trades Exhibition lived.

'It is!' my father replied.

'Oh good!' exclaimed the well-dressed man. 'I have a Hairwaver stall on the Fairground here and I've a job for her after the Exhibition closes, if she's interested, and if she's at liberty.'

My father informed him politely that I wasn't either interested or at liberty, but thanked him for his enquiry. The well-dressed man voiced disappointment, raised his pale grey homburg and departed.

With a cheery, 'I'm off, see you later!' my dad went to work.

At dinnertime my dad was sitting in his chair scrutinizing a copy of *The World's Fair*.

'Ye Gods!' he burst forth, 'listen to this!'

My mother and I obediently stopped what we were doing and heard him read out the following advert. 'Don't miss this fantastic offer! Metal Instantaneous Haircurlers with tube and clip, one shilling and two pence a gross! With trade name stamped on tube, two shillings a gross! Order now and avoid disappointment!'

Crumbs! And I had been informing the trusting public that, as a 'special concession', we were offering not *one* curler, not *two* curlers but *three*, in the small pink box for one shilling!

'Well,' announced James Henry, 'as you are so good at the demonstrating lark, I've a good mind to send for some. We could run our own stall on the Fairground – 'Hird's Instantaneous Hairwavers!'

He looked up at the two women in his life, to discover us standing there almost as if we had been petrified!

'Well? What do you say?' he smirked. My mother came out of the trance first.

'What do I say?' she asked as she put the cruet down in the middle of the dining table. 'I'll tell you what I say!' She moved towards the back kitchen door then did a beautifully timed stage turn and executing a perfect imitation of my dad, she said, 'Bloody Haircurlers!'

I completed my assignment for Mr P. – and collected my fifteen shillings.

The 'real' patent leather shoes were greatly admired at both Sunday School and Chapel and I faithfully rubbed the toes with Vaseline and stuffed them with newspaper after I had taken them off. The shoes were 14s 11d – so I had a penny left out of my 15s wages. I gave this to my mother.

After she died we found it in her jewel box, carefully wrapped up in tissue paper along with Neville's rather yellow halfcrown.

I would like you to know that for many years Mr P. requested my services 'for demonstration purposes' when he had a stall at the Trades Exhibition. Faithfully he would call at 6, Cheapside, but I was never 'at liberty'.

I would also like you to know that when my father informed the 'well-dressed enquirer' I was not 'at liberty' he was telling the truth, because that very tea time he said to me, 'How would you like to work in the office on the pier, this season?'

I was delighted and said, 'Oh, thanks Dad – my night school shorthand and typing will come in useful and you'll be able to see *how well* I'm doing!'

He looked at me with a twinkle in his eyes and said, 'Never mind about my seeing how well you're doing – I'll be able to see *what* you're doing!'

21

Oh my Papa – to me he was
so wonderful!!

Hecky plonk! Have you ever worked for your dad? I'm
only joking when I say that – it was great really. I used
to report for duty at nine o'clock each morning and
finished at five o'clock.

I remember one morning my mother asked me to go
for some bread before I went to work. When I arrived at
Gibson's in Euston Road, it was to be told 'It won't be a
minute, Thora – we're just taking another batch out!'
Oh, the aroma of hot bread, isn't it marvellous?

I waited about five minutes and then looking at my
watch (*THE* watch, I told you about!) I thought, 'I hope
it won't be long or else I'll be late for work!'

Being late for work, or late for anything, as far as
James Henry was concerned, was the unforgivable sin!
I must say, I never knew my dad to be late for anything.
Mind you, I admired him for it and it was wonderful
training for us. He used to say that if you were late, let
us for argument's sake, say, one minute – that you were
as many minutes late as the number of people you had
kept waiting. Hence, once when I was a minute late for
rehearsal when he was directing the Morecambe
Warblers Amateur Operatic and Dramatic Society, he
admonished me in front of everybody and informed

169

me that as there were sixty-three people at rehearsal, I was sixty-three minutes late! Red of face and very ashamed I apologized to the whole cast. I was never late again I'll tell you that!

It's a good job I had that training really because I'm married to a man as bad – or good – as my dad! If Scottie and I are going on a journey by train, he has the car hire at the front door so early that by the time we arrive at the station we could comfortably catch the train prior to the one we've gone for! Forgive me for telling you that I am never late for rehearsals, anyone I have worked with will substantiate that. Good old Dad, good old Scottie! My working life runs very smoothly.

Anyway, I've been standing in Gibson's Confectioners waiting for the bread a long time, haven't I? Sorry! As I came out of the shop it was two minutes to nine – oh, crumbs! get your running pumps on, Thor! I ran home, flung the hot bread on the table, kissed my mother ta-ta and flew up Cheapside like a scalded cat! As I approached the promenade the clock tower came into view, its hands were pointing to nine and twelve and gave the appearance of a policeman stopping the traffic, they looked as though they were saying, 'STOP! It's no use you running like that, you should be there now!' and to prove it as I crossed the road on to the promenade the clock boldly struck NINE! Oh I sprinted – thank the Lord, I used to sprint for the school – along the prom, past the Children's Corner and up the slanting forebay of the pier, through the big wrought iron gates at the entrance of the pier, which old Artie Gott had opened – and with a breathless

'Morning, Mr Gott' I whizzed past him up the pier. I was a bit at the panting stage as I flew into Dad's office. Putting my handbag in my desk drawer with one hand, I whipped the cover off the typewriter with my other hand and sat down. I was about to say 'Sorry I'm late, Dad' but I didn't get the chance.

'You're late!' he informed me as though I didn't know.

'Well, I'm sorry, Dad – only a few minutes though, and I had to wait for the bread!'

He wasn't cross or anything, don't misunderstand me, he was what you might call, FIRM!

'Bread!' he said, 'And what's the bread got to do with it – you work HERE and you are late!'

'Well,' I said, 'my mother asked me to go for the bread and it wasn't out of the oven and I had to –' he looked at his watch on his wrist as he interrupted my weak explanation, I'd put the 'My mother asked me' line in, not to put the blame on her, but to add the homely touch. I mean, I was speaking of the woman he loved! I needn't have bothered because it didn't work.

'It's now six minutes past nine and you're supposed to be here at nine o'clock remember – so don't be late again please!' With that he walked out of the office. When my coffee arrived for elevenses I noted that instead of the usual two finger biscuits on the little plate, there was a chocolate eclair! The waitress from the café put the tray on my desk, pointed to the eclair and said with a grin, 'That's from your dad!'

As that particular season on the pier drew to a close, I experienced the same feeling that I do now when a show is near its end. I was sorry it was over. However much I try to console myself with the fact that I have done a job of work to the best of my ability, I am unable to stop myself thinking for an odd moment, 'Oh heck, that's in the past now and won't ever happen again!' It's stupid I know, but nevertheless it's part of the way I am made so there it is. Although I knew I could go back to the Pier Office the following season, I was sad the present one was finishing.

One afternoon whilst I was at work on the pier, there was a knock on the door of number six Cheapside and upon answering it my mother was confronted by a gentleman who had a Drapers and Milliners Shop in Euston Road, which ran parallel with Cheapside. He didn't waste words but came straight to the point. He did the flattery routine by telling my mother he thought I was a very smart and alert young lady and he and his wife would like me to work for them as a shop assistant. And that was how, when I finished on the pier, I went into the General Drapery Business.

22

The EPNS wedding

My parents' Silver Wedding was approaching and Nev and I were in a bit of a quandary as to what to present them with, as a mark of esteem and love from their devoted son and daughter.

We were in an even bigger quandary as to what we were going to use for money!

I was commissioned to 'have a look round the shops for something nice'. Now the 'looking round' bit was easy – and the 'something nice' bit was easier still – it was the looking round for something nice *that we could afford* that was tricky.

Needless to say, the first shop window I planted myself in front of was James Hargreaves, Jeweller. True enough – once again in the window – there was something I thought beautiful (not as beautiful as the watch I was wearing at that very moment and *had* worn every moment since I acquired it!) but what I saw was beautifully suitable for our 'mark of esteem', at least so I thought, and after all Nev hadn't mentioned any article specifically.

It was an oak salad bowl resting on a base of oak, bound round the rim with silver. (It was EPNS really, but I thought it was silver!) The servers were in EPNS

with oak handles – like skipping rope handles – *and* –
and this was what appealed to me – there was a small
EPNS shield on the front of it, absolutely begging to be
engraved on.

As I stood there, the old imagination set to work once
again and in my mind's eye I read 'To Mum and Dad on
the occasion of their Silver Wedding – love from Thora
and Neville!' Oh, I could see it! Not only could I see the
engraving on the shield, I could see the whole works,
salad bowl, servers and engraved shield, on top of our
piano! Oh yes – that was the very gift, no doubt about
it!

So once again I dashed into Jim Hargreaves' shop
and, as always, he was understanding and helpful.

'How much is that oak and silver salad bowl in the
window, Mr Hargreaves, please?'

He smiled as he replied, 'Just a minute, Thora, I'll get
it out of the window and see!'

As he unlatched the glass door at the back of the
window and then moved two or three articles to reach
the salad bowl, I was thinking, suppose someone else
buys it – I'll never see another one just like that, with a
shield on.

He brought it to the counter and turning it upside
down perused the price on the little ticket that was
stuck on the base. I held my breath!

'Thirty-seven and sixpence!' he said, adding, 'it's
very nicely made, isn't it?' I agreed it was.

'There is quite a nice white porcelain bowl inside it,
you see, for the salad!'

Cripes! white bowl inside it as well, to protect the
real oak!

As I have told you before, we knew Mr Hargreaves, he was 'our' jeweller, so I was able to ask him if he would kindly 'put it on one side'. I told him what Nev and I wanted it for and he agreed that it would be a very nice and suitable gift for Mam and Dad.

So far, so good – we'd decided on the gift. All we had to do now was to get thirty-seven and sixpence. Nev and I had an extraordinary general meeting and decided that as we had some war saving Certificates the ideal thing would be to draw out one each and make the rest up out of our bits of odd cash.

This sounds easy enough, but the saving certificate books were in my dad's drawer and it was an under-stood thing in our house that Nev and I never – I re-iterate, *never* – opened my mother's or father's drawers unless, of course, we were told to. Come to think of it, by the time Nev and I reached our teens, we always regarded the cupboards or chest of drawers in each other's rooms as private.

So how the heck were we going to get hold of the books of certificates? We tried all the obvious approaches, such as, 'Shall I get you a clean handkerchief, Dad?' or 'Can I get your tie for you, Dad' all to no avail until one day, by the grace of God, Dad said to me, 'Nip upstairs and get me my cuff links will you please, love?'

Quick as a flash, Nev said, 'I'll go, Dad!'

I'll admit it took him a bit longer than it should have. In fact, Dad called out, 'Can't you find them, Neville? They're in the leather stud box in the corner of the drawer!'

When Nev replied, 'I've got them Dad!' I was very relieved, I knew what else he'd got as well.

We went to the post office, but of course we couldn't get the money straight away. After signing an application for repayment each, we were informed that a warrant would arrive at our home address and if we took *that* one to the post office, we would get the cash. Crumbs! that meant that the OHMS envelope would arrive in the post at 6, Cheapside!

I wish you could have seen the scurrying, willing and obliging Thor and Nev who, so thoughtfully, each morning when the postman knocked, sprang up from the breakfast table with a cry of, 'I'll get it!' We managed it, I'm happy to say, and in the lunch hour we collected the cash – one pound each! Good egg! We could afford to have it engraved – and buy a nice card as well!

As Nev went off, I shot along to 'our' jewellers and informed Mr Hargreaves about the engraving. I also paid for the salad bowl even though he suggested I should settle up for the lot when the engraving was complete. No fear, I thought, let's get rid of the two pound notes!

So with the halfcrown change in my purse, and the salad bowl paid for I left the shop in a gay and light-hearted mood. I was anticipating the look of wonderment, pleasure, surprise and incredulity on my parents' faces, when the day arrived for us to present them with the oak and 'silver' salad bowl and servers, complete with engraved shield.

My mother finished the ironing that evening and duly put the handkerchiefs on a dinner plate to air on the ledge over the fireplace. Later, when she felt the 'noserags' were aired enough for use, she put them in separate piles and requested me to, 'Take those up and put them in our respective drawers, will you, love, please?'

God bless her for saying that! I nipped upstairs. Nev was in his room and, opening his bedroom door, I hissed, 'Pst! pst! the books, the books!' holding my hand out for same.

As I put Dad's hankies in his drawer, I replaced the saving certificate books under the rubber band that held the remaining ones. It was with love and devotion that I placed the handkerchiefs in the corner of the drawer – well, that's what I thought it was – but it was really with *relief*!

I can laugh at it all now, although, come to think of it, 'old habits die hard' and I still say to Scottie, my husband, 'May I go into your drawer for the nail clippers?' to which he never fails to reply, 'Of course, you don't have to ask!'

The great day arrived. The gift was on the breakfast table, the expressions of wonderment, delight and incredulity were all as anticipated, with the addition of one we had *not* anticipated – as my mother wiped her eyes she enquired, 'Wherever did you get the money for that?'

And believe it or not – we told them!

23

The end of the world

When you were young and the weather was 'thundery' and the sky took on a dark-grey kind of pewter colour appearance, did you ever say to your schoolfriends, 'Oooo, it's the end of the world!' Did you? We did!

And did you get an excitement of sorts when some spooky-minded friend said, 'Oooo-er, all the ghosts will come out of their graves!' We did! Which all goes to prove, and with pride I announce, that I was as daft as any other youngster! And I'm very happy to admit it!

But it wasn't thunder or ghosts or anything ethereal that was responsible for 'the end of the world' in my young life. It was something much more material. My 'End of the World' was brought about by two Bradford businessmen, who owned the Central Pier!

I've related how the Pavilion Theatre had been miraculously changed into the Pavilion Ballroom, and how this prosperous end product was due to the brains, inventiveness and never-ending work of my father. Right! You know all that, so 'new readers start here!' I have no intention of sounding bitter about the following or about the person my father 'tutored' as far as pier management was concerned – because that same person was always very kind to Nev and me, and indeed, he admired my father greatly – so please don't misunderstand or get the idea I am running him down. I'm not! And it really wasn't his fault that he knew nothing about running a pier, until my father patiently and unselfishly taught him. He would admit all that himself! He's dead now, so God Rest Him – it was with sincere respect I went to his funeral.

Things were running very smoothly at the Central Pier. The ballroom was a big success, the bars were always full, the 'spondoolicks' was rolling in and everything in the garden was lovely! It was at this prosperous period that the two Bradford businessmen, dreaming of even greater wealth – and having picked my dad's brain – offered him 'half his wage' if he wished to stay on as assistant to his protege!

My father informed the two Bradford businessmen where they could insert the two small domes of 'The Northern Taj Mahal!' One each!

'Oh, what a lovely smell! what are you baking – gingerbread?' I asked my mother, as I took my coat off. She was in the kitchen and, as she didn't reply, I thought she hadn't heard me.

'*Is* it Gingerbread?' I enquired as I went into the kitchen – and then I saw the expression on her face. There were little tears in the corners of her eyes and she looked so sad that within a second my arms were round her and I was appealing, 'What is it, Mam, what's the matter?' She was rolling a piece of pastry out to cover the top of an apple pie during the above conversation – and why is it, that when a person is upset but continues with the job they are doing, they always look more pathetic than if they just give way and burst into tears? Have you ever noticed that?

As she covered the prepared apples in the dish with the piece of pastry she said, 'Your dad has told the two Mr So-and-So's where to stick the two small domes off the Pavilion – and he's finished on the pier!'

My dad finished on the pier! Impossible! He couldn't be! He *was* the pier! *We* were all *part* of the pier! It had been such a big part of our lives! Hell! It *was* our lives! Nev and I knew every plank of the pier deck, every flagpole and flag, every automatic machine, flower tub, kiosk, bar and deckchair!

And what about the Pavilion? We knew and loved every dressing room, staircase, the ballroom floor and everything? What about the fountain my dad had thought out? What about the six nude women who held the boxes up? They were practically relatives!

My dad finishing on the pier? It was the end of the world – *that's all*! *The End*! (I was always a bit dramatic y'know!) How about dancing in the open air and the dozens of pals I took on there – for nothing? How about Nev on the Lime Perch, and the Spot Dances in which, if the music stopped and the Lime was on you, and you had a current copy of *Answers* in your hand, you could win a canteen of cutlery or a clock? And how about my private Ladies' Toilet with the marble wash basins and the lovely little mirror that informed you 'Mene Towels' were 'for Ladies'? Oh God – it was – *yes it was* – the end of the world!

Have you noticed the selfish touch in all I have just written? My first thoughts were about things Nev and I would have to forego. On the other hand, and I speak in defence of Nev and I, we did love every inch of the Central Pier, it had watched us grow from little children into fairly responsible teenagers, my father had willingly given it fourteen years of his life and knowledge; he had been a slave to the pier, each morning from eight thirty until eleven or twelve o'clock at night. Even in the winter he went back at night to see that everything was safe.

He'd walk round the entire pier and buildings to see that nobody had carelessly dropped a cigarette, he would check and light the warning beacon at the very end of the pier, which involved climbing up on to the high diving platform once used by Madame Rosa Vere. On nights when there was a gale my mother had suffered agony until he returned home safely. And now, suddenly, he was finishing on the pier! What I hadn't realized at the time was that by telling the Bradford businessmen where to put the domes, my father had effectively put himself out of work!

When I grew older I often thought about all I have just told you. I would think of how conscientiously my father had worked, the honest way he always put his job first, and how there was nothing he didn't do. No, I take that back. My Dad just missed doing one thing. He should have told those men from Bradford where to stick the large dome as well!

24

Not guilty, yer honour

Dad had left the pier and I was about to start working in a draper's shop . . . it was a debatable point which was the bigger tragedy. I shall call the shop Glumdell's, that wasn't its name but it will suffice.

The shop structure comprised two large bay-type windows and the floor of the recessed entrance was of coloured quarry tiles in a pattern. The narrow double doors had the usual big brass latch. Upon entering the shop, the counter was on the left and facing it was the millinery department with a large mirror on the wall, surrounded by hat stands, the type that are wall fixtures and welcome a hat popped on them. There were large, deep millinery drawers from where the mirror finished to the floor. Through an archway was the back shop, three walls of which were lined with shelves and packed with boxes of goods. The right-hand wall boxes were huge things covered in dark green American cloth. They pulled out by a big brass handle. There were thirty-four of these handles. I know because I cleaned them each morning.

On the morning I arrived at Glumdell's to take up my duties, the very first thing that impressed me – or *de*pressed should I say, was where we hung our

As the Frau in **The Big Blockade** (*a one-day part*),
Ealing Film Studios. Perhaps I was the cause of the war!

Above: In **Once a Jolly Swagman** starring Dirk Bogarde. I played his mother (*I look old enough to play anybody's mother!*)

Below: My first film appearance, **The Blacksheep of Whitehall**, starring Will Hay (*he let me share the Liquorice Allsorts*).

This was the first film my daughter Janette and I appeared in together (**They Came In Khaki**). She was four, but I was a bit older.

As Mrs Holmes in **Flowers For The Living**, the play
that did everything for me.

This was my first starring part in the West End:
Emmie Slee in **The Queen Came By.**

This is one of the many and various charladies
I played - Mrs Coot in the film **Fools Rush In.**

'Mrs Gaye with an E'. The play was called **No Medals**, but this is from the film which was retitled **The Weaker Sex.**

Above: Mrs Doorbell in the film **The Cure For Love.** I was also playing in the theatre at night, and I had to peel the rubber make-up off my face in the car en route from the studios. I was so happy in this film with Robert Donat, it was a shame to take the money - but I did!

Left: Rosa in the film **Madness Of The Heart** (*'as nice a woman as you'd meet on a day's march'*).

outdoor coats. It was in the passage of the house that was attached to the shop, and ran behind and above the premises. One side of the passage housed a long oak stock cupboard and we hung our coats on pegs on the opposite wall. Everything was spotless, and I mean spotless, but it was the 'smell' that upset me and I couldn't think what it was. I soon found out, the big oak stock cupboard was full of Fustian trousers – all sizes! Phew!

My first duties were explained to me. I had to go into the back yard and get the mop bucket and mop, which they kept in the outside 'loo', bring it in and fill it with hot water and disinfectant then proceed to mop the shop floor, starting at the back of the shop and working my way out backwards through the shop door so that I would mop the entrance to the shop as a final gesture.

It was then explained to me that I must wring out the long mop tightly and wipe the woodwork under the windows 'where the dogs had been!' Right, next item, empty the bucket and don't forget to rinse it out with clean water before returning it to the outside 'loo'. My next artistic task was to clean, with metal polish, the brass latch and letter box on the shop door 'and be careful not to get any metal polish on the paintwork.' Then I had to clean and polish the resident brass yard measure that was secured to the back of the counter. My 'big finish' was cleaning and polishing the thirty-four brass handles on the big boxes at the back of the shop, 'and be careful with these, if you get polish on the boxes it won't come off!'

Behind the counter were the usual shelves filled with cardboard boxes, but in the centre at the same height as the counter was a little display of various haberdashery goods.

Ruling supreme over everything else was a display of steel hatpins; they were stuck in half of an unbustable ball, which had been cut in two and the flat piece used as the base which supported the half dome that was pierced by the hatpins. But these were no ordinary hatpins. Even *then*, when *I* was fifteen and a half, they were period pieces. Mind you, they were lovely, each was about eight inches long and the heads on them were magnificent. Massive, but magnificent.

I can remember the head of one was about the size of half-a-crown (of course, even a halfcrown is a period piece now, isn't it?) with a pastoral scene on it, another one had a cameo head on it, and so on. I'll bet any television wardrobe department would give the earth for them now.

I was told to put a piece of paper on the counter top and emery paper the hatpins! 'Because they soon go rusty being steel, and we don't want that, do we?' I will admit I didn't mind. I thought they were being preserved because they were antique. Not on your nelly! I had to clean them in case anybody came for a hatpin!

Now who in the name of goodness would want an eight-inch-long hatpin, in steel, when everyone was wearing toques? Never mind, I emery-papered them each morning, gradually wearing the steel away. By the time I left Glumdell's the steel pins were so thin I was afraid they would break. Nobody had ever purchased one.

You'll notice I said, 'by the time I left Glumdell's?'

Well that isn't quite correct. I was *sacked* from Glumdell's – for *stealing*! Put on a record of 'Hearts and Flowers' and I'll tell you what happened.

On a Saturday night it was Glumdell's who 'shut Euston Road up!' We were always, without fail, the last shop to close; we would be mopping out the entrance and wiping down where the dogs had lifted their legs long after every other shop had closed and their assistants had gone home. It was a very prosperous business, but, even so, during the last hour we were open on a Saturday very few customers came in.

I had been working there just over a year, so was about to take some 'Iron Tonic' in preparation for my second Christmas at Glumdell's. We really did work like mad preparing for Christmas. There were only two assistants and 'himself'. 'Madam's' contribution was to come and stand under the archway, her hawk eye watching that we never stopped, and saying, 'How do you do,' to the customers.

One job I was not mad about was making balls of cotton wool, about the size of sago, and sticking them on the Millinery mirror with spit to form the words, 'A Merry Christmas to all our Customers!'

The Benefit Boot shop was opposite Glumdell's on the other side of Euston Road, and I had seen a very pretty pair of red bedroom slippers right in the middle of their window – four and elevenpence halfpenny they were. I wanted to give them to my mother as a Christmas gift, so about a week before Christmas I asked the Manageress to keep them for me.

Our uniform at Glumdell's was a navy blue serge dress, which reached nearly below our calves; it was embarrassing really, because the short skirt was in fashion then, and although we requested to have the length shortened 'Madam' wouldn't hear of it. What, she asked, would it look like if you had to go up the steps to get a box from the top shelf! I'll tell you what it would have looked like – the black hole of Calcutta, that's what, because we wore black knickers and stockings!

Over the long serge dress, to preserve it, we wore a black sateen 'pinarette', yes, that's what they were called. It was an apron with a bib top. There were two pockets in the pinarette that were neither use nor ornament because they were so shallow. It was because they were so shallow I was sacked for stealing! Let me explain.

We were very busy on Christmas Eve and I hadn't collected the red bedroom slippers. I'd been over during my teatime but the shoe shop was packed, so I thought I'd pop across later. I did, and paid for my mother's present with two halfcrowns, which I had brought to work out of my savings. The halfpenny change I put in the shallow pocket of my pinarette.

As I came back through Glumdell's shop door I saw we were busy, so I rushed and put the slippers with my outdoor coat in the smelly passage. I didn't waste time by taking my purse out of my coat pocket and transferring the halfpenny from my pocket to the purse, but went straight back behind the counter to serve. About half an hour later I was serving a customer and, as she had bought rather a lot of goods, I needed a large sheet of brown wrapping paper. This was something else that embarrassed me; we always used large sheets of brown paper that goods had been wrapped in when they came from the warehouse; they were always creased and crumpled, so we were never able to make a tidy parcel. I always thought it was a cock-eyed way of doing things. Bending down to get a piece of crumpled brown paper from under the counter where it was kept, I heard something drop out of my pinarette pocket and roll into the back shop, I realized it was my halfpenny change from the five shillings I'd paid for the slippers, so I didn't bother to go and find it immediately because I was serving. I could find it later.

The slippers were a big success and my mother was delighted and, of course, I was delighted that she was delighted. The loving incident I will now relate happened on about the seventh of January on a Saturday morning. We were into a new year and as per usual I was going into the back yard 'loo' for the mop bucket and long 'mop' I was on my way back into the shop when 'Madam' halted me.

I must admit, she terrified me – honestly. I was frightened to death of her, so you'll appreciate that when she ordered, 'Just a minute!' I nearly dropped the ruddy bucket! She then proceeded to say that a customer in the shop had noticed 'some money' fall out of my pocket on Christmas Eve when I was bending down to get some brown paper, and had thought it was strange that an assistant should have loose cash in her pocket and so on and so on and so on.

As I looked at her, I *knew* no customer had ever said anything of the sort. I could tell by her face, don't ask me how, but I could.

In retrospect, I know that as she said what she did, I

changed as a person or perhaps it would be more correct to say that it was a changing point in my life.

Suddenly, I was no longer frightened of her. I stood there clutching the handle of the long mop, I could have cried, but I wasn't going to – *how dare she*? She was as good as accusing me of being a thief! *Me*! I'd never taken anything that wasn't mine in my life and I'd never wanted to – and I never would! Clutching the mop handle until my hand hurt, I said, 'Are you calling me a thief?'

It was her reply that *did* it, she said, 'Well, *I'm* not but it's very funny that this – er – customer should remark that some money fell out of your –' she got no further, because I heard somebody say – and it must have been *me* because there was only me there, 'You bloody bad old bitch!' I thought she was going to faint! I thought I was going to as well, when I realized it was me who had sworn at someone for the first time in the sixteen years I had lived up to then! Need I say that, as I was given my meagre wage packet that night, I was also given my notice! I was out of pocket as well – because I never found my halfpenny!

You are bound to wonder why one of my parents didn't go to Glumdell's and knock Madam's teeth in! Well I'll tell you why.

When I went home for my dinner on the day of the accusation I hadn't got my coat off before my mother enquired, 'What's the matter?' I unashamedly admit I burst out crying. 'Oh, love,' my mother murmured as she embraced me, 'whatever's happened, what is it?' In the comforting safety of my mother's arms, I told her. I think it was a 'changing point' in her life as well because she immediately seemed to become a *tigress* protecting her young.

'*She said what*?' she demanded. 'Right, you sit down and have your dinner. I'm going round there *NOW*! How *dare* she, the old faggot! Accusing one of *MY* children –'

All this was being said as she unhooked her coat off the peg on the partition. It was at this juncture I started to plead, 'No, don't go round, Mother, please, I'd rather you didn't, it will only cause more trouble and . . .!'

James Henry came through the front door, before I'd finished. You can imagine the following five minutes of our lives, can't you? He was furious! My mother was told she could take her coat off because *he* was going to see Mr and Mrs Glumdell! By God! They would be sorry they had accused me of the lowest crime on earth when *he* had finished with them, by God they would. His children had been brought up to know the difference between right and wrong, we were a family that was well respected in the town and to dare accuse his daughter . . . on and on he went, I was crying and pleading, 'Don't go, Dad, it will make it worse for me, *please, please* don't go!'

Well, he didn't go, not because he didn't want to, but because I was so upset at the thought of him doing so. I assured them both that I was no longer afraid of Madam, so things would be different. Even so, he only refrained from the attack on the understanding that when I had dutifully finished my work that evening I would give in my notice. I have already told you – I didn't get the chance – *they* presented *me* with it!

I started to work my fortnight's notice without any

embarrassment, I was a changed young lady, albeit I worked harder than ever, if that was possible. Jobs that were automatically done each day I did with gusto, adding many other little jobs to them.

It would be untrue to say there wasn't an atmosphere because there was, but the fact that I never stopped doing *something* did leave a bit of egg on their faces.

Actually, 'himself' was sorry I was leaving and told me as much as I helped him to dress the window. As we artistically arranged 'Ladies' combinations, with bust inserts' he told me, 'It's nothing to do with me, you know.' 'I know,' I said, using an inflection that left him in no doubt I knew he was frightened of her as well! Poor, henpecked old soul!

On the Tuesday, which was only the second day of my 'atmosphere fortnight', he enquired, 'What do you think you will do?' He asked this rather sadly, really, and I felt a bit sorry for him.

'Do? Mr Glumdell,' I exclaimed, 'I shall find another job, of course!'

He looked at me, then looked at the floor as he said, 'That won't be too easy – without a reference!'

25

'Change please'

'Wanted, young lady cashier for the Queen's Square Branch of the Lancaster and District Co-operative Society Limited – *must be eighteen.* Apply in own handwriting to the secretary, etc. etc.'

The above advertisement appeared in the *Morecambe Visitor* on the Wednesday after I had received my notice at Glumdell's. I applied immediately.

On the Friday morning I received a letter asking me to be at the Co-op offices in Lancaster at 7.30 that evening. I was there. So were another million hopefuls! The big room was full of long tables and the applicants were instructed to sit down. It was then explained to us what we were to do. In front of each person were papers and pens, and piles of 'gum sheets'.

For anyone not familiar with the system that was used at certain Co-op Societies, I will explain. A 'gum sheet' was a long narrow piece of paper about three inches wide and about eight to ten inches long, gummed on one side. After each purchase made, the member was given a narrow slip of paper, called a check, stating the amount they have spent, the shillings amount being written in words and the pence amount in figures. These amount slips were stuck on the gummed sheet and, when full, the member took it to one of the Co-op shops or offices, where it was added up and the full total written on an orange-coloured slip and stuck on the top of a new clean gum sheet, and off you went again, sticking your checks on. In my Co-op days, at the end of each quarter, your gum sheet was taken to the office and you received two shillings in the pound dividend on all you had spent, and sometimes a twopenny bonus as well!

On the night I am telling you about, the pile of 'gum sheets' in front of each applicant had to be added up and summarized on a sheet of ruled paper which was provided. All I can add to that is – there seemed a lot of 'gum sheets'!

At the 'off' we all started, heads down and pens at the ready – it was just like a school examination. All was silence with the exception of the scratching of pens on paper and the near silent murmurings of lips as the adding up took place.

I was enjoying myself; I wasn't bad at arithmetic and here was the opportunity to use a little of my book-keeping and accounts knowledge I had acquired at night school. Oh, yes, the thin red line!

Eventually the sound of chairs being pushed back could be heard as first one and then another future Chancellor of the Exchequer took their papers up to the little gentleman who was presiding behind a desk at the far end of the room. I was to discover he was the Lancaster and District Co-op Secretary.

Everybody present finished before I did. It wasn't because most of the amounts to be added up were written in words, although that can be quite difficult until you get used to it. It was because I was so anxious to make the end product neat and businesslike. I might still have been sitting there, if a quick glance at the old-fashioned clock on the wall hadn't reminded me that the last applicant had left the room twelve minutes previously!

Using a pencil as a ruler I drew a final thin red line under the grand total. I looked at my effort, then added another thin red line under the one I had already done. Yes, that looked better, much more professional! I blotted it carefully and then gathered my papers together and took them as an offering to the gentleman, who was still sitting waiting patiently behind the desk at the end of the room.

'Thank you,' he said as he accepted my papers. 'It took you rather longer than anyone else, didn't it?'

This was not a reprimand, it was just a quiet statement of fact, and even whilst he was saying this his eyes were taking in my efforts.

'This is all extremely neat,' he stated, his eyes leaving the papers and looking up at me.

'Thank you, sir,' was all I said.

He turned to the last page where the final column was penned, and as I saw his eyes start to move down it, I realized he was adding it up – so I added it up as well, to discover that where I had put three farthings in the grand total, it should have been a halfpenny!

Before I could stop to remember 'my place' I had touched his arm and then pointed to the total.

'Oh! excuse me, sir – that should be a halfpenny, not three farthings,' I dared to volunteer. He looked at me so very kindly and said, 'You went up that column of figures very quickly!'

In normal circumstances I might have been tempted to say 'No I didn't, I went *down* it!' but I refrained. He thanked me for attending, said he was sorry it was so late and wished me 'Good night.' *He* was sorry. It was my fault.

I caught a bus in Dalton Square and went back to Morecambe. By the end of the following day I would have worked one week of my notice at Glumdell's. One gone, one to go!

On the following Tuesday a letter arrived asking me to go for an interview on the Wednesday evening, same place, same time, with references. These were acquired by my father from a JP in the town, my Headmistress, the Headmaster at night school and our doctor, who was also a JP. My father was prepared to provide one re my office work on the pier, if necessary.

When I arrived at the Co-op Head Office there was only one other young lady there, so I thought perhaps as we were rather early the rest would arrive later. A Co-op official (they all look alike, don't they?) collected our references and asked us to wait in a small ante-room – we did, for ever it seemed.

There were only the two of us for the final round. My opponent was a very pretty girl and certainly looked more intelligent than I did. She told me she worked in the Borough Treasurer's Office in Lancaster Town Hall (goodbye job, I thought!) – but as she suffered from every kind of travel sickness she wanted to work in Morecambe were she lived.

She was summoned to the inner sanctum first – it was the committee room. I sat there waiting – it didn't half feel lonely! I had put my long hair up into earphones for the occasion, as I thought it would make me look a bit older, remembering the advertisement had stated *must be eighteen*! Eventually my pretty challenger came out of the committee room, and smiling very kindly, she wished me 'Good night and good luck!'

In I went. The scene was a large comfortable room governed by one of the biggest polished mahogany tables I had ever seen – I was later to appear in plenty of rooms like this one when I played Councillor Sarah Danby in *The First Lady* on the telly. About twenty Coop committee members were sitting round the table – I won't bother to describe them, they all looked alike, and at the far end sat the Secretary of the Lancaster and District Co-operative Society, my former kind inquisitor, with what were obviously my references in front of him. I was asked to sit in a corresponding chair to his – at the opposite end.

After general Good evenings, the Secretary explained exactly what the job entailed, and then out came the first question, 'How old are you, Miss Hird?' Just as quickly as it was asked, I answered, 'Sixteen, sir.' I wish I could describe the intakes of breath, the heads turning to each other, the mumblings of derision! It was reminiscent of a Labour conference! The Secretary kept his eyes on me – that was all he did, it was enough.

'Er – we did state in the advertisement that we required a person of eighteen – it was stated very clearly,' he said. 'I know, sir,' I defended myself, 'but I think I can do the job!' There were a few more mutterings at this point.

'Your references are excellent, but this position

involves handling large amounts of money and you appear rather young – are you working at the moment?' I replied, 'Yes, sir, but I finish on Saturday.' 'Why?' he asked. 'Why are you leaving your present position?' I took a deep breath and then I swallowed – here goes, I thought, don't waste words, Hirdie, you've nothing to be ashamed of.

'I've been sacked, sir!' I heard myself say in a firm voice. Hecky plonk! The mumblings and mutterings all started again and were only silenced by the Secretary tapping on the table with his pencil. All went quiet, he looked down at my little pile of references, cleared his throat and informed me, 'There doesn't appear to be a reference here from your present employer – why is that? What are you being sacked for?'

By now, the 'might is right' chorus were looking at me with steely eyes, and a couple of them were looking at their watches with some impatience. I suppose they had every right to feel I was keeping them out of the 'Cross Keyes' but wasn't their slogan 'Equality for all?' All right, I'd tell them why I was being sacked. They had every right to know.

Looking at the full table as though it was a full house in a theatre I said, 'For stealing, sir.'

You could have heard a pin drop! God 'strewth! Some of them nearly slithered under the table!

'I . . . er – I think you had better explain,' said the Secretary after he'd regained his composure – and I did – and I told them the whole story, every detail. As a matter of fact, if it hadn't been so serious, I could have almost felt I was telling a bedtime story to a lot of little children, so attentively did they listen – but it *was* serious, and I *knew* it was, so after strenuously defending my honour I finished off by saying, 'So you see, gentlemen, I have nothing to be ashamed of – *I* know the money that fell out of my pocket was my own.'

At this point you could have heard another pin drop! – and then – 'Thank you, Miss Hird,' this came from the Secretary, quite quietly really. I was politely dismissed and thanked for coming along. With an equally polite, 'Good night, and thank you,' I left the room.

I cannot remember the journey home on the bus, but there must have been one.

As I hung my coat up on the varnished partition in our living-room, my mother asked me, 'How did you get on!' She was preparing a cup of cocoa for me.

'I don't know,' I replied as I pushed a dislodged hairpin back in place, 'I told them why I had got the sack – that seemed to shake them a bit, but I did tell them everything!'

'That's a good girl,' my mother said proudly as she poured the hot milk into my cocoa mug.

It wasn't until I was in bed, that I suddenly realized I hadn't told them everything, I hadn't told them that I had called Madam Glumdell a bloody bad old bitch! Which was probably the *real* reason why I had got the sack!

On the Saturday morning, my last day at Glumdell's, a letter arrived at 6, Cheapside, requesting me to report for work at the Lancaster and District Co-operative Society's Queen's Square Branch, for duty, at eight thirty on the following Monday morning! I'd got the job as cashier!

As I unhooked my coat from the rail in the Fustian-smelling passage, Madam stood like a wardress in the shop. I buttoned up my coat as I proceeded to walk out of the shop for the last time. I opened the door with the big brass latch I had cleaned so often as she called after me, 'I can't see you getting another job in a hurry, we are not giving you a reference, you know, so don't bother to come back and ask for one!'

I turned and looked at her, and with all honesty I said quietly, 'No, Mrs Glumdell, I won't do either – good night!'

The door of Glumdell's closed behind me for the last time.

In my fan mail on 9 October 1970, was a charming letter from an equally charming lady, I should think. She added a postscript which read, 'I believe that when you were in your teens, you worked in my aunt's draper's shop in Euston Road, Morecambe. I gather you were the only one she couldn't boss! Hearty congratulations!'

Thank you, dear lady, but you have been misinformed. Your aunt *did* boss me, which I suppose she had a right to do, as she was the boss. But she also awakened in me the knowledge that I had a life ahead of me that would probably hold many undeserved accusations and rebuffs, in fact, she really assisted me to grow up! At least I'm grateful to her for that!

26

'Fierce flames are raging'
(Il Trovatore)

I stood on Morecambe Promenade on 31 July 1933, as the Central Pier Pavilion burnt down, watching a very happy slice of my life go up in flames.

As the small dome on the left-hand side pathetically crumbled like a deflated paper bag, the little balcony in front of it collapsed in sympathy and disappeared.

'That's our mustard and cress balcony,' I thought.

The gallant centre dome stood proud and magnificent, trying to defy the flames as they curled round its base, but the orange and red arms of fire reached greedily upwards and embraced it in a cruel bright red cloak. The big dome was soon entirely ablaze and as the massive flames reached to the sky it looked as though it was frantically trying to cling or clutch on to something – or perhaps it was raising its arms to the audience on its final curtain.

With a heartbroken wail of agony, it collapsed, and took the small dome on the right with it for company. The balcony where we'd kept the doves went, too.

A tumult of memories rushed through my mind as I stood there amongst dozens of people, but alone, 'Programmes, threepence each – perfumed with Amo-Del!' 'Two more jellies, please!'

'Oh no, this is not I!' sang Miss June, in her navy blue costume and panama hat!

'Sorry I'm late, Dad, but my mother asked me to go for the bread!'

Regardless of my thoughts, the fire didn't stop to think, it was greedily eating into the Pavilion and unashamedly belching black smoke. The place where Devilshoof had carried me over the scenery rocks was devoured quicker than it takes to record.

I ached with sadness as I wondered how much longer my Vestal Virgins could hold the boxes up! Of course, they had never held up the boxes really, had they? I can remember thinking – I'll bet they are valiantly trying to hold them up now! But the inferno was too much for them and the part of the Pavilion they had graced so well, crashed as I thought of them lovingly.

Within a few minutes the entire structure was a mass of flames.

The papers reported that it was Morecambe's biggest fire to date! How like the Central Pier! Nothing but the best! 'Everyone on stage for the finale, please!'

The northern Taj Mahal in true Indian fashion had held its last rites on a burning funeral pyre.

It was there. It was there no longer. All in ninety minutes!

As I sadly walked away, I was thinking of my dad. He was in Lancaster that day so was spared the devastating sight I had just witnessed, I was grateful for that.

I knew the question I would ask him, 'D'you think some silly devil carelessly dropped a fag end, Dad? If you'd been there you'd have found it, wouldn't you?'

I ambled along the promenade, dejectedly pushing against the wind, thinking, 'The domes have gone – it's no use my dad telling anyone where they can stick 'em any more!'

I looked at the raging sea, it pounded deafeningly against the sea wall, madly furious at the disaster it had witnessed during the past two hours. As it thundered its way up the ramparts it suddenly pulled back savagely, leaving its white spume running down the walls like giant tears. I held on to the promenade railings and looked at it. Dark grey, almost black. It was already wearing mourning for the late lamented Central Pier Pavilion!

27

The drummer boy

When the Winter Gardens, Morecambe, was taken over from the Broadhead Circuit in 1933 by a group of wealthy northern businessmen, it was given a face lift, an uplift and every other lift you can think of. The old place was really transformed.

Credit where it is due, it had been looking like a poor relative, which is always a sad thing to write about, especially when one can remember the glittering years of variety and dancing there. However, unlimited money was spent, splendid ideas used and the result was worth all the praise showered upon it. It was back in its place as a first-class variety theatre and ballroom.

The new orchestra, under the leadership of Cecil Hodgkinson, was installed in the band pit and it was to become so popular that the Theatre would be full at seven o'clock, just to enjoy the music prior to the curtain going up at seven-thirty. I was invited to the exciting opening night. It really was a wonderful evening, the entire place had been redecorated, the seats renewed, everything gilt had been regilded and there was a wonderful atmosphere of opulence.

If I tell you that I didn't really notice the drummer in the orchestra, that would be a big fat lie. I did. But it wouldn't be a big fat lie to say that although I noticed him I didn't suddenly think, 'Ah, there is my fate!' It was quite a few months before I thought, 'I *think* that's my fate!' by which time, you will have gathered, we were 'going out' together.

Anyway, I won't recall in detail the three years we saw each other every day but I will tell you that after three years we became engaged and I was taken to Forfar in Scotland to meet his father. (It's usually the other way round, isn't it? Only as Scottie had had his supper at our house for three years one might say he already knew my father and mother. And they knew and loved him as I did.)

If ever Scottie had a rival it was his father, 'The Chief', because from looking at his dear face for the first time, that night long ago, on Forfar station, my love for him increased daily, as his did for me, until he died. See what I mean about being born lucky? A wonderful set of parents of my own and a loving father-in-law as well. (Scottie's mother had died when he was seven.) When he came to live with us, by popular demand, I could do no wrong and he always stuck up for me. This was counterbalanced, however, by my mother, in whose eyes my husband could do no wrong and she always stuck up for Scottie. A wonderfully balanced arrangement, you must admit.

There was something else that was very lucky for us about my parents and Scottie's dad . . . they all got on extremely well because they had so very much in common.

By this time I had begun to work in the theatre, and Scottie and I used to have a favourite stroll after our respective curtains had come down. If his Winter Gardens show was down earlier than mine at the Royalty, he would collect me at the Theatre. If my show was down earlier than his I would wait at my mother's and he would collect me from there ... all very convenient.

We agreed that this little stroll was a good way to clear the theatre air out of our lungs – but who am I kidding? We were young people in love, and, quite honestly, didn't give a damn about clearing our lungs!

Our walk or stroll was only about half a mile, if that, and ended on a little hill known as Woodhill. I suppose there had been a wood there at one time and that is why it was so called. I had known it since I was a little girl and used to picnic there, with my lemonade bottle full of milk, and my brown bread and banana sandwiches, but I could never remember it as anything but a sort of meadow on a hillside. A meadow that smelt of fresh grass and clover. As I grew older I discovered that the full moon shone on it, too! Smashing!

Most of the surrounding area around had been built up, and part of Hodgson's Meadow, another of my picnicking spots when I was little, was by now a road of spick-and-span new semi-detached houses.

Perhaps it was the moon – or perhaps we'd cleared our lungs of theatre air – perhaps it was because Scottie was in digs, but whatever it was, he once again got on to the 'marriage chat'.

How do I explain that although I knew he was the one destined to be 'the one that *didn't* get away!' I was not mad keen on getting married too soon. I had a wonderful family life at home into which Scottie was welcomed and I loved him dearly, so I said, 'I'll marry you if you'll have a little house built for us, on this hill!'

I suppose it was about two months later that, as we arrived at Woodshill one night, I saw that the foundations of a house had been dug! In the middle of the well of earth and clay there was a small piece of wood stuck up, and nailed across it horizontally was a smaller piece of wood bearing the word, 'Sold'. The 'S' was the wrong way round, which made it look a bit sad, but it fitted with my mood as I said to Scottie, 'Aw, what a shame! There you are you see, someone has beaten us to it!'

My man is very undemonstrative really, but on this occasion he put his arm round my shoulder and said, 'Did you ever think you would *have* to get married?'

'No I didn't!' I shot back, 'and what a thing to say!'

'Well,' he laughed, 'you'll have to marry me now, because this is *our* house!'

I flung both my arms around him! Within three minutes I knew what sort of curtains we would have and which tree, in the non-existent garden, we would sit under!

An obliging cow had 'dropped its card' in the foundations. Muck for luck, I thought, and it was!!

We called the house, 'Prompt Corner' (but of course) and it cost the amazing sum of four hundred and ninety-five pounds!

Scottie and I returned from our honeymoon on a train from Forfar that arrived in Morecambe around lunch time. As the station was midway between my parents' house and our own brand new little house, you may wonder why we made for 6, Cheapside, first. Well, that's easy to explain. I wanted to see my parents and tell them all about our honeymoon (well, not *all* about it – but at least about the lovely scenery!). And also, as it was lunch time, I was anticipating a 'free nosh!'

I shall never forget the aroma of roast lamb, mint sauce, and new potatoes rolled in butter, that wafted up our nostrils as we opened the front door.

After loving hugs all round, my mother informed us that they had already eaten. 'We had lamb chops,' she said, 'and I would have prepared some extra if I'd known you were going to call here on your way from the station, but there are plenty of new potatoes left and some mint sauce. So why don't you nip round to the butchers and get a couple of lamb chops? You can grill them here and we can hear the rest of your news while you eat them!'

Quite simple and straightforward, really, only she didn't know that the newlyweds had but three shillings and eight-pence between them! Which had to last until the Friday. (And it was only Monday!) Never mind, I bought two lovely thick chops for *tenpence* (doesn't *that* sound like a bit of ancient history!), reducing the housekeeping cash to two shillings and tenpence!

There was apple pie and custard on the table so after we had eaten the two succulent chops I said to Scottie, 'Apple pie and custard, love?' as I cut him a generous wedge. As I was about to put his plate in front of him my mother said, 'It's threepence a portion!' I nearly dropped the plate on his lap but then started to laugh as I said in a very assured way, 'Yes, I'm sure it is! 'But it *is*!' protested my mother with a very straight face. In fact, she was so serious that I asked, 'You're kidding, aren't you, you don't really mean that you're charging us for it?'

'Yes. Two portions will be sixpence!' she assured me.

I gave her sixpence, and didn't enjoy my three-pennyworth at all. My own, dear, generous mother, who gave everything, charging *me*, her own flesh and blood, her own loving daughter, blasted threepence a portion for blasted apple pie and custard! Ah well, you live and learn, I thought.

As we walked to our new house, poor Scottie had to suffer my martyr-like moanings, such as, 'I'd never have believed it!' 'My *own* mother charging us for a sweet!' etc., etc. However, I can honestly say that as we entered our newly-painted front door for the first time as Mr and Mrs James Scott, I was so happy that I wasn't bothering about anything . . . not even how I was going to manage until Friday on two shillings and four-pence housekeeping money!

Scottie returned to work at the Winter Gardens that same evening and as I wasn't playing in the rep. company that week, I met him after his work. We called at 6, Cheapside, to say 'Goodnight' as we were on our way home.

In the centre of the dining table were two large plate pies, a savoury one and an apple one. My mother started to wrap them in greaseproof paper and burst out laughing as she did so. I pretended I didn't see the joke, but as it was hard to keep a straight face because my mother's infectious laugh had started Scottie laughing as well.

'It was worth it to see your face at lunch time,' my mother explained.

'Well, there was no need to charge me!' I retorted.

'Oh yes there was, you're a married woman now and you'll have to learn to make your money spin out . . . if you want anything badly enough and can't afford it, you'll just have to wait until you've saved up for it!'

How right she was, and how often Scottie and I have saved for some special item, enjoying the anticipation of buying it as much as the actual purchasing!

We unwrapped the pies when we arrived home, to discover that the apple pie had a centre decoration. Nestling there, as though it had laughed itself into my mother's fabulous pastry, was my sixpence!

28

The pioneers

It was a great moment when we discovered that 'The two James's' (my dad and Scottie's dad were both called James) had both at one time been managers for Pooles. Not Vernon's Pools or Littlewoods' Pools but the original Charles Poole, the pioneer of the Panorama, Cyclorama and Mirrorama, which were the forerunners of the film industry.

A Panorama, to describe it as per dictionary, is a continuous revolving landscape, circular or semicircular view, inside of a cylindrical surface painted with scenery.

To describe it as per Thora, a Panorama was two massive rollers like tall pillars and the scenic canvas was wound from one to the other by means of a big handle. (By the way, I know I'm not twenty-one any more but neither am I old enough to have seen one of these wonderful contraptions in action. All my knowledge of same was gleaned from my father.) When the aforementioned progressed even further it was called a Cyclorama. The next step was the Mirrorama and by the time it reached this stage it was really something! Scenes were projected from a magic lantern on to the revolving canvas. There would be moving clouds going one way, while cut out figures, carriages and horses, fixed to a gauze, would be moving the other way. 'The Siege of Mafeking' was produced quite realistically by adding gun noises, flashes, and a background of smoke. A gentleman would stand at the side of this living miracle and describe to the open-mouthed audience what each scene depicted, pointing out various interesting details with a billiard cue.

There is no doubt at all that this was the forerunner of the modern motion picture industry, and our parents were in at the conceiving, just as they had both operated Lumiere cinematograph machines at the dawn of the twentieth century. How interesting they were to listen to and how patient when we would ask them to describe some intricate detail more fully.

James Henry even appeared in a film in those early days. The part he played demanded that he should ride up into the clouds on a bicycle! This effect was achieved by laying a sky-and-cloud painted backcloth on the ground and riding across it normally. Clever stuff eh? and the beginnings of trick photography and stunt men all rolled into one!

When I first started in films, I was greatly befriended by Thorold Dickinson and his wife Joanna. It would require a separate book to record their many kindnesses to me.

One night when I was dining at their house, we were discussing the early days of filming and I told them about the two JAMESES and their involvement with the 'industry'. Thorold was so interested, that he asked my father to write about his experiences during those pioneer days, which he (Thorold) eventually incorporated into an article in a film magazine.

I have already told you that my father moved along in the entertainment business from artist to manager. Parallel with that, Scottie's dad moved on to the musical side and was to become Musical Director at various theatres. He also taught the cello, which he played very well himself.

So there you are. Scottie's dad played the cello and my dad played the banjo. A great pity they didn't meet years earlier. What a double act they'd have made! 'The two Jimmys'. From Schubert to Jazz: open for offers for summer season or Royal Albert Hall Concerts!

29

'Morecambe's Royalty'

Although my father had left the Royalty Theatre so many years before, it continued to be quite a part of our lives. I was in my teens when I made my debut into 'rep.' at the Royalty, it was during the time I was a cashier at the Co-op. What happened was, the repertory company was presenting a play that required a larger cast of artists than they had in the resident company and they asked me 'would I oblige?' I did. It was the thin end of the wedge. Eventually, as I've mentioned, I appeared in rep. there. At first the parts I played were always very small (come to think of it, the parts I played were *always* very small, but we won't go into that), so, consequently, I was off stage more than I was on, but even that had its advantages because by the time I had joined the rep. the dressing rooms were under the stage, my childhood hunting ground, so whilst all the artists with the big parts (pardon the expression) were acting their socks off, I would wander around my old haunts happily reminiscing! You are well aware by now that the stage door to the Royalty was in Cheapside, so what better door to venture through when I went into rep? A stage door in 'our street'. Of course I had been through that door hundreds of times before but never as a wage earner.

My first part in rep. was in *Yellow Sands* by Eden Philpots. I played one of the twins. As one twin says most of the words and the other is only an echo, the Morecambe Repertory Company weren't risking their reputation when they cast me as the echo! It was great fun really, because the other twin (poor soul) had to study all her lines but all I had to do was wait until she had said them and then echo the last two words – e.g. if she said, 'Happy birthday, cousin Jennifer', all I had to say was, '. . . cousin Jennifer!' If she forgot to speak, I was laughing bags because I couldn't echo nothing! It was money for old rope really. Come to think of it, a bit of old rope is about all I could have bought out of my wages. One pound a week I got. On my first pay day I celebrated by treating myself to a bottle of L'Onglex nail varnish . . . it was sixpence.

I could easily fill a book about my experiences in rep. but I'm not going to. All I will say is that they were great days and nights and hundreds of funny things happened to me. I shall have to refer to my rep. days during one or two of the little stories I want to tell you, so that will suffice.

It's extraordinary how one looks forward to, anticipates and talks about, one's first wedding anniversary, perhaps a little more than, let's say, one's third, eighth, or fourteenth. Most wives will agree with me, I think, that a couple of weeks prior to the first anniversary one is inclined to say in a rather offhand way or manner, 'Just imagine, in *two weeks* we will have been married for a *whole year*!' or 'It doesn't seem *nearly a year* since

we were married, does it?' or 'Who'd have thought . . .
it's our wedding anniversary in *two weeks* . . . hasn't the
time flown?' The husband usually agrees with all the
aforesaid remarks because it is the safest and easiest
thing to do. He's also very grateful that the little
woman has reminded him! In plenty of time!!

There's another thing about the first wedding
anniversary, too. The bride of last year is rather
inclined to look at the clock (which was a wedding
present), sigh nostalgically and breathe, 'A year ago
today, at this very minute, I was putting my wedding
dress on and being zipped up the back!' or 'I shall *never*
forget, I laddered my new nylons as I pulled them on
(titter-titter), I thought I should never be at the church
on time!' Little did she know that within a few hours
the brand new bridegroom would throw his 'L' plates
away and with fumbling fingers would be frenziedly
and legally laddering 'em again!

Any road up – that's enough of that sort of talk – as
my mother would have said!

About a couple of days before our first wedding
anniversary, Scottie said to me, after I had brought the
subject up, accidentally on purpose, about a dozen
times, 'Good God, is it *really* a year?' It struck me at the
time, that he used exactly the same expression he
would have used had he said, 'Good God . . . is it *only* a
year?' But we'll pass over that!

There's an expression, common to the north, 'We
haven't much money but we do see life!' Well, that
applied to us!

On the day prior to the anniversary, Scottie asked
me, 'Would you like a mink coat or a diamond solitaire

ring?' I add quickly, there was a twinkle in his eyes as he said it! I replied that I had so many mink coats and diamond rings that it would be ridiculous to buy me any more!

Then we both burst out laughing. You see, this was the wonderful period when everything we wanted had to be saved up for. We hadn't a bank account but we weren't in debt either . . . except for the house, and we religiously put the thirteen shillings and eight pence halfpenny rent away each week so that it was there to pay the mortgage on the specified date. I had a series of empty cigarette tins in the top drawer of the desk, each one labelled neatly and clearly. I can remember those tins like old friends. The fags they had contained were called 'Ashton' and they were thirty for a shilling. I've still got one of the tins amongst my 'treasures'. The great advantage about them was, the lids were half red and half white, divided obliquely, and, if one so desired, one could print the description of the contents on the white half instead of going to the trouble of making labels of stamp edging. The tin I still cherish has 'Papers' printed on it, but that doesn't mean it contained toffee papers, the Aspen papers, curl papers or cigarette papers – oh no, it meant that it was the receptacle for the weekly money for the newspapers. The money was put into the tin each Friday when we were paid our respective wages, so that it was *there*, waiting to pay the newsagent.

Another tin displayed the word 'Windows'. I used to put fourpence a week in that tin, because Edward Fern, the window cleaner, used to do our windows, front and back, inside and outside, every fortnight, and he charged eight pence! (*Eight pence*! I haven't as many windows in our present house and it costs two pounds and the bloke only does the windows outside! There's another thing, apart from the price, where our present bloke can't compete with Edward Fern – Edward was an artist at his job who always 'got in the corners!').

'Clothes', 'Insurances', 'Garden' (that was for seeds, etc.), 'Rates', everything was covered by my 'tin system'. But my favourite tin was the 'Weekend in the Lakes' tin. It meant, of course, the Lake District, and every time Scottie did a broadcast with the orchestra, and there were many, the money was put in that particular tin. You'll notice, if you please, I had put 'Weekend' in singular, so that we wouldn't be disappointed if we only managed to go once!

'Weekend in the Lakes' sounds as though we were going to take our shoes and socks off and 'paddle or stand in the middle of Lake Windermere for the weekend. Doesn't it?

Right! Now where the 'ell was I? Oh, I know, Scottie had just asked me whether I wanted a mink coat or a diamond solitaire ring for my first wedding anniversary present and I had replied in a rather facetious manner that I had too many minks and diamonds!! Well, after we had stopped laughing, and I think there had been a bit of a kiss and a cuddle, I asked him, 'Would you like – and you have a choice – a navy blue Hillman Minx with a gilt "S" on the door, or a three and elevenpenny ha'penny evening shirt from Greenwood's in Euston Road?' He thought for a minute, then (melodramatically acting out his indecisions) finally said he would prefer the shirt because he needed a new one to wear in the orchestra.

On the great day itself, I presented him with the shirt, carefully gift wrapped in a piece of fancy paper. I'd also bought a most beautiful card for three pence . . . honestly . . . *THREE PENCE*! He in turn presented me with some flowers and a card, which I've still got (the card I mean, not the flowers).

During lunch, he remarked that he wished I would tell him if there was some little thing that I would like that he could give me because he didn't feel the flowers were enough. 'Right!' I said, 'there *is* a little thing that I would like that you could give me!' 'Good!' he said. 'What is it?' 'A baby,' I answered, as I chewed on a chip. 'And I want us to make it tonight!'

The doctor called me into the surgery. I knew her well and I knew her dad before her. Her dad had known me very well too, he'd brought me into the world, and you can't know anyone better or more intimately than that!

'Now then, Thora, what's wrong?' she asked, lighting a State Express 333 and offering me one.

'Nothing,' I replied, 'I'm just in an interesting condition, that's all!' She bounded up from the desk, said how happy she was for Scottie and me and my mother and father, and then instructed me, 'Get on there!' 'There' was that dark green, leatherette covered couch thing. She turned away from me to put her cigarette out in an ashtray on her desk and whilst her back was still to me she asked, 'How far?' 'Three days,' I replied confidently.

'Three da . . . ! Get off there and pull your skirt down. *Three days*! Come back and see me in a couple of months.' 'All right,' I said, ' . . . but I'll bet you one hundred State Express 333 . . . that I am!'

'Right!' she said, 'and I'll bet you . . . one hundred . . . Players it is you smoke isn't it? . . . that you're not!'

I got my hundred Players and *we* got a wonderful baby girl. Doctor Jo delivered both. 'It was,' as I said to her, 'it was daft of you to take the bet on – you see I know Scottie better than you do and when that lad makes up his mind to do a job – he does it properly!'

On our seventh wedding anniversary I gave Scottie a navy blue Hillman Minx with a tiny gold 'S' on the door. A lot more working water had to flow under the bridge before I got my mink coat, and when I *did*, for my twenty-fifth wedding anniversary, I lent it to someone before I ever wore it myself.

When the curtain rose on the biggest drama of our lifetime, the war, Scottie joined the RAF and for the first time since our marriage we were parted. I had the comfort of our ten-month-old daughter, but, like most people I wanted to 'do my bit' in some way.

I went to the Clarendon Hotel, which was the RAF Headquarters and Billeting Office and offered my services to help win the war. I became a civilian clerk. You will obviously assume that it meant my finishing in the repertory company. Not at all. The parts I played were so small, it was arranged that I could rehearse in my lunch hour!! I worked things out to the second; I would leave the office at 12.30 – rush across the road to the bus stop in time to catch the 12.32 from the Battery, which was further back along the promenade. It was only a short journey to Euston Road Central and I'd be on the Royalty stage at 12.42! Not bad, eh? On arrival at the theatre, the rest of the company, very accommodatingly rehearsed the bits that concerned me, and Bob's your Uncle!

As my parents still lived next door to the theatre at 6, Cheapside, I was always sure of a bit of 'nosh', free, gratis, and for nothing (although I always offered my meagre share out of the rations I got on my own and the baby's ration books, they were never accepted – that's parents all over, isn't it?). It also meant I could see our baby daughter who was contentedly being loved and cared for by her doting grandparents during my working hours. If my role in the play involved more than two entrances my mother kindly provided me with sandwiches wrapped up in greaseproof paper, which I would eat when I got back to the office. The sandwiches I mean, not the greaseproof paper.

30

'Ring down the curtain – I can't sing tonight'

The old Victorian Music Hall song with the above title is inclined to get a laugh in 1975 and remarks such as 'The show must go on' and songs such as 'There's no business like show business', 'Laugh Clown Laugh', 'Close the Shutters, Willie's dead', 'Smile though your heart is breaking' are a bit mushy and I've laughed and made jokes about 'em as often as anybody else.

All the same there *are* occasions when it would be both comforting and convenient if one 'hadn't to go on' – the stage I mean – but one does 'go on' because – excuse the expression – 'The show *must* go on!' I recall, very vividly, the day my mother died. I was in rep. and, would you believe it, on my first entrance in the play we were doing I was attired in black for a funeral, and my opening line was, 'If we're going to mourn the departed, we must do it completely!' Nobody could or did love their mother more than I loved mine and the fact that I played that night will be understood by all my fellow workers. I wasn't playing 'a big important part' – it was very rarely that the repertory company cast me in such a part – but you see, there are no 'understudies' in rep., and in any case my dad, Mr Professional, said 'Go on, love, go to work, your mother would have wanted you to!' So I did. The strange thing was that, as I walked on to the stage and said the line, I said it without any additional emotion; in other words, I said it as I had rehearsed it, it was the *rest* of that wonderful band of players who could hardly speak. When the final curtain was down, I went to my dressing room, excuse the *my* dressing room bit, I *shared* a dressing room – and my dad was sitting there. 'Hello, Dad! What are you doing here, love?' I asked ever so brightly. 'I don't know,' he answered. 'Well, just let me clean off and we'll go into the Rat Pit and have a drink,' I replied.

'The Rat Pit' was the pit bar at the Royalty Theatre, and the artists had access to it from under the stage. It was aptly named, we had to pass the gentlemen's urinal to get to it and believe you me the effluvium was enough to make anyone join the 'Blue Rubber Band' or 'The Band of Hope' and cry off drink forever! But we didn't notice 'the perfumed passage' much that night.

As we walked home (I had insisted that James Henry stayed on for a while with us because my mother had died in our house, 'Prompt Corner') a lump of pain, like a brick, formed under my ribs. I suppose the same thing has happened to lots of people reading this. In my case it *stayed* there for five whole weeks until one day, after carefully saving my meat coupons for weeks (because this story happened in 1942), so that I could give Scottie a mixed grill for his lunch when he arrived home on leave from the RAF, I gazed at the little kidney, the weary sausage and minute piece of steak and the bit of shrivelled bacon, that were all huddled together on the plate as though they were ashamed of

221

their size, and I can remember thinking, 'Oh, he *will* enjoy this!' As I grabbed hold of the plate, my anticipation of Scottie's joy was so great that I forgot to use a towel or an oven glove and as the red hot plate burned my fingers I dropped the blasted offering – it fell upside down on a piece of coconut matting! The brick under my ribs started to dissolve and I cried for two hours!

My darling Scottie sat at the dining-room table in his RAF uniform, picking coconut matting hairs out of the mutilated sacrifice, faithfully eating the 'surprise' I had cooked for him and saying, 'Don't cry, love, it's lovely – *really*!' He knew, of course, I was crying because I'd lost my mother five weeks before!

I am never likely to forget the week we played *As You Are*. I was cast in the character of the mother-in-law, Emma Pearson. She was a woman of sixty, so after I had made myself up, complete with paste nose, I nipped out of the back door of the Theatre, ran the ten yards to our back yard door, and into the house. There, confronting my mother, I appealed anxiously, 'How do I look? I've not overdone it, have I?' She assured me I had done very well, as she smoothed a rather harsh line of greasepaint, which I had applied to give the effect of wrinkles, with her little finger. You see, that was just one of the lucky and wonderful assets I was blessed with; I mean, how many actresses have the advantage of nipping out of their dressing rooms and within a count of twenty are able to be in their own living-room asking their very experienced and professional mother, 'How do I look? I've not overdone it, have I?'

When the curtain was about to rise, the buzz was going round the company, 'George Formby's in front!' and quite a bit of excitement prevailed, because he was a big name. The leading man said to me, 'I'll bet he's in a box,' and I said, 'I'll bet he hasn't paid!' (I said this with a laugh and not with disrespect, I assure you!)

After the show, the manager of the Threatre brought Mr and Mrs Formby down under the stage because they had asked to meet me. I was just taking my paste nose off when I was informed that they wished to speak to me, so with my paste nose pointing towards my left ear I was introduced.

I won't bother to tell you what they said about my performance but I will tell you that I heard him saying he was going to make a film of *As You Are* and that he would like me to repeat the part I was playing on the stage in it. He then said he would arrange for me to go to Ealing Film Studios for a film test.

I was dumbstruck but I managed to thank them both very much. I stood there like someone in a trance.

I was still standing there with my paste nose pointing towards my left ear after they had gone, when it really dawned on me what George Formby had said. I didn't know whether to laugh or cry. Instead I gave a great sigh, and as I did so my head went back and my eyes looked up. I was standing underneath 'the grave drop'. '*I* know *you*, don't I?' the grave drop seemed to say in our Nev's voice of years ago.

Then I *did* cry!

Opportunity knocked on the Monday and on the Friday night while I was removing my makeup after the show, there was a knock on my dressing-room door. I called out. 'Come in!' but nobody did, so, grease towel in hand and face covered in cold cream, I opened the door.

I'm not one for flattering, but the gentleman standing at the door really *was* well dressed and very smart, added to which, he was very handsome as well. I didn't know who he was so I just smiled through the cold cream, whereupon he enquired, 'Miss Hird?' 'Yes,' I answered.

He gave me his card. I'm short-sighted anyway, but it doesn't help much when one's eyelashes are sticking together with cold cream. Anyway, I managed to read 'Gordon Hamilton-Gaye, Casting Director, Ealing Film Studios.' The casting director! And me covered in cold cream! Sod it! Then I suddenly thought, as I'd never kidded myself I was in the front row when good looks were being given out, perhaps the cold cream was covering a multitude of sins!

As Morecambe is a seaside resort, my first thought was that he was on holiday, so, like an idiot, I asked him, 'Are you here on holiday?' 'No,' he replied, smiling, 'I travelled up from London especially to see you!' 'Just to see me?' I stammered. 'Yes, just to see you!' My mouth was open a bit, I was nervous, I was dithering, I was embarrassed because of my greasy face and I was young, so perhaps it is understandable and forgivable that I just looked at him and gasped, 'But the fare is three pounds seven and nine!' Hey, d'you know, I couldn't imagine anyone going to that expense to see me! He didn't half laugh. I wonder whether he would have laughed had he paid the fare from London today!

If things go on as they are doing, it's going to cost three pounds seven and nine to travel from Marble Arch to Oxford Circus by tube.

'Is there somewhere we could go to chat for a few minutes?' he asked. As I was sharing a dressing room I replied 'Yes – er – well – er – where would you like?' (What a daft thing to say.) 'Well,' he said, and this was the moment when I knew I had a friend for life, 'What about the prop room?'

Sitting amongst the props, he voiced his own love of prop rooms, having been connected with the live theatre before he was in the film business and as I sat and listened to him, I wiped the remaining cream off my face.

I looked around the room, a room that I knew so well, a room that had given so much pleasure and was now witnessing the germ of something that could end in a lot more pleasure. I'm not going to excuse myself for feeling like I did. I felt I wanted to say, 'What shall we play at being now, Nev? Film stars?'

Years later, when I was the subject of *This Is Your Life*, Gordon Hamilton-Gaye was one of the mystery guests. When I heard that voice off-stage say, 'But the fare is three pounds seven and nine,' I didn't need to guess, I *knew* who it was!

31

As Dick Whittington said, 'Ten miles to London? Come on, Puss!!'

So, hey up Metropolis, here I come! Now just hold on a minute whilst I describe the ensemble I was wearing. The main bit was, of course, the suit, it was from the 'Fifty Shilling Tailors', it was navy blue with a white pin stripe, my blouse was made of white pure silk, I wore white gloves, black patent leather court shoes and my hat was in navy felt and rather large. Nothing about that outfit to cause alarm or make you laugh, is there? Not yet, but read on please.

My Auntie Molly and Auntie Martha (who weren't relatives in any way, only their back yard door backed on to our back yard door), were dear, kind neighbours and I loved them both very much, hence the title of Auntie. God bless 'em!

They had each of them just acquired a black, silver pointed fox fur and with their usual generosity they insisted that I should wear *both* furs for my debut into the moving picture business!

My mother said, certainly not, it was most kind of them both but they had saved up for the furs and supposing anything happened to them, she would never forgive herself.

Both furlenders said I must wear them. My mother

said I mustn't. The furlenders said they would like me to wear them and it was nothing to do with my mother. My mother said she *wouldn't* like me to wear them and it would have plenty to do with her if I lost them. I just stood and listened. At the end of the final round, the referee's decision was a draw. All the aforesaid argument had been in the most friendly way.

Both fox furs had a snap-clip mouth so one mouth could clip to the other, rather as though they were eating each other, and the two bodies and brushes could hang down my back, nothing about *that* to make you laugh either if I happened to be tall and willowy, but I am only five feet and one inch tall and the brushes of the luxurious furs were hanging well below my bottom, so the effect was er . . . well er . . . rather top heavy and grotesque.

The gates of Ealing Studios opened to welcome me (well, that's not quite correct, the *small* gate at the side of the big gates was pushed open by me) . . . the air raid warning sounded as I did so, everybody started running so I did as well, I had no idea where we were all running to but I guessed it was a shelter. It was and we sat there for over an hour. A woman sat next to me shelling peas for the restaurant as though she always went there to shell peas!! There was a lot of joking and rude remarks passed about what should happen to rotten old Adolf!

A film test is not like a driving test, a breath test, or an eye test, it's like er, well, er, a film test, and I am here to tell you that 'not nobody nowhere' knew less about a film test than I did! Which I will prove!

After being made up and costume I was taken on to

the set, where I was looked at, talked about and photographed and then tested as the sixty-year-old mother I had played in the play. After all that it was decided to send me back to make-up where I was to be given 'the glamorous treatment' – it seemed to take hours (which is not surprising, with my face!), false lashes, hair styled, all little bits of curls over my forehead and the prettiest of 'juvenile lead' dresses.

When I returned to the set I was informed that I was to be tested as Lynda (who was the female lead in the play and daughter-in-law of the part I had played). They had employed a young actor to play, for the test, the part that George Formby would play in the film.

He was standing in the middle of the little set they had built, looking distressed. I had to walk on, looking equally distressed, whereupon he asked, 'Where will you go, Lynda?' and I had to reply, 'I shall go to London!', and then exit. Not much, you will admit, to give 'em an idea of whether you can act or not. We did the scene about ten times, so I'm sure you'll understand when I say that I thought we kept on doing it because I was doing it wrongly. I'd no idea that they were shooting close-ups, medium close-ups and long shots. The young director of the test was very kind and helpful and after the tenth attempt came up to me and said, 'Splendid, now in this next take, I want you to say the line with more anger, sort of, "I shall go to London and bugger you!" Get it?' I said I would try.

By now, I was convinced that they were just being kind and patient. On I went for the eleventh time, my young leading man asked me, 'Where will you go, Lynda?' and I replied, 'I shall go to London, and bugger you and bugger everything because I don't think I'm any good at this . . . if I haven't done it right after ten attempts I never will, after all I was *asked* to come down here, *I* never asked if I could, I was quite happy in rep, I mean, I'm sorry but *you* did ask *me*!' At that moment the director said, 'Cut!' As I didn't know what that meant, I just stood there with egg on my cupid-bowed lips, false eyelashes, and curls-over-my-forehead face!

I was requested to go and change into my own clothes, and I was glad to escape for a breather after my pathetic outburst. I was then tested as a secretary.

After all that, I was thanked most profusely and everyone treated me very kindly.

I was staying the night at 'Kenmare Cottage', which was only yards from the studios. It was a wonderful old place, all authentic old oak beams and ingle-nooks. Great food. But great or not, that night I fell asleep at the table during the soup.

The following morning I had to go to the studios to see the result of the test. I arrived and was directed to the Rushes Theatre. Quite honestly I didn't know what rushes meant and wondered whether I should have to rush into the theatre and rush out again. The place seemed full of people, mostly men, but as soon as I spotted Gordon Hamilton-Gaye I felt a bit more at ease. I was introduced to Mr Shandos Balcon and sat on his left.

Then it all started. The screen flickered and the first person I saw on it was the clapper boy, holding the clapper board and saying, or announcing would be a better word, 'Screentest-thorahirdtakeeleven!!' Then he clapped the board.

I can't really describe the next bit adequately, because I had gone sort of numb all over as I saw and *heard* myself on the silver screen.

The curls on my forehead were bobbing up and down, my false eyelashes were being blinked at the rate of knots and my cupid-bow mouth was saying, 'I shall go to London and bugger you and bugger everything because I don't think I'm any good at this, if I haven't done it right after ten attempts I never will, after all I was *asked* to come down here, *I* never asked if I could, I was quite happy in rep., I mean, I'm sorry, but *you* did ask *me* – A quiet voice interrupted me with the word, 'Cut!' and the screen went blank. The lights went on. I was sitting there petrified, clutching Mr Shandos Balcon as though we were in the back row of the cinema! There was quite a bit of mumbling and subdued laughing. I felt *awful*!

Hamilton-Gaye came up to me, encouraging as always. He looked at me, rather seriously I thought, and said that Mr Michael and Mr Shan would like to see me in their office. I went, feeling just like one felt at school when the Headmistress requested, 'Stay behind after school please, I want a word with you!'

I knocked on the door of the office of Messrs Michael and Shandos Balcon feeling as though they might tell me to write, 'My name is Thora Hird and I must not be rude' five hundred times. A quick and very businesslike 'Come in!' changed my thoughts completely to, 'Thank God I have my return ticket home!'

The Brothers Balcon were marvellous, businesslike but marvellous! Before I had a chance to apologize, Mr

Shandos explained why I would not be playing George Formby's mother and how one can get away with so much more, make-up wise, on the stage than on the screen. *I was too young!* (What a wonderful thing for an actress to be told, I can't recall anyone saying it to me recently!!!)

I swallowed hard hoping that he wouldn't notice, and by now I was *more* than grateful that I had my return ticket home. Giving me no time to feel sorry for myself, he continued in the same businesslike way to tell me that, all the same, *they were putting me under contract*! – *Under Contract*!!!

He explained they would pay me ten pounds a week whether I worked or not, plus ten pounds a day when I worked on a film. I thanked him very much but added that I didn't think it fair to them if they paid me when I didn't work and that I would return to the repertory company in Morecambe until they needed me. I also added that as the repertory company only paid me one pound for a week's work why should he and his brother pay me for doing nothing?

His face was a picture! He looked straight at me as if I were a specimen of rare imbecile he had never seen before. Then he turned and looked at his brother Michael as though he wanted confirmation that he had heard me correctly. Putting his hands on my shoulders he gently steered me into a very large and beautifully carved chair. 'Thora Hird,' he said, quietly but firmly, 'don't ever let me hear you saying a thing like that again. You are going to go a long way in this business and I have not the slightest doubt that some day in the future you will be in this office, *not* to tell us we are paying you too much . . . but to argue that we are paying you too little!'

Years after that day I *was* sitting in the same office. Our daughter, Janette, was ten years old and under contract to Associated British Picture Corporation. Ealing Studios were interested in her for a film. I reminded Michael Balcon of the day I had told Mr Shandos I thought they were paying me too much! He remembered, and jokingly informed me that he didn't particularly notice me arguing that Jan's fee was too high! I was sitting in exactly the same chair that Mr Shandos had steered me into many years before.

Mr Shandos is dead now, God rest him, and Mr Michael is SIR Michael, and deserves to be.

Thank you Brothers Balcon, you obviously agreed with something my Dad had told me years before: 'If you work for nowt you're worth nowt!'

32

Many happy returns

Right then – after my three day stay at Kenmare Cottage next to Ealing Studios, a film test, the offer of a contract and fifteen air-raid warnings, I made my way to Euston and caught a train back to Morecambe. I was weighed down with good news and Auntie Mollie's and Auntie Martha's silver pointed fox furs.

I sat in a window seat of a third-class carriage, thinking. I tried to put my head back but the large brim on my hat prevented this, so I sat up straight. Had I been in the carriage alone, I would have taken my hat off and put it on the luggage rack, but the carriage as well as the luggage rack was full and I hadn't the nerve to take my seven and elevenpenny model off because I was afraid my hair might look untidy. Earphones and figure eight coils were all right without a hat, but a hat always mussed them up!

Aye dear, what a chump I was, wasn't I? I mean, what the 'ell did it matter how my hair looked? I didn't know any of the passengers, and they didn't know me, I doubt if any of 'em had given me a second glance, so who would have cared? *I* would – that's who.

Of course – er – and pardon my mentioning this – they were totally unaware that, sitting in that third-class window seat was a woman of wealth, a plutocrat, an actress with a promised film contract, two borrowed silver pointed foxes and a pair of patent leather court shoes that were crippling her! But that, of course, was their loss.

As we pulled into Crewe station, I asserted myself and with all the assurance of a 'Ten pounds a week if I didn't work and ten pounds a day if I did,' I stood up and pulled the carriage window down and hailed the tea trolley attendant. Putting my 'lace curtain voice' on, I ordered a cup of tea (twopence) and a pork pie (threepence). I took a red ten shilling note out of my purse and offered it in a nonchalant manner, and as I did so the two foxes slowly slithered off my shoulders as though they were doing a high dive, and ended up on the platform in a heap one on top of the other, as though they were copulating.

I returned to Morecambe, I returned the silver pointed foxes and I returned to the rep. company. According to everybody I met, I was now a film star. The repertory company put up my wages by five shillings but although my wages increased the size of the parts I played didn't.

Before long I was requested to return to Ealing Studios to 'appear', which is about all I did, in a film. It was known in casting jargon as a 'two-day part' and I would never have got it had it not been for the persistence and perseverance of Gordon Hamilton-Gaye. (I shall refer to him from now on as Gordon H.G. I mean I *can't* keep writing Gordon Hamilton-Gaye, it sounds too bombastic for such a lovely person – God rest him.) The film was called *The Black Sheep of Whitehall* and starred Will Hay.

Over a dozen young, well-known character actresses had been tested, but apparently, though capable, they weren't exactly what Will Hay had in mind for the part of 'Joyce', his secretary in the film. After each unsuccessful test, Gordon H.G. would dart in with the request, 'Will you see the test of this girl from the North, Will?' Each time he got the same reply, 'No Gordon – because I want an established actress in the part!' Any road up, after more tests, of established artistes, Gordon H.G. said, 'Just see her test, I'm not asking you to give her the part.' So, Will Hay saw the test. According to what I was told, it had only run about half a second when he turned to Gordon and said, 'What a face – who is she? Send her a telegram!'

I think I should point out that the test he saw was where I'd been 'glamoured up', and it's best not to dwell on what he might have said had he seen me in my natural beauty!

So, thanks to Hay and Gay, I played in my first moving picture. My pattern of living after that was to return to my home in Morecambe and appear in rep. between film 'engagements' until I was recalled to the studios. The second film I appeared in was with Frank Cellier and Michael Redgrave in *The Big Blockade*. I was a barmaid at a German railway station buffet. I had about eight words to say. My own hair being a good length, the hairdresser plaited it and wound it round my bonce to help me look like a Frau.

My contribution to the film took only one day to complete. So however you add up, my first film role was two days' work, and my second, one day's work. Was I slipping? Watch it, Thor! Happily, my third film role was a good 'un. It was a film made by the Studios about security on the 'Careless-talk-costs-lives' theme, and it was directed by Thorold Dickinson who was a joy to work with.

However, back to the film. We all worked for half pay, and the studios contributed handsomely, as part of the war effort. I knew the finished film was to be shown to the forces as well as to the public, and I thought to myself, 'Oh good, Scottie might see this!' He did. Seven times, because the forces were *forced* to see it!

The above makes it sound as though it was a rotten film. Well it wasn't. It was a good film. What I mean is, although he was pleased to see the celluloid me once or even twice, seven times *is* a bit much, isn't it?

Once when we were visiting our daughter in Beverly Hills, she and I watched a late, late film – *The Big Blockade*. How we fell about at my plaits and my 'Frau' accent!

33
Way out West

My first appearance in the West End was in *No Medals* at the Vaudeville Theatre. The stars were Fay Compton and Frederick Leicester, and the play ran for nearly two years. This all started in 1944/45. I played Mrs Gaye, the comedy charlady, a cockney woman of about sixty, so it gave me a chance to apply the 'slap' (make-up) to the best of my ability.

I enjoyed playing the part and equally enjoyed playing it in the film version, which was called *The Weaker Sex*.

Looking back, I cannot honestly say they were two of the happiest years of my life. How could anyone be perfectly happy when one's husband was in the Air Force, one's four-year-old daughter in Lancashire (albeit she was being expertly and lovingly cared for by our nanny Vera). Thank you, Ve, I shall never forget the care you took of our little girl and neither will she. You really were the best Nanny in the world, whilst you yourself, personally, were living alone for the first time. 'Alone in London.' Hecky plonk! That sounds like a chapter heading in a Dickensian serial! Well it does, doesn't it? Apart from which, I don't like my own company and I'm not the sort of person who will go to a lot of trouble over meals if I'm only cooking for myself. But of course that never came into the routine of things during the war, being rationed to one ration book.

What I mean is, well take a 'ferinstance', on the rare occasions that Scottie is in America and I am here in England, although I will grill myself a steak or poach myself an egg or something like that, I will prepare a salad rather than bother cooking vegetables, whereas Scottie, if he is alone will grill himself a pork chop, automatically make stuffing and apple sauce, cook two veg and spuds, follow with a sweet or cheese and find it no trouble at all. Mind you, he's a smashing cook and the lad does enjoy a spot of good food. No, it's not that I'm lazy, God forbid, I'll take time and care to set myself a table plate or a tray nicely, whereas Scottie will probably eat in the kitchen off the top of the fridge, even so, if marks were being awarded for self preservation he would deserve the most!

Oh dear, I went off the subject again, didn't I? Sorry! Now where was I? Oh, I know, 'Alone in London!'

Anyway, there's one thing I will say, and that is, although it wasn't the happiest time of my life, I made a lot of very good friends and I've still got 'em!

I have no intention of making this book one of those 'when I was appearing at such and such a Theatre'. Let me just tell you some of the amusing anecdotes that come to mind.

One night when I was going into the Vaudeville Theatre stage door (I was appearing in the play *No Medals* at the time) a rather large dog paused and appeared to read the billboard. Then it lifted its leg, and wee-weed all over my name, which was in very small print at the bottom of the bill. There were a few other names as well but it appeared that my name was the bull's eye, because that's where most of the wee-wee had hit before running down. Laughingly I said to one of my fellow artistes as we entered the theatre, 'I don't think that was meant to be taken personally, do you?' That night as I made my way to Trafalgar Square tube station through blackened Maiden Lane and the Strand, I thought about the dog christening me, and I started to laugh. I was on my own remember, but it's something I am very guilty of, having a bit of a laugh to myself. By the time I arrived on the platform for the tube, I had forgiven the dog and excused it by telling myself that it wasn't its fault that my name happened to be in 'the wines and spirits' at the bottom of the bill.

Please believe this next bit. As I stood there with my gas mask jauntily slung over my shoulder, I looked round and there was a day bill advertising *No Medals*. I found myself hypnotized as I watched the smallest Yorkshire terrier I have ever seen pull on the lead its mistress held and go up to the bill and have a sniff. It started the sniffing routine at the left hand lower part of the bill, moved with a sniffing motion to the right, found my name, read it, lifted its little three-inch hairy leg, and, direct hit, it wee-weed all over it. I couldn't believe it! Twice nightly! I started to laugh, and I laughed so much that the owner of the dog moved away pulling her dog with her. I think she thought I was drunk or had air-raid shock.

34

Lease and Lend

I have been taken for a mug many times. I have been taken for a ride, as far as lending money is concerned, many times. I have been taken advantage of (in the nicest possible way) many times . . . but I have only been taken for a prostitute once.

It happened on a particular night, when, as part of the war effort I had been to the Nuffield Centre to do a show for the Service lads after our show *No Medals* at the Vaudeville finished. I was living in Ealing at the time, and as I arrived on the platform of the underground station to get my tube home, I saw the usual camp of citizens: some in bunks, some bedded down on the platform itself, old people and tiny babies sleeping, middle-aged people trying to sleep, and young mothers keeping vigil and not bothering to sleep at all. The brave undefeatable people of London, who are so capable of setting an example to any other country in the world, had taken food, thermos flasks of tea and coffee, and bedding along with their wonderful sense of humour and were calmly defying Hitler to drop anything that night! At the end of the platform, where I went to stand and wait for the train, there was only me and a weighing machine. I was wearing a bright red coat, my hair was nearly the same colour, and I wore it in the fashionable Veronica Lake style which was, as people my age will remember, a side parting with a slight wave covering one eye! It was a silly style, really, but one might as well be dead as out of fashion, as the saying goes, and anyway, come to think of it, the present fashion for hair is like curtains that cover both eyes!

Anyhow, there I was, complete with gas mask in case slung over my shoulder, ready to defy Hitler, Goering or anyone else. Well – so I thought.

Down the flight of steps at the right hand end of the platform weaved a GI, rather 'under the influence' – if you follow me! He was smoking a huge cigar.

Let's be fair, it would have been impossible for him *not* to have seen me with my bright red coat and matching hair. On the other hand, and with the greatest respect for our lease lend friends, he couldn't in any event have been called shy or retiring. With a slight roll to starboard, he came up to me, took the cigar out of his mouth with stiff fingers, and enquired, 'Hiya, Red?'

Let me record here and now, I have always been afraid of drunks. Nervously, I moved from one side of the weighing machine to the other. (What the 'ell protection I thought *that* would be I don't know!) Not in the least put off, he followed me and, sticking the cigar back in his mouth, he once again enquired, 'Hiya, Red?'

With British politeness I requested, 'Will you go away please!' (Honestly, can you imagine a more barmy request to an inebriated GI?) But, he had no intention of going anywhere, except with me. 'Hey,

Red!' he repeated, 'I'm *talking* to you!'

'Well, I'm not talking to *you* and I don't *want* to talk to you,' I informed him – which was a stupid remark because I *was* talking to him – I mean, I was *compelled* to talk to him to tell him I didn't *want* to talk! I then heard the distant rumble of the train and immediately assumed a courageous façade! As the train pulled into the station he said, 'Waal, don't talk – jus' tell me, wadda yew charge?'

The tube train doors slid open, and as I stepped into the comforting safety of a full compartment I turned and replied, 'I haven't the faintest idea – what do your mother and sister charge?'

'Lady!' he answered, 'my mom is the greatest!'

The doors hissed to – shutting him out and leaving him protesting on the platform, cigar in hand – nearly in tears at my mention of 'the old Rocking Chair'.

As the train rumbled on I began to feel a bit sorry for him – he was a long way from Tobacco Road or wherever it was he came from. But so was my husband who was in Belgium with the RAF.

I suddenly sat up very straight as I wondered what *he* was doing at that moment!

In 1948 a play called *Flowers for the Living* by Toni Block was to be put on at the New Lindsey Theatre, Notting Hill Gate, and I was asked to go along there to see Frederick Piffard who was presenting it and John Oxford who was directing it.

Now there used to be a very good shoe mending shop at Notting Hill, so, as I'd been 'resting' for quite a few weeks, I thought I'd take the shoe mending (a pair of Jan's and a pair of mine) along with me, therefore using the same three halfpenny bus fare to cover both jobs!

The foyer of the New Lindsey Theatre was very small and looked even smaller because it was packed like sardines with actors and actresses. At this point I had no idea that I had gone for an audition. Suddenly, a dark-haired young fellow came bustling through the doors that led from the auditorium – he saw me and handing me a script he requested that I read pages five and six in act one, page twenty-three in act two and pages fifty something or other in act three. I thanked him very much and opened the script at page five to discover that most of the dialogue on that page was for a character called Shirley. Turning to the front of the script, I read the description of the characters and discovered that Shirley was the fifteen-year-old cockney daughter of Mr and Mrs Holmes. Well, hell, I know that 1948 is twenty-eight years ago, but in all honesty I cannot claim to have been only fifteen even then. So I closed the script, picked up my basket on to my knee and sat waiting patiently to give the script back to the dark-haired young man the next time he burst through the doors, which he did almost immediately.

'Miss Hird please, can you come through?' I could and I did. Sitting in the auditorium were Messrs Piffard and Oxford who greeted me most kindly. I explained that I felt rather long in the tooth to play Shirley, but they hardly let me finish before Freddie Piffard interjected, 'No, no, you're not here to read Shirley, we want you to read Mrs Holmes!'

Now just let me tell you this next bit. I was wearing a

cream tie belt overcoat and my hair was still *à la* Veronica Lake.

The description of Mrs Holmes (which I hadn't read) went something like this: Mrs Holmes is a shabby, hard-worked, middle-aged cockney woman who looks as though she is going through the change, etc., etc.

Well, I might not have been fifteen but I wasn't that old either! However, back to the New Lindsey auditorium and Messrs Piffard and Oxford.

I approached the stage and stepped up on to it, it was only about a yard off the floor. I faced out front and I started to read the part of Mrs Holmes. Not having seen it until that moment, I wasn't prepared for the sadness of this poor woman. As I read, I cried. (I'm a real silly maggot and easily moved.) I tried to stop crying but I'm afraid by the time I'd finished, my nose was running, my mascara was running and *I* felt like running. There wasn't a sound in the auditorium as I stepped down from the stage and walked up to Messrs Piffard and Oxford, handed 'em the script which they took, and said, 'Sorry about that. May I suggest that you tell whoever you give the part to not to bother to act it – just feel it!'

'That's why we are giving it to you,' they replied as they handed back the script to me.

'How did you get on?' asked Scottie as I walked in home. 'Hey – I've got it!' I replied, my face covered with a grin as I put my basket down. 'Er – what about the shoe mending?' he enquired. Oh cripes! I'd forgotten to call at the cobblers. Never mind, I could afford another one and a half penny bus fare now I was in work.

I've called the cobblers' shop 'the shoe menders'. I suppose some people call it the shoe repairers, but it doesn't matter does it, whichever it is – it's all a lot of cobblers.

Flowers for the Living was really my Cinderella story, and I shall always be grateful to Frederick Piffard for risking me in the part of Mrs Holmes. Everything seemed to stem from that. My contract with J. Arthur Rank, the many plays and film parts I was offered. My dad came to London to see the play and I particularly asked him not to come to the opening night because although he had taught me everything I knew about the business up to that point, I felt I wanted him to see me give a performance worthy of his care and patience, and I knew that wouldn't be on the first night.

After he had seen the first night notices, though The New Lindsey was only a little theatre it was one of the best shop windows for a play possible and all the London critics were there, my dad asked, 'Do you think I can come and see you tonight?' 'I'll tell you what,' I replied, 'come tomorrow night, Dad, and I'll try and be ready for you!' That was agreed upon.

After the show the following night we went into the bar. Everybody was being very kind about my performance and I watched James Henry trying not to look too proud.

When we got back to our little mews house, Dad was full of praise for the performances of the rest of the cast. I can remember thinking 'It's any minute now, he'll say I was all right.' There was no feeling of conceit about this, it was merely that I valued his opinion more than anyone else's, because my dad had never ever said to me, 'Oh, you are good!' or, 'You were the best.' He had always given me constructive criticism and had always told me I could do better. When no word of praise was forthcoming I began to wonder if everyone else, critics included, had been wrong.

He got up from the chair, saying he was going to bed. As he went through the lounge doorway he half closed the door and then pushed it open again. Looking straight at me with those smashing blue eyes of his he said, 'You're a wonderful artist. I've lived to see you perform like you did tonight. Good night and God bless, love!' And he closed the door gently.

I was so happy to know he was pleased with me that I laughingly called after him, 'Hey – can I have that in writing?'

He died early the next morning.

During our final week at the New Lindsey, I was requested, 'Don't bother to clean off – Mr Sydney Box is coming to see the show tonight and can only stay for a few minutes afterwards to have a little chat with you in the bar!'

I did clean off – Mr Box stayed three quarters of an hour – and he was the instigator, the thin end of the wedge, or whatever you like to call it, of my being put under contract to J. Arthur Rank! *Flowers for the Living*, eh? I just wished my dad could have been there.

R. F. Delderfield had written a play about life in a general draper's in 1887, Queen Victoria's Jubilee Year, and the play was called *The Queen Came By*. You know, I've been very lucky really, I keep telling you this, don't

I? But I have. The part of Emmie Slee is an actress's joy – I played it at the Embassy Theatre in Swiss Cottage prior to us moving into the Duke of York's in the West End, and I have played Emmie on the two occasions the play has been on television.

During our run at the Duke of York's, our very small daughter Janette was allowed to watch the play one matinee. I can see her now as she came to my dressing room to have tea. She was wearing a kilt of my husband's family tartan and a little tailored tweed jacket with elkhorn buttons, her long plaits sporting tartan ribbons. The play had upset her because she didn't like me being ill at the end.

There is a loving little girl in the play called Kitty Tape. I say little girl, actually she's about sixteen or seventeen. The feeling between her and Emmie is such that when you come out of the theatre you may think that Emmie may or may not be her mother and either would seem acceptable. That all sounds a bit Irish, but you know what I mean, don't you? Well, Jan just loved the character of Kitty and told me over her sandwich in my dressing room that when she grew up she was going to play Kitty Tape. I explained to her that by the time she was old enough to play Kitty, sadly, the play might have been forgotten.

Years later, in 1955, I played Emmie when *The Queen Came By* was done on BBC television. Happily it was successful. They invited me to play in it again the following year, but I graciously refused because I thought it was too short a time since we had done it previously. It was postponed and the following year I was again asked to play Emmie. This time I accepted.

About a week before rehearsals commenced, Jan rang me up and in conversation said, 'You're doing *The Queen Came By* again on telly, aren't you, Mummy?' I said I was. 'Who's having first billing?' she asked, laughing. 'Who's what? Well, *me* I should think, why?' There was a real burst of laughter and then she said, 'Why? Because I'm playing Kitty Tape, that's *why*!'

My breath went. I was *delighted*. Then it dawned on me that it was Janette Scott – *film star* who would be appearing, by kind permission of Associated British, as well as it being my own daughter who had, as a little girl, informed me that she would play Kitty Tape when she grew up. I really was overjoyed. 'Mummy – are you still there? I was only joking about the billing, darling, I mean, nobody could ever star over you in that play!' That was daughter talk, but I got first billing anyway at least, we shared, we both starred. It was the only play we ever did together and it was probably as good a bit of work as either of us has ever done.

35

'Upstairs – Downstairs'

(With apologies to that splendid series)

So, once again, as one door closed, another one opened, and as *The Queen Came By* passed by, I went back to the land of the silver screen. *Fools Rush In*, *Boys in Brown*, *The Conspirators* and *Cure for Love*.

I've just remembered something about one film I was in, I won't bother to tell you which film it was because that's neither here nor there and I don't suppose the director of that unfortunate epic is ever likely to read *this*, but if he does – he'll know the name of the film all right.

We had two American stars in the picture and the poor director had no skin left on his hands through stroking them (the stars I mean). It was pathetic to watch him, honestly, but you see, those sort of situations start me off tittering and I used to enjoy the performance he gave. He also sported an American accent! *An American accent!* He was an East-end cockney! I could understand him wearing a trilby on the back of his head, *à la* Bogart, because he was bald. I could understand his chewing gum and the 'Yeah! sure – okay, baby – roll 'em!' But what I couldn't understand was the way he treated the small-part artists.

On the first day of the film we were all assembled to

start on yet another happy adventure. I was in the very first shot. I had to walk down a beautiful staircase, supposedly in the hall of a house in Belgravia, and answer the doorbell. By the way, I was playing the housekeeper-cum-everything. I've forgotten the script, but whatever it was it had to be spoken as I descended the staircase. 'Shall I start to speak as soon as I'm in shot?' I enquired, most politely I thought. 'Oh, just say the speech as you come down the stairs,' he threw away. So that's what I did. I said the speech as I came down the stairs! 'Stop! Not like *that*!' I heard him bawl, 'Oh God – don't – start – to – speak – until – you – are – halfway – down – the – stairs – now go back and start again!' These dictated to me as though I was a stone deaf idiot!

Now bear in mind, I was only about four stairs down when he stopped me with his bawling, so after his dramatic performance, I continued walking down the staircase (rather majestically I thought), all five feet and one inch of me, and kept on walking until I was standing in front of his nibs who was sitting in a chair with his name on.

'Don't speak to me like that, please, and don't shout at me either, I'm not deaf!' I said quietly. 'If you will kindly direct me as to how you wish the scene to be played, I will try and do it to the best of my ability. Just because I have a Lancashire accent doesn't mean I'm a fortune teller with a tent on the sandhills at Blackpool, y'know. I can't foresee what you want!' And with that I went and sat in the chair with my name on. The unit applauded! They'd worked with him before. The director and the small-part player got on like a house on fire for the rest of the 'twelve days over seven weeks!'

That was the only occasion I ever 'had a few words' that I wasn't paid for in any film studio. And considering I chalked up my hundredth film a couple of years back, that's not bad going is it?

I don't know how familiar any of you are with the play *Tobacco Road*. Come to think of it, I don't know how familiar any of you are, period. But just in case you don't know anything about it at all, please allow me to 'fill you in'.

Tobacco Road is situated in Georgia in the 'Deep South' – yes sur! To depict this, the stage of the Playhouse Theatre was covered with fine sand about eight inches in depth. The Lester Family lived *in* a broken down old shack and *on* turnips. Jeeter Lester was played by Mervyn Johns and Ada Lester his pellagra-ridden wife with the twisted crippled foot (due to pellagra) by yours truly. Ada Lester had seventeen children, if you read up any Tobacco Road history you'll find that there's not much to do during the winter months!

Now I am not going to decry the play – like almost everything else I do – I enjoyed being in it, but I must hurry and get to the bit I want to tell you about. You couldn't, in all honesty, have called any of the poor pellagra-suffering Lesters, *bright*. In fact, they were all a bit dim, due to the continual diet of turnips (because pellagra is a deficiency disease which is probably the reason their brains were a bit deficient as well). So it came as a shock to nobody when one of the sons, Dude (whose sexual desire had been unleashed by Sister Bessie the preacher), having acquired an old motor car, backed it into poor old Mum, knocking her flat, then continued backing over her stomach until she *is* flat. (All good stuff.)

At this point I must make a little admission. If I have to scream in a play I always ask my understudy to do it for me. I just cannot scream without my voice going after I have done so, honestly!

Right, so back to flat Ada Lester having been run over by her sex-ridden son 'Dude'. All that motor car business was done off stage and my understudy used to let out a piercing scream as she held out a saucer on which lay about an inch and a half of Gordon Moore's red toothpaste. You've probably used it at some time or other to make your gums nice and pink. It's very good. However, it's also very good to give the effect of 'spitting blood' and after I had scooped it off the saucer with my little finger and put it in my mouth, I had to sort of crawl on to the stage on my flat stomach, clawing at the sand (you're getting the picture, aren't you?), and that is one of the reasons we had seven or eight inches of sand so that one could claw at it or walk on it and not reveal the wooden stage underneath.

So, having crawled along into my final position which was almost centre stage, I would try to look up at Jeeter (brave little woman) and at the same time release the red toothpaste which would very obligingly spurt out and then dribble down the side of my mouth. When I felt the audience had seen it, I dropped my head on one side in the sand and expired.

Jeeter had a speech that seemed to last for ever after

I'd 'popped off', but it was easy enough for me to lie there until the final curtain. Well, as a rule it was.

I forget how many cats they had at the Playhouse and it really doesn't matter because, let's face it, it only needs one cat to use the sand to cover up its 'buried treasure'. Phew, mate! D'you know, it became a nightly challenge for me to expire, and if, as my head dropped on the sand, I realized my nose was within an inch of one of the theatre cats' deposit accounts, I would add a death twitch which would move me slightly away.

By the time the play was ready to fold, and because the sand of *Tobacco Road* was the same sand we had opened with, my death twitches were becoming increasingly numerous, because it was difficult to find an unpolluted spot.

Oo, I love being an actress, it's all so *glamorous*.

36

What'll you have?

During the Festival of Britain year, 1951, Jack Hylton presented the play *The Happy Family* at the Duchess Theatre. Henry Kendall and I starred in it and one day, during the rehearsal period, we were lunching in Rules Restaurant in Maiden Lane, when Henry happened to bring up the subject of birthdays, and, would you believe it, we discovered we shared the same birthday, 28th May. We opened at the Duchess on 14th May, so the play would have been in production fourteen days when our birthdays came around.

I shall never forget Henry coming to my dressing room and saying, 'Well, I suppose we shall have to give the company a drink.' Now don't get the idea that he said this in a mean way, Henry Kendall was a generous man and a very clever man and I liked him and respected him a lot. But he did have the ability to make me laugh even when he was being serious, which explains why every time I think of the following story, I burst out laughing.

It was decided upon that we would invite the company into the Stalls Bar after the show the coming Saturday night for a glass of 'Champers'. 'We're not having any cards printed or invitations or anything,' announced Henry. 'Well there's no need,' I replied. 'We'll get the young ASM (assistant stage manager) to invite the company through the tannoy (public address system) at the side of the stage.' Agreeing with all this, Henry left it to me to see the ASM which I promised to do when I went down to open the next act. This all happened on Tuesday night, 24th May. On Wednesday night we were in our dressing rooms during the interval when we heard the tannoy click and then the ASM announce, 'May I have your attention, Ladies and Gentlemen, please. Miss Thora Hird and Mr Henry Kendall invite you to a glass of Champagne in the stalls bar, after the show on Saturday night next. Please come and join them in celebrating their joint birthdays – thank you!' Click. Henry and I agreed that the announcement was most satisfactory.

Most satisfactory? Hold on a minute whilst I tell you what happened.

After the show on the Saturday night, I changed quickly and cleaned most of my stage make-up off, leaving only sufficient on as a base which I powdered. Adding a touch of fresh lipstick, I was ready for the fray. Jack Hylton had given us a large, square, iced cake – in fact, he had rung me up that very morning and *enquired* how many candles were required. He was a Lancastrian as I am and I think I understood him very well. I told him one hundred. His words were, 'Why's that then?' and I informed him that Henry was eighty-five and I was fifteen!

On the Saturday night, Scottie came along to my dressing room after the show with a friend of ours called Kay. As we left my dressing room we were joined by Henry and, getting into the lift, we descended to auditorium level. The happy little birthday boy and girl!!

Of course we ought to have known that something was amiss when we had difficulty in opening the doors of the Stalls Bar. But we didn't think. The bar was packed! Champagne corks were popping at the rate of knots, and gay, abandoned laughter greeted us from the happy throng. Henry's face was a picture. Grabbing me by the arm he tried to pull me to one side but there wasn't an inch of spare room anywhere so he hissed into my ear, 'Good God, how many guests have you invited!' 'Only Kay and Scottie,' I shouted back. The noise and gaiety was your full Victorian naughty house. POP! Every time, a cork popped Henry flinched.

At that moment a couple of ladies pushed their way through the masses to thank me most sincerely for inviting them. They had come from Southall because they had never been to a party like this before. They kindly pointed out a batch of people who had travelled all the way from Beckenham, specially. One of the ladies added that she thought she and her friend and neighbour were very lucky to have been in the Theatre on Wednesday, the night that the invitation was announced, and had the announcement been made every night this week? Oh, cripes, it dawned on me what had happened. However, to make sure, I bawled out at her, 'What invitation?' To which she replied, equally loudly, 'The invitation in the interval on Wednesday night, we were in the stalls.'

Well – let's be fair – they had been invited! 'May I

have your attention Ladies and Gentlemen please – Miss Thora Hird and Mr Henry Kendall invite you to a glass of champagne in the Stalls bar, after the show on Saturday night next, please come and join them in celebrating their joint birthdays – thank you.' The tannoy had been plugged through to a theatre full of people as well as the dressing rooms!! I mean, you couldn't blame the uninvited guests for thinking they were invited could you? 'Cos they had been.

Although I saw the funny side of it all, Henry didn't. He pushed his way out of the bar through the doors that led into the empty auditorium and sat on the front row of the stalls looking at the curtain, which was down. I joined him, trying my best not to laugh. 'Well I'm not paying for this lot!' he exploded. 'It's that stupid bloody ASM's fault,' he said. 'Fancy having the thing plugged through to the auditorium!' 'Never mind, love,' I comforted, 'it is our birthday!' And then I started to laugh and couldn't stop.

He didn't laugh, he didn't want to laugh, he tried not to laugh but then he *did* laugh. So we returned to the bar and to the popping of corks and to the host of people we didn't know but who felt they knew us, and we cut the cake!

Everybody raised their glasses and shouted 'Happy Birthday!'

It cost us – oh mate, it cost us! But you can't help laughing can you?

After *The Happy Family* I played in *This Same Sky* (by that clever actress Yvonne Mitchell) I certainly enjoyed playing Momma Brodsky to Frederick Valk's Poppa

Brodsky and it was this play that took me to the Duke of York's Theatre for the second time. The only difference was that number one dressing room had acquired its own 'convenience' which was you'll agree, very convenient! Then I played in *The Troublemakers* by the American author George Bellak, who also directed it. During this time I 'partook' in numerous films – well, it's true, you name 'em, I was in 'em! Of course, many of the parts were just a cough and a spit, and frequently the same sort of coughing and spitting. The wardrobe departments at various studios took to calling me prior to my going to the Studios to say, 'Same sort of thing as usual, Thora, wrapover apron, head scarf and curl pins?'

Then, in February 1954 something happened that I shall never forget. I met Charlie Chaplin! Magic! There's no other word to describe it. He is now Sir Charles Chaplin, which I think he should have been years ago, but that's beside the point. I was in America during the period they gave him an Oscar and as I watched the ceremony on television, I could have wept, well I *did* weep and I'm not ashamed to admit it. I remember sitting there thinking, 'What took them so long?'

How did *I* meet him? Well I'll tell you. Our daughter, Janette, was an important asset of Associated British Film Corporation and Mr Chaplin had a script he wanted to make into a film in England. After the initial chats with ABPC, his secretary rang us from Switzerland to say that Mr Chaplin was coming over and would be staying at the Savoy and that he would like to meet Janette. Scottie had looked after Jan's business matters since she was nine years old, which was really splendid because it meant she had had affection, she was obedient (good old Dad), and she also had a good education.

When the appointment was being finalized, the secretary said that Mr Chaplin would like both Jan's parents to go along and have tea with him and Mrs Chaplin. So the three of us went.

It really was a fantastic afternoon. He was very anxious for Jan to play the part in the film of the fifteen-year-old Irish girl who eventually became a saint. We all sat like children at bedtime whilst he told us the story and as he read every character in the film for us, he literally turned into that character before our very eyes. He even played the part of the young girl, it was almost unbelievable. During tea, we talked about his early days in England and we listened enthralled, practically ignoring the paste sandwiches and the scrumptious cream cakes.

He told us how he came to write the music of 'I'll Be Loving You Eternally' (I think the title is 'Eternally', isn't it?). How he had thought of the notes of 'Won't you buy my English Lavender?' which are very similar to the opening bars of 'Eternally'. But it was something else that was unforgettable. While he was singing the notes he was using his fingers as the legs of a ballerina and those magic fingers were dancing along the tea tray. Each time I see his film *The Gold Rush*, and I do so whenever possible, I am reminded of that afternoon. Most of you will have seen it at some time or other, and you will remember the scene where Chaplin sticks a couple of bread rolls on two forks and manipulates them so that they do a tricky little dance ending in the splits! Well, as I watched those magic fingers I thought, 'Hecky plonk! I'm actually watching this genius at work!'

It really was a smashing afternoon and as we rose to leave he took Jan's face in his hands and said, 'If I can't get you for this part I won't make the film.' Unfortunately there was some kind of unpleasantness and trouble at the studios (not ABPC studios; the studios where Chaplin wanted to make his film). So, of course, it never got off the floor. To be more correct, it never even got *on* the floor!

Never mind, we did have those few illuminating hours for which we thank you very much, Sir Charles and Lady Chaplin!

37

'World premiere'

When Walter Greenwood died at the end of 1974 the world lost an extremely clever author and playwright and I lost an extremely intelligent and humorous friend. Walter could make me laugh and equally make me cross; and though we could and would argue like mad about a line in any of the plays he wrote for me, we never fell out, and there never was a time when we weren't speaking. His knowledge of English history was fabulous, and there was nothing I enjoyed more than listening to him when he was on the right side of a couple of 'whiskey all-ins!' He talked of our historic island in the same truthful and colourful way he wrote about Lancashire, mingling sadness with humour. I was in America when he died, and I learned of his death through an obituary in *The Times*. I shall miss you, Walter – our loss is the other side's gain, and I'll bet you have already told whoever is on the other side that *Love on the Dole* was returned to you thirty-nine times before it was published and that you didn't become the proud owner of an overcoat until you were nineteen. Oh, and another thing, you will have found out whether Richard III did or did not send those little Princes to the Tower. You always swore blind he didn't!

(I always felt that was on account of your Lancashire softness coming out, y'know, because he was a hunchback.)

Saturday Night at the Crown, surely one of his funniest plays, seemed to punctuate my life for many years. The first time we presented it was at Oldham Rep. I went up there to rehearse with the resident company and stayed at The Grapes. The people who ran the place were wonderful to me, informing me that, 'You've got the bedroom and sitting-room Nellie Wallace had, you know!' (And I can't blame Nellie for staying there; she was no fool, every Lancashire comfort including fantastic grub and a big coal fire in my sitting-room!)

When I saw the billing in front of the Theatre, I nearly collapsed laughing, there in large letters it said: WORLD PREMIERE OF WALTER GREENWOOD'S *SATURDAY NIGHT AT THE CROWN* STARRING THORA HIRD.

World Premiere! In Oldham!! Now don't think for one minute I am running down Oldham, I'm not, I love Oldham, but the World Premiere bit struck me as a bit ambitious. However, walk tall, as they say.

Mrs Kathleen Williams, who did all the bookings for the Blackpool Tower Company came to see the show on the Saturday night (the world premiere was only there for a week), with George and Alfred Black, the impresarios. In the first interval Kathleen came into my dressing room and said, 'Oh, we're having this for Blackpool!' At the end of the show George and Alfred confirmed it. All in happy mood we went over to The Grapes.

In the second act of *The Crown* (I shall refer to it in

that manner from now on because it's such a long title to write and I shall have to keep mentioning it because so many funny things happened to me during my life as Ada Thorpe). Well, as I said, in the second act of *The Crown* we talk for the entire act about Annie Cross and Fanny Butler, who never appear in the play but are certainly a big part of it. They are ensconced up in the 'Singing Room', which, as we all know, is the room in the pub where the small stage is, for the 'turns' who appear to entertain the customers whilst they 'sit and sup'.

Now The Grapes had a smashing singing room – and at this point allow me to mention that in 1955 not every pub boasted one; but The Grapes did and the singing room was in full blast as Kathleen, The Blacks, Walter and I entered the pub itself for a celebration snifter. Kathleen was very keen to see it – the singing room, I mean – because of the singing room in the play, so we took our drinks and just stood in the doorway.

A man on the stage was belting: 'Hone-lee a rose, hi give yew' from *The Vagabond King*, and as he burst into the second line of the song 'Hone-lee a flow-wer . . .' the master of ceremonies put his hand on the singer's arm and stopped his vocal efforts.

Pushing the singer gently to one side, the MC spoke into the mike as follows, 'Ladies and Gentlemen, excuse me for that [meaning stopping Caruso in the middle of his aria], but there is somebody wot has just come in this room who, and I think I speak on behalf of us all, we love very much [cough]. She has been in Oldham for the past two weeks entertaining us in a play at the Coliseum, so I'm going to ask her to come up on here [the stage], which I'm sure she will, and say hello and goodbye to you all, because she is going home tomorrow, ladies and gentlemen [at this point his hand and arm were sort of beckoning me on to the platform]. It gives me great pleasure to present – Janette Scott's Mother!'

Do you wonder I have never had any conceit?

P.S. One morning recently I was listening on the radio to Pete Murray's *Open House*. He played one of Mel Tormé's records and announced afterwards, 'And that was the velvet voice of Thora Hird's son-in-law – Mel Tormé!'

See? Everything evens out if you wait long enough!

The Love Match was written by Glen Melvyn, a clever writer, a wonderful comedian and a helluva nice fellow. It seemed like fate that eventually I would have to be part of *The Love Match*. Glen asked me to be in it so many times, but each time I was busy. However, the moment arrived when I was able to accept his offer. First of all we did a week at Wimbledon. It was a treat! We then did a short tour. Jack Hylton saw us play in Brighton, and presented us the following year at the Grand Theatre, Blackpool, for the season, my introduction to that lovely theatre.

After a very successful season in Blackpool, Jack Hylton decided to bring *The Love Match* into the West End. We opened at the Palace Theatre, Cambridge Circus, playing twice nightly. I travelled to Manchester every Sunday morning for six weeks to be part of a radio show with Ken Platt and Billie Whitelaw, appeared in a film called *Tiger by the Tail* then started on the Norman Wisdom film, *One Good Turn*.

John Paddy Carstairs directed the Wisdom film, and anybody who ever worked with John Paddy will tell you what a love he was, never lost his temper and could get the best out of anyone. Little did I know then that when Freddie Frinton and I started the television series *Meet the Wife* he would direct the first batch. Come to think of it, little did I know then that I would ever be asked to do a television series.

I enjoyed making *One Good Turn* very much indeed . . . never a dull moment, by the time it was finished we were ready to start the film of *The Love Match*.

We had transferred from the Palace, Cambridge Circus, to the Victoria Palace by the time we started to film the play.

When at the end of August, we finished the film I was free to do one of my candid cameos in the film *For Better or Worse*. In my spare moments I used to nip to a recording studio to do my 'voice over' for 'Mother's Pride' bread, which was a job I had for many years. I've been known to catch a London train from Blackpool or Bournemouth on a Sunday, when I was playing a season, record, 'I'm the Mother in Mother's Pride, y'know!' on a Monday morning, and catch a train back to wherever I'd come from in time to play the first house at six-fifteen. I was never bored – I had not time to be.

Doing 'bits of parts' in films has always been fun – I don't mean 'bits of parts', 'parts that were bits' would be more descriptive. I loved 'em because when one did as many as I did, it was always a challenge to try and alter the way I played a charwoman or a daily or a land-lady, and I must confess, I was always treated well and with quite an amount of affection at the various studios.

I hesitate to say 'Of course things were better in those days.' I mean, who knows if they were? I'm quite sure there are thousands of people today who enjoy their work as much as I do and are treated just as well as I was and am. I'm not referring to the folks who think the world owes 'em a living. Life's too short to waste time writing about them.

All right then, I'm still treated well and kindly in the television studios, in the theatre and in the film studios. Oh, and I nearly forgot, sound radio. Well, I think I am anyway. Perhaps it's because I am very old fashioned and believe in giving a fair day's work for a fair day's pay. Hey, I sound like a union leader don't I? Well I'm not. I'm not rich enough for a start, and I only own one house, I've no telephone in my car and it took me a much longer time than it did them to get on to the telly!

38

'SNATC'

Saturday Night at the Crown. In the spring following the 'World Premiere at Oldham', G.B. and A.B. (everyone who knew or worked for the Blacks lovingly referred to them in that way while they in turn called me 'Thorird', because they said that was the way Northerners always referred to me) took the play out on tour. This enabled us to tighten it up a bit, and it also enabled a lot of comic bits to be added. In the last act of the play Ada, the character I played, is definitely the worse for wear, having consumed quite a few glasses of stout. I had to eat a pork pie, and during the week we played the Alhambra, Bradford, a little incident happened. I would break the pie in half very carefully so that the half I gave to Herbert, my husband in the play, was only an empty crust. You ought to try that sometime, it really is possible, with care, to leave all the meat in the half you keep for yourself! Well, one evening, a little piece of my meat fell on to the stage. I bent over and picked it up, wiped it on my coat, took the piece of empty crust off Herbert, stuck the bit of meat inside and gave it back to him! It stopped the show. So of course I dropped a bit of meat every performance and it always had the same effect. I am unable to write about the added business in a way that is convincing enough to prove to the reader how very funny some little things that happen by accident can be. All I can say is, that by the time I played Ada Thorpe for the thousandth time, and that happened to be in Australia, most of the big 'business' laughs had 'gone in' after we originally opened with the World Premiere in Oldham. Most actors and actresses will agree, I think, that the perfecting process of a character in a play is really quite exciting. Well, *I* think it is, for the simple reason that however often you play a part you are always striving to make it just that one toot better.

So, we prepared for the tour. Let's be honest, apart from the tightening up effort we all hoped to make a bob or two. Fond though I was of G. and A. Black, I knew they hadn't got where they were through putting shows on just to tighten 'em up a bit!

Mr Harold Boyes was their business manager, he was one of the keenest and shrewdest business men I have ever met, I admired him tremendously and we were and are very good friends. Now we had no reason to think we would play Blackpool that season, because a show was already booked there for that year. However, unfortunately for the show that opened it didn't do the expected business and folded after five weeks, so our tour was cut short and we took over. No artist really likes doing that, y'know – I think most of my fellow rogues and vagabonds feel a twinge of sorrow when their 'in' means someone else's 'out'!

So, Blackpool here we come! Wotta season. The part of Ada Thorpe, which I played, is as long as Hamlet. I was drinking ten glasses of Dandelion and Burdock (five each show we played twice nightly) until we got the prop glasses, which of course look full but aren't. As I wished the company good luck on our first night in Blackpool, I finished up with the request, 'If you love me will you please, when the curtain drops for the interval, wait to go to the toilet until I've been. Thank you!'

Incidentally, Dandelion and Burdock pours out looking like stout, but it's non-alcoholic and I think if you are drinking ten glasses a night you should go easy on the Beechams and Senna Pods. I'm not certain of this, I'm just speaking personally.

Blackpool is only thirty miles from Morecambe, my home town, so can you wonder that I enjoyed playing a season at The Grand Theatre so much? It's a lovely theatre, designed by Frank Matcham who designed the Royalty Theatre, Morecambe, which is now a memory. The clever Mr Matcham must have known what he was doing acoustically, because I have worked in three theatres he designed, The Royalty, Morecambe, The Grand, Blackpool and The Kings, Hammersmith, and in any of those theatres you could literally whisper on the stage and be heard quite clearly at the back of the gods!

On Sunday a few of us had gone over to Morecambe to see various friends, and Walter Greenwood and I decided to have a long walk! We started out at the Golf Club at *Bare*, walked the length of the promenade past the Battery Hotel onto Sandilands promenade and finished up in lovely Heysham Village. We refreshed ourselves with a glass of nettle drink – it used to be called nettle beer when I was a kid, but somebody put the kibosh on that. 'Right!' I said, 'shall we get a bus back?' 'A bus!' exploded Walter. 'What's up with walking!' We walked, and I'm glad we did because if we hadn't, I wouldn't be able to tell you this typical 'Greenwoodism'.

As we strode out along Sandilands Esplanade, the picture of the bay was really wonderful. You don't have to be born in Morecambe to appreciate the breathtaking views across the bay, the sunsets, and the shrimps. The afternoon was closing in, the tide was out and the ripples of sand were broken up by small pools which reflected the dying sunlight. A few birds hopped about amongst the screeching seagulls. We stood by the esplanade railings and looked at the purple and gun-metal hills across the bay backed by the soft pink and orange of the sinking sun's rays. 'I'll bet you don't know what *that* bird is!' stated Walter, pointing to a little thin-legged creature that was stamping its little clawed feet up and down on the wet rippled sand as though it were doing a Spanish dance.

'Well, as a matter of fact, I do!' I replied. 'Remember I was *born* here, I'm a sand grown'un y'know, it's a sand piper!' 'Yes – well – just watch it a minute!' he ordered, 'You'll learn a lesson well worth remembering.' This was typical Walter Greenwood talk and I always enjoyed it.

'What have I to watch?' I asked. 'There . . .' jumped in Walter, 'you see it hammering on the sand with its beak?' I said I did. 'Well now, watch.' At that moment the sand piper was standing like a statue staring at where it had been hammering, then, with a swift downward movement of its head, it collared a worm and stood dead still again, only this time with the wriggling worm in its beak. It was standing there posing as though it was trying to say, 'How about that then, look what I've found!' 'So what's the lesson – God helps those who help themselves?' I asked. 'No – it's not,' replied Walter, quietly but definitely. 'The lesson *is*,' he continued, 'when the sand piper hammered on the sand with its feet (as soon as he said "feet" I started laughing), the nosy worm underneath thought, "Hello, what's going on there, what's that knocking?" and it poked its head up through the sand to have a look, didn't it?'

'Yes!' I agreed, '. . . but –'

'Well, there's the lesson to remember,' he said. 'What?' I asked. 'If that worm hadn't been so bloody nosy it would still be alive!'

However you look at it, he was right!

39

'The Crown'

There were so many small anecdotes about *The Crown* and I really would like to write about them all but that's not possible – because if I do this book will never come to an end! – so I'll just slip in the one about the night a woman in the upper circle at The Grand, Blackpool, laughed so much her false teeth fell out and hit a bald-headed man in the pit! It's *true*!

At the end of a wonderful season G.B. and A.B. asked me would I play Sunderland (Oh Gawd!) and Manchester Palace. I was very tired but the word Manchester revived me! I had never played Sunderland so I thought, 'Well, I'll have a go – it will be an experience!' It was.

Bernard Fox, who is now very happily married and very successful in America, and lives about half an hour from our daughter in Beverly Hills, was playing Harry Boothroyd in *The Crown* and playing it very well may I add. He had a Mercedes car that I reckon was an antique *then*, but that's beside the point, he offered to run me to Sunderland and believe you me it can be a really beautiful drive. We arrived at the theatre and entered the stage door just as the stage door keeper was filling his kettle. He ignored us until it was full and on the gas ring and he'd found the matches, struck one, lit the gas, blown the match out and chucked it on the floor. Then he turned and looked at us. It was a look of pity.

I noticed that his pullover had about three four inch wide 'ladders' in it as he said, 'What number?' (meaning what number dressing room key did I want). 'Oh good morning!' I replied. 'Er – number one I should think, at a guess!' I was being far too bright and it was getting me nowhere. 'Two as well please whilst you're there,' requested Bernard as his nibs went to the key rack. He passed us the keys, looked us up and down as though we were hobos, shook his head slowly from side to side, did a couple of 'Tut-tuts' and said, 'Oooo, you'll do nothing here!' He was right! We didn't. But we made up for it the following week in good old Manchester.

After Manchester we put *The Crown* to bed, but it rolled over and woke up again in 1957 and we went into the Garrick Theatre in the West End where we played twice nightly happily and successfully.

I had a line in the show referring to the Halle Orchestra, which was written as follows: 'Herbert doesn't care for that kind of music,' which I altered to, 'Herbert doesn't care for that kind of music, that Sergeant Malcolm and his band!' Well, one night Sir Malcolm Sargent was in front. I didn't know he was, but he thought I did, because after the show he dashed round to my dressing room, delighted that I had mentioned him. Before I had a chance to inform him that the Sergeant Malcolm line was in every performance, he requested that I put the line in the following

Friday, second house, as he was bringing the Prince and Princess of Denmark and a couple of members of the Bowes-Lyon family to see the show.

Well, of course, the line tickled them pink, they all came round after the show and had a drink in my room. I'm glad he thought I had put the line in specially for him the first time he saw the show and I'm glad I didn't tell him I hadn't, because if ever there was a gentleman, 'Flash Harry' was he.

After *The Crown* closed its doors at the Garrick we thought we were about ready to shout 'Time Gentlemen Please!', but in 1960 we took the play to Scarborough for the season where one little incident occurred that I'd like to tell you about.

Two theatres stand next to each other on the promenade: The Arcadia, where we played, and The Futurist, where The Black and White Minstrels were appearing. The same stage door is used for both theatres and the parting of the ways is just inside the stage door – a case of our company going to the left, and the other to the right.

The minstrels were a great band of people and our small company got to know them very well. Their season ended a week before ours, and on their final Saturday night, I was sitting on our stage during Act III getting on with my drunk scene, when the door was flung open to admit the Black and White Minstrels in their entirety, singing, 'Thora, how we adore her' to the tune of 'Ida, Sweet as Apple Cider'. It really was an unforgettable moment. When all that lovely lot in white tail suits and white tall hats made their entrance on one side of the stage, the applause started and went on and on while they crossed in front of the audience and made an exit on the opposite side – I wouldn't know exactly how long it all took but what a compliment they paid me!

Talk about 'Follow that!' When the ovation died down, we'd nearly forgotten where we'd got to in the play before they came on. The actor playing Harry, the landlord, looked at me and said, 'What about that then, Ada?' to which I replied, 'Lovely, Harry, most touching – and I have no colour prejudice!' Which got another round of applause. Oh! Happy Days!

And that was the title of the next play Walter wrote for me: *Happy Days*. We'd had quite a few meetings about the title and suddenly Walter said, 'You always put "happy days" before your name when you give an autograph. Let's call it that!' So we did.

Coliseum, Oldham, here we come with another World Premiere! George and Alfred Black again made a pilgrimage up north, saw it, liked it, bought it, and by arrangement with the Blackpool Tower Company, presented it the following season at The Grand, Blackpool. Great, twenty-two weeks, twice nightly and never an empty seat.

It was during that particular season that our daughter got married, and one day G.B. and A.B. and I were going into the Opera House Restaurant for lunch when I said, 'Er – there's something I want to ask you. Do you think I could. . . .' They didn't let me finish. I can't remember whether it was A.B. or G.B. who said, 'No, sorry Thorird!' I informed them that they hadn't the slightest idea what I was going to ask for, but they informed me they had because they read the newspapers as well. I wish I was clever enough to capture with a pen the humour of these two gentlemen, you see, they laughed through all that last bit of print you have just read. They *knew* I was going to ask if I could possibly have a certain Saturday off to go to my daughter's wedding, just as they *knew* they couldn't give it to me. I was starring alone, and it *was* a Saturday in Blackpool. And here is the strange thing, I *knew* they were right.

All right then, on the wedding morning I felt like any other loving Mother feels on the day her child (an only child in this case) is getting married, but I must say our daughter made me feel I was in London because from seven thirty in the morning she rang me about every ten minutes until nine o'clock. Lovely bits of chat like 'I'm just putting my dress on, Daddy says it looks lovely!' and 'I wish you could be here, Mummy!'

Now I must explain that in the play *Happy Days*, my husband, Peter Sinclair, who played Andy Mactagget, and I, who played Maggie Mactagget, celebrate our silver wedding. I think he's forgotten it, and when a telegram arrives from our son, Malcolm, I burst into comedy tears whilst I am reading it and rush off the stage. Right, are you with me so far? Well, while I'm off stage (drying my eyes), I discover a fur coat and twenty-five red roses (in cellophane, so that they would last for the entire run of the show!), and I burst back on to the stage wearing the coat and hugging the roses. On the particular night we are talking about, my husband had been to the wedding in London, and managed to get back to Blackpool for the end of the second house and was literally standing in the wings as I ran off crying. I had two dressers because my quick changes during the show were just that, *quick*! As one dresser passed me some tissues to blow my nose and wipe my eyes, the other dresser put my free arm in the fur coat sleeve and as I threw the tissues down and put my other arm in the other sleeve, the first dresser passed me the roses. Phew! I don't know about you but I'm tired out just thinking about it!

Well, as I said, Scottie was standing there as I made my exit crying. He was holding Jan's wedding posy of tiny little rosebuds, lily of the valley and forget-me-nots. As Florrie, the dresser, handed me the twenty-five extremely life-like red roses, Scottie said, 'Take this on, Jan sent it for you!' And he handed me the posy, which of course I took on.

The audiences in Blackpool are a joy – that isn't only *my* opinion, but the opinion of very many artists who have played to them – on that particular occasion, however, they surpassed themselves. As I started my curtain speech, I held the posy and when I told them, 'We have had a wedding in our family today' – the roof went off. I'll never know whether the applause was because they loved Jan or because they knew I hadn't been able to be at the wedding or whether it was because they just felt like it – or what. I went on to tell them that I usually brought red roses on for the final scene, but that my husband had rushed back in time to give me the posy from Jan. Handkerchiefs were being flicked out of breast pockets, women were opening their handbags to root for a tissue, noses were being blown. If ever I felt the understanding of an audience, it was that night. The curtain came down, went up, came down and went up to tumultuous applause and whistles. On the final curtain the stage director, Chris May, dashed on stage and threw his arms round me, the company were just as loving and it dawned on me as the audience trooped out of the theatre to the recorded music of Syd Phillips' *Happy Days!* that there are a lot of kind people in the world. I can't finish this chapter without telling you that every member of the company bought me a small gift that day – it was as though *I* was getting married. The young ASM came to my dressing room with her present – a small punnet of strawberries and a carton of cream. And I still have three very pretty little white china angels that three of the girls in the company bought for me on that day. I wonder if Pat Phoenix remembers she was one of the donors? I remember!

Each time 'the end of a season' in Blackpool approached, I always had a little heartache, whether it was because I was leaving my lovable Lancashire, whether it was because whenever I finish a job, I feel it's a part of my life I can't enjoy again, or whether it was because I always used to wonder when I left the theatre whether I'd ever play there again.

We only played once nightly during the final week, which was a piece of cake, and, as it was usually October by then, the shops were displaying Christmas goods – so you could buy your Christmas crackers if you felt inclined to do so.

We didn't ever buy crackers, but we always arrived back in London with a great hunk of Lancashire extra-strong farmhouse crumbly cheese. (Did you notice

Janette, aged four. The day she had this photograph taken she was offered a film contract which we refused, 'because we did not want her to go into the business'.

Above: In **One Good Turn** with Norman Wisdom.

In television's **Dixon Of Dock Green.** Where would we be without
the talents of 'Wig Creations', the make-up department and the
wardrobe department? One only has to learn the words! (BBC)

Above left: **The Good Old Days!** (BBC)

Above right: 'Vivienne' took this photograph - I wish I could look like this when I get up in the morning.

Below: Here he is - my lovely 'Fraid' (*the late Freddie Frinton*). We laughed our way through many happy years in **Meet The Wife.**

Above: With Bill
Owen in the BBC
sound series
**There's One Born
Every Minute.**
(Radio Times)

Left: 'Hello, baby,
how's nurse?' Me
as the nurse in
BBC television's
Play of the Month,
Romeo & Juliet.

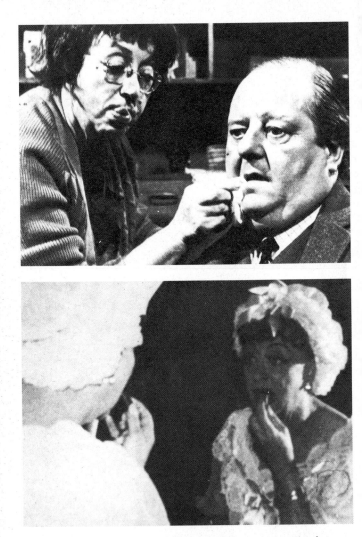

Above: I've happily worked with John Sharp many times in plays, films and television. This was one of the happiest, the television play **A Thing Called Love.** (London Weekend Television)

Below: In my dressing-room at the Palladium, where Freddie and I were appearing in **Meet The Wife** sketches and assisting in various extravaganzas.

This is him! That fella! My husband, Scottie. He's just been cueing me with my words. It looks as though I know them. (Keystone Press Agency)

Avez-vous un cuppa? - Cheeky monkey!
(Keystone Press Agency)

that? 'Cheese and crackers' in one sentence.) Oh mate, that cheese! And I can't get it anywhere in London. If you really want a feast for the gods, try some of the aforementioned cheese on an oven-warm barmcake that has been liberally spread with farm butter!

Excuse me, whilst I go and make myself something tasty to eat – the thought of all that has set me off!

40

'Emergency ward – Sfax!'

I often wonder if it was the piano copy of 'In a Persian Market' by Albert Ketelby that did it – or, of course, it could have been Rudolph Valentino in *The Sheik*, or the bit in the overture of *Samson and Delilah*. Any road up, whichever it was, from quite a tender age I have been hooked on souks. And it makes a happy state of things that Scottie is also hooked on souks, otherwise perhaps I should never have been able to visit so many.

'Souk', described in the dictionary as 'an Arab market place'. I love a souk. Well, perhaps *love* is the wrong word, so I'll say I enjoy a souk tremendously. We really have visited very many and always found our trips most interesting and entertaining – with one exception. It happened like this. We'd been 'souk sight-seeing' in Tunis and travelled on to Djerba, that little fly speck of an island off the northern coast of Africa in the Mediterranean. One afternoon after sunbathing we entered our room for a siesta. Scottie flopped on to the bed and I went to have a quick shower. It was as I stood under that welcome cool spray, soaping my birthday suit, that I thought to myself, 'Aye, Thor, your stomach is sticking out a bit!' In fact I was so convinced that it was sticking out more than it should, that I turned the

shower off, wrapped my protruding abdomen in a bath
towel, went into the bedroom, exposed myself and
enquired of Scottie, 'Should my stomach look like this?'
I must quickly explain that after thirty-eight years of
being married to me, that sort of question doesn't
surprise Scottie – and although we hadn't been
married more than about twenty-four years the afternoon I made the stomach enquiry, it didn't surprise
him. But my domelike abdomen did.

'Have you got any pain?' he asked, quickly sitting up
in bed.

'No – well – er – I don't think I have,' I answered.
'You're not constipated are you?' he enquired. 'Quite
the opposite after all that couscous,' I said. 'Well, I don't
know what to think,' he sort of muttered, gazing at my
navel as though he'd never seen one before. 'There's
one thing for sure, you're not pregnant! Ha! Ha! I mean
you're *not* – are you?'

I assured him that there was no chance of the patter
of little feet.

We sat outside and had a cup of tea (Pardon the
expression! Tea! made with one teabag and warm
water) and I began to feel 'not so well'. By six o'clock I
felt 'not so well at all,' and enquired if the hotel had
such a thing as a hot-water bottle. All right, I know it's
like asking for a refrigerator in an igloo but believe it or
not within thirty minutes there was a knock at the door
and there stood the hotel porter, grinning all over his
happy face and looking like an advert for toothpaste.
He was holding his right arm and hand up high
displaying a little pale blue rubber Teddy Bear which
also acted as a child's hot-water bottle, obviously left

behind by some previous guests. 'Yes please?' he smilingly enquired . . . 'Yes thank you,' I gratefully agreed and, took the bottle from him. It was filled with cold water which had probably been in the little blue Teddy Bear since the previous patrons absent-mindedly left it behind. Poor old Teddy, all that cold water in his tummy – and poor old Thor – all that rotten pain in *her* tummy.

We left Djerba the following morning at seven o'clock. As usual, I was looking madly attractive and sexy, I was wearing a white tailored coat from Simpson's, Piccadilly, and clutching a bottle of Vichy Water in my right hand. My coiffure was – well how can I describe it? Rather as though I had been pulled through a hedge backwards. The reason for this unusual style being, I'd been so ill the previous evening I hadn't bothered to 'put my curlers in!' We arrived in Sfax at four o'clock in the afternoon.

Scottie settled me into bed in our hotel and then set about getting a doctor. The heat was suffocating. My pains were spifflicating! Was I glad when the bedroom door opened to admit Scottie and the Sheik of Araby. Well, of course, it wasn't the Sheik of anywhere but he was an Arab doctor who only spoke a bit of French (thank God for Scottie in that case). Why, oh why, did I always play noughts and crosses during the French class at night school? Though I had passed my French exam, because I was able to mime, '*Voici le tableau. Le tableau represente le grand-père, la grandmère, le père, la mère, le fils, la fille et le bébé.*'

He, the Sheik, was wearing a white overall buttoned at the side of the neck and, ill as I was, I remembered that the first overall like that I had ever seen was worn by Mr P. on the 'Instantaneous Hairwaver stall' at the Trades Exhibition at Morecambe. All in my past! Oh dear, the pains, was I to see a future? The Sheik wore what I believe are described as butterfly-wing lensed tinted glasses.

After prodding at my tummy he turned to Scottie and said, 'Apen-dee-cite kron-eek!' and went on to tell Scottie to go out and buy an ice bag. *An ice bag in Sfax*!! He added that if I was no better after the application of the ice bag on my tum, we'd better get in touch with him again. Scottie argued that something ought to be done at once, but to no avail. The Sheik rode off into the desert night eating his piece of Turkish delight.

Will you believe it that Scottie was able to purchase an ice bag in Sfax? Well you'd better, because he did, but even that didn't help much and Rudolph Valentino had to be recalled. He gave us the choice of the native hospital (straw palliasses on the floor) or his own private clinic. Need I tell you where we went?

I was taken into a twin-bedded room. As I was already in my nightdress, all the nurses had to do at that point was remove my coat and sandals. The next bit was off-putting. They produced from nowhere a rather rusty old safety razor. One nurse shot my nightdress round my waist, whilst the other one started to give a 'short back and sides' on my most intimate possession! Right, we all know those things happen prior to an operation but dear God, when she started blowing the cut curls away in the same manner one blows used india rubber away after erasing something, I thought, 'What would the London Clinic say!' By now

I was 'very poorly', but on her last 'blow' I looked at her lovely black face and winked and managed to say 'Hi Jean!' (hygiene). She didn't see the joke.

They got me off the bed and in my bare feet walked me down a long passage. I can vividly remember the biscuit-coloured, brown-patterned tiled floor. At the end of the passage we entered a room which I thought was a laundry because there was an ironing board standing in the middle of it. With Arabic sounds they guided me to the ironing board which had three little white steps at the side of it, and holding my elbows they gently guided me up the steps and laid me on the board. Between throwing up and wondering where the hell I was, it suddenly dawned on me that I was lying on an operating table!

On my right (in the blue corner), was an Arab doctor all of six feet four inches tall, and on my left (in the red corner) was a shorter Arab doctor who had a very kind face and looked to me just like Robert Lennard, Casting Director for Associated British Pictures. I'm not suggesting that Robert Lennard looks like an arab, but Bob has a kind face! The tall one fastened my right ankle to the board with a leather strap and buckle, and one of the nurses fastened my left ankle likewise. Honest! Meanwhile Robert Lennard appeared to be sticking something in my arm but I didn't mind because he was smiling at me with his kind brown eyes, but I *did* mind the ankle strapping lark because it reminded me of the silent film days when Pearl White was left strapped to the railway lines until the following week's episode.

Robert Lennard and the six-foot-four gent must have

only been 'small part artistes', because there was no sign of the Sheik of Araby. I suppose once I was strapped to the ironing board he would make a big entrance! Chord on, please – ta-rah!

At this point I lost interest. In other words, I don't remember anything more until I came round in one of the twin beds about 3.30 in the morning. Scottie was in the other bed; he had never returned to the hotel. As a matter of fact he only went back to the hotel once and that was the following day, to collect our luggage which he brought to the clinic, where he stayed with me until I was fit to travel back to the old country.

On the night I was admitted, the Sheik of Araby had taken Scottie out on to the balcony of the clinic and informed him that I had peritonitis and a gangrenous appendix and he would operate on me for two hundred and fifty British pounds – he was very curious to learn if Scottie *had* that amount of money on his person, which between you and me, dear reader, Scottie had *not*. However, having married me for better or worse and having promised in the Wesleyan Chapel to endow me with all his worldly goods, Scottie implored, nay, ordered, the Sheik to operate at once, thinking that the following day he would find a bank and get some spondoolicks. Little did that Scottish lad realize that Ramadan had started that very evening and that he had no chance of a bank being open for the next few days. So what did our brave lad do? By various means he discovered where the British Vice Consul could be found – and he found him – in a little shack full of tins of dried milk on the side of a harbour – and he was a Maltese. Rule Britannia! Any road up, the

Vice Consul was able to send a frenzied cable to our National Provincial Bank manager, who came out of his wardrobe and acted immediately so that the money arrived just in time to stop the Sheik of Araby pushing my appendix back in and stitching me up!

I will say this – and I mean every word of it – I shall always be grateful to the Sheik because he obviously saved my life, and to prove it he carved his name in Arabic as an operation cut! As God's above that's the truth and any London doctor who has had to examine me will tell you that after the 'shock' of seeing my operation scar, and the remark 'Wot the 'ell's that?' I have explained fully.

When I was in Perth, Western Australia at the Theatre Festival, I did a television quiz show called *What's my Secret*, and my secret was that I had 'The Sheik of Araby' cut on my stomach. Of course, as I've already said, he *did* save my life so I'll keep him anonymous. When I tell you that his first name was Mohammed you'll appreciate that I carry a longish scar, kid!

Isn't it amazing what the human body can stand? Six weeks after the little drama I have just related, I was to open in Blackpool for a season, and here we were next to a Mosque hearing them call to Allah and wondering what we were going to do. A cable arrived from A.B. and G.B. which read: 'Hey Thorird what are you doing out there – hurry up and get well and come home – Fond love A.B. and G.B.' I wept.

Scottie arranged for a taxi to drive us to Tunis Airport where an invalid's chair would be at the ready. What he hadn't arranged was how I was going to get out of bed to make the four-hour journey on shell pot roads. You see I had all these drainage tubes hanging out of my stomach! He awakened me at 5.30, well that's not quite true – at five thirty we were both awake because of the wailing of a man whose wife had given birth to twin *daughters* – daughters! not even one son!

I had only been out of bed once, for five minutes, and although I was not really fit to travel, the Sheik was quite anxious that I should get to London because his admiration of English doctors and hospitals was really sincere.

No way can I describe the next few hours – Scottie trying to dress me, getting me to the taxi, where I was in such pain I couldn't move a muscle, and couldn't bear to be touched. Arriving at Tunis Airport, they wheeled *me* to the Caravelle first and made Scottie wait until the healthy passengers boarded.

The pilot radioed Orly Airport to have an invalid chair standing by. And they had. They were marvellous. The next pilot radioed London Airport with the same request, but unfortunately when we touched down at Heathrow Airport we had to sit in the plane for twenty-five minutes after everyone had disembarked – and wait.

Eventually a little green van came scuttering across the tarmac and pulled up at the bottom of the staircase leading up to our aircraft. By this time it was almost eleven o'clock at night and I would have been quite content to sit in that plane for the rest of my days, because by that time I was nearly beyond caring about anything.

After carrying me down the stairs, or steps or ladder

or whatever it's called, they put me in the invalid chair
and pushed me up a ramp into the van. I can only make
a rough guess that the feller who had been told to get
the chair and the van and bring it to the aircraft was *not*
a fan of mine! As he pushed me up the ramp, he pushed
me and the chair into the side of the van – bang! No
apology – Scottie was furious and by now was looking
almost as ill as me. But not quite. You see, I had the
'ether scabs' all over the lower part of my face, due to
the fact, that, although the Sheik was a clever surgeon,
such things as 'pre-op' pills' and all the clever things
we use here prior to an operation were not part of their
plan of campaign. All they did was bung a schimmel-
busch mask over my nose and mouth and pour ether
on to it. I'll admit it was in a beautifully shaped glass
flask, but that's no help is it? Consequently I was a real
old 'scabby chops'.

Where was I? Oh, I know, being banged into the side
of the little green van. As we arrived at the buildings
about half a minute later, our Christian driver pushed
the chair and me out of the back of the van, held his
hand out with the palm upwards and announced, 'I
don't go no further than this, see, 'cos I ain't allowed.'
Scottie had to put hand luggage, his and mine, mackin-
toshes and various other objects on the ground to
enable him to get a hand free to dip into his trouser
pocket for a tip. Ill as I felt I can remember thinking,
'What's he tipping him for? All he's done is almost
knock the tubes out of the Sheik's autograph!'

Picking up all the articles he'd put down, Scottie
managed somehow to hang everything on himself – he
looked like a loaded camel. With a, 'Never mind, love –

we're home now,' the caravan moved off the thousand miles' trek to customs.

I know our customs officers are acknowledged to be the best in the world, but the one who recognized me under the scabs was brilliant – and humorous with it – well, he made *me* laugh when he asked, 'Anything to declare, Miss Hird?'

So there you are – I opened at Blackpool, tubes hanging out of the 'Sheik's autograph' and all! I had two rehearsals only, in the dress circle bar at the Grand Theatre, and played twice nightly for the season. The only thing that was 'cut out' of my part, in the play I mean, was where, during a Curry's Water Scene in the bathroom, I had to sit on the toilet lid and a spout of water lifted me four or five feet into the air. A.B. and G.B. wouldn't let me risk that! I was inclined to agree with 'em!

By the way – and I nearly forgot to tell you this – while I was in the Sheik's Clin-eek, one of the nurses presented me with a very large glass tube. She was sort of pushing it at me and I was pushing it back at her. You see, the contents of the tube looked, well, a bit nasty. Will you believe, the contents were my *gangrenous appendix*!!! The Muslim religion does not believe in one being buried incomplete, and they thought I would want to keep the tube with its enclosed souvenir until such time as . . .

I gave it back – besides, my charm bracelet is full!

41

'The best laid schemes'

You will have gathered by now that I was always a fan of my brother with regard to his humour. All right, perhaps I was a little biased because he was my brother; but it's a fact that anyone who knew him well will verify that he was a real funny devil!

Scottie and I had often remarked that he should write a comedy, not particularly for me; but that he should use his talent in this direction by putting pen to paper. Well he did, and he called it *The Best Laid Schemes*.

When I was preparing for a summer season, the play I was going to embark on was usually decided upon by the November prior to the June I would open in it. The Brothers Black had got hold of a comedy that I won't mention by name because, quite candidly, I thought it was about as funny as a dose of mumps. I was invited to lunch at the Pastoria by Harold Boyes and I knew he was going to hand the play to me.

Neville had finished his play and, honestly, it was very, very funny. And, of course, he knew me so well that all the situations he had written with me in mind I felt capable of handling. I didn't feel, and neither did he nor Scottie, that I could push his play because he was my brother, so we took a bit of my Dad's name, James

Henry, and a variation of my mother's maiden name, which was Mayor, and Neville Hird suddenly became Henry J. Meyer. It looked good and it sounded good.

Mr Boyes had entertained me to a splendid lunch and during coffee he said, 'Oh, take this play with you and read it again will you?', meaning the not very funny play. Nev's play was in an envelope at my side, so handing it to Harold I said, in a very couldn't care less tone, 'Have a look at this one will you, Harold, when you've time, and let me know what you think of it!' He took the envelope, slid the play out, looked at the title and the name of the playwright and said, as only dear Harold could, 'Henry J. Meyer, who's he? Never heard of him!' I agreed, but added, 'No, well, you won't have, it's his first play but *I* think it's very funny. Anyhow, just have a read and tell me what you think, will you?' He said he would – when he had the time.

It was about a quarter past three as I got into a taxi to come home, and as Harold closed the taxi door on me he requested that I read the 'funny as mumps' play again because they all thought it could be hilarious with a few alterations here and there. As the taxi moved off I put my head out of the window and shouted, 'Yes, and you read that one because I think it's very funny *without* any alterations here and there.' And that was that. At six o'clock that same evening Harold rang me, the first words he said were, 'Who is he?' 'Who's who?' I enquired, as if I didn't know, 'The fellow who has written this comedy?' Let me state here and now, there are two things I am NOT: beautiful or a 'stranger to the truth'; so without lying I replied, 'Oh, it's a chap who has known me – well – all my life' to which, to my great relief Harold said, 'Well, never mind who he is, he has written a very funny comedy.'

It was at this period that A.B. and G.B. asked me how I would feel about Freddie Frinton being in the Blackpool show with me, explaining that he had worked for them in variety but would like a 'little go' at the acting lark. I agreed immediately. I'm no fool. Now it had come to pass that in *The Best Laid Schemes* Nev wrote a drunk scene for the husband. Well, who better to cope with that than Freddie? I mean to say, it was a piece of cake for him, and he was a great asset to the show.

And so, my friends, *The Best Laid Schemes* was chosen as the show for the Blackpool Season, 1962. But tarry awhile – at that stage nobody knew that Henry J. Meyer was my brother! What I mean is, nobody except Scottie, Nev's wife, his agent and me!

As the season progressed and, do forgive my saying this, we played to two packed houses every night, whenever A.B. or G.B. nipped into my dressing room for a 'sip', one or the other of them would always remark, 'Hey, Thorird, it's a funny thing that Mr Meyer hasn't been to see the show, isn't it?' and I could always truthfully answer, 'Oh he has! He booked six seats for last Tuesday!' or, 'He booked four seats for last Friday,' which was true, he never had a complimentary seat all the season, and he couldn't have had if he'd wanted to, which he didn't, because there weren't any!

On the very last night of the show, Neville and his wife Lily were in the little sitting-room attached to my dressing room. They had brought large boxes of chocolates and flowers for the company and as I looked at the

'Admiral' sitting there having a mug of beer I thought, 'You clever thing, our Nev. I'll tell 'em tonight who Henry J. Meyer is!' Believe me if I'd rehearsed 'the revelation scene' for a month it couldn't have played better.

I have a habit of always, on the last night of any show I'm in, seeing to it that my dressing room stuff – make-up, covers, etc. – are all packed before the last act. It suits me that after the final curtain there is none of that rather depressing business to do. Right, I changed into my going home clothes, and my dresser took my last act dress, shoes and coat up to wardrobe. So there I was in the empty dressing room as G.B. came through the 'drapes' from my sitting room with a whisky in his hand.

'Well, Thorird,' he said, 'the end of another good 'un eh?' 'Yes – thank you,' I answered. 'You'd have thought Meyer would have come in tonight wouldn't you?' he questioned, with a real twinkle in his eyes.

I was about to spill the beans when he added, 'Of course, he *has* been in hasn't he? I know who wrote it y'know!' I was just going to say 'Do you?' when he continued, '*YOU* did!' 'I didn't, y'know,' I assured him. 'Oh, yes,' he continued, '. . . nobody knows you well enough to write like this for *you* but *yourself*, do they?' And he started laughing. At that very moment Nev walked in to join us and I was able to say, '*He* does. Mr Black meet Henry J. Meyer.'

That lovely George Black, who should have lived for ever, looked at Nev, whom he knew, shook hands with him and said, '*Are* you him, Nev? Well get your pen out and write another!'

It goes without saying that Neville – ahem – sorry – Henry J. Meyer – did just that!

42

'The Bed'

We took *The Best Laid Schemes* to Torquay for the season following Blackpool, and it was there that Ronnie Chesney and Ronald Wolfe came down to see me and Freddie about a television script they had written called *The Bed*. Freddie and I felt that the idea was just up our streets.

It was arranged that we should make *The Bed* more or less as a pilot for a comedy series. For the uninitiated, that means it would be shown in the *Comedy Playhouse* series and then, if the comics were comic enough and if the television company could manage to find a slot for it, we might be given a series. We *might*!

We finished the season at Torquay and came back to discuss rehearsals of *The Bed*. We started to rehearse on Sunday 1st December at Sulgrave Boys' Club where I was to spend a lot of my life in the following years, and we went to BBC Birmingham on 9th December to play it to an audience and 'put it in the can'. I shall never forget that day. Freddie had been rehearsing *The Bed* from 9.30 to 2.30 each day, then driving back to somewhere or other to appear in Pantomime in the evening. Well he was *so* tired he could hardly keep his eyes open, and as most of *The Bed* took place *in* bed, you can imagine the difficulty I had in keeping him awake. Every time we stopped for anything during the recording, Freddie would drop off and I had to keep nudging him with my knee or my foot and whisper, 'Wake up, Fred love!' We laughed very often when we recalled that first recording.

Regardless of all that, the BBC must have been satisfied because the result of *The Bed* was to be the very happy and successful television series, *Meet the Wife*. Of which more later.

43

'This is your life –
No it's not – It's his!'

During dinner one evening after we had returned from playing the season at Torquay, Jan enquired, 'Mummy, can you keep the most *secret secret* you've ever heard?' to which I promptly replied that I could. I'll tell why I replied promptly – because I *can* keep a secret! D'you know, when I was a school girl aged ten, a friend of mine who was couple of years older than I, told me a secret and with our little fingers locked I swore I would never utter it to anyone. And I never did – torture wouldn't have dragged it out of me, money or jewels couldn't have bought it, because you see we'd locked our little fingers and sworn an oath! I met this old school friend a couple of years ago, and I was proud to inform her that her 'secret' was still safe with me. She's a good sport and she said, 'D'you know, Thor, I remember us hooking our little fingers but I can't remember what the *secret* was!' I lowered my voice to inform her, 'You had got the *curse* – started on your periods!! Sh!' We exploded with laughing. When we'd contained ourselves, dried our eyes and blown our noses, she informed me that I was freed from our finger-hooking secret as she had just 'gone through the change!'

Sorry – I sort of went off the subject again didn't I?

Right! Jan had asked me whether I could keep a secret. Well, the secret *was* the BBC were about to do a *This is your Life* and the culprit, sorry I mean subject, was David Frost, and I was the chosen body to get him to Shepherd's Bush Theatre by hook or by crook – if I could.

A few nights later we were again having dinner (we don't care, y'know, we often have dinner), and David, who was dining with us, was munching away when I said, 'Hey, David, we were having a discussion at rehearsal today and someone remarked that as we made our living on television, we really ought to visit each programme that plays to an audience and see the various methods of producers, etc. Do you agree?' Before he could get rid of his mouthful of food and answer, I continued, '*I* do – I mean, for a start, *I've* never been to a *This is your Life*, have you?' By now he had cleared his mouth of food and informed me in no uncertain terms that he hadn't and had not the slightest intention of ever doing so! 'Oh, come on,' I wheedled, 'let's go and see one made. I'd love to, honest.' Eventually he agreed.

I excused myself from the table and ran into the lounge to look at the diary. I *knew* which date they wanted him there because I had it marked with a sort of spy-like sign, so I had to use my histrionic ability a bit more. 'I can only go on the so-and-so,' I called out. 'It's the only night I have free when they'll be doing one – is that all right for you?' He took out his pocket diary – scrutinized it and very begrudgingly agreed, that yes, it was all right for him. Tee-hee, I thought, little do you know Frostie, that it's *you* they're doing. So that was that.

When we returned from Torquay I did quite a few little bits – the *Vic Oliver Show* on sound, *Woman's Hour* and so on, and – I'd started to rehearse the play *All Things Bright and Beautiful*. The famous 'David Frost. This is Your Life' day came during the rehearsal period, so I would need to leave rehearsal early on that day.

As we say in the north, 'I took the director on one side' and explained to him that many are called but few are chosen to convey the subject of *This is Your Life* to the appointed execution ground! I did *not*, repeat, *not*, tell him who the subject was. The director, John Moxey, agreed immediately to let me leave early. In fact, he started to direct my means of getting across London to the hairdresser's by suggesting I order a taxi for three o'clock and so on. On the day it all happened beautifully.

Arriving home from the hairdressers, I put two voluminous bath caps over my 'shampoo and set' and had a quick bath. I had the house to myself because Scottie was out at a Masonic Luncheon and Jan was at Pinewood filming *The Beauty Jungle*.

David's mother and father had come from Beccles to spend a few days with him (tee-hee, little did he know *why* they had chosen these few particular days!) and were to come to our house, with David, and collect Jan and me around five-forty. About five-thirty a Rolls-Royce pulled up outside our front door. Jan got out and burst into the house looking (excuse me, as it's me daughter) gorgeous! I was ready. I cannot ever remember up to that point in our lives, Jan *ever* saying to me or Scottie, 'Let's have a drink shall we?' And that's the truth.

But that evening she said, and I shall never forget it, 'Oh Mummy you *do* look nice shall we have a drink?' All in one breath! So we did! David and his parents arrived in another Rolls-Royce, so Jan sent hers away. David had a sherry and his parents orange juice (his Dad was the dearest of Wesleyan Ministers, and God will rest him), after which the caravan prepared to move off.

As we drove along the Bayswater Road and approached Shepherd's Bush from Holland Park, David said, 'Well this is all very nice – I wonder whose life they are doing tonight – some poor soul is, at this moment, totally unaware of what the future holds!' We all laughed – as I, 'cleverhead', nudged Jan on one side of me and Mona, David's mother, on the other! *Some Poor Soul*! Tee-hee, it won't be long now, I thought.

We arrived at the Bush and got out of the car and, as arranged (secretly), we just walked in like anybody else – but we were put on the front row. The moment arrived. Eamonn Andrews appeared, to loud applause, and started on his spiel. He was standing in front of us, more or less. He chatted away and gawd knows there is nobody better than he at this particular kind of thing. David was looking round and whispered to me, 'I can't see anyone behind us who it might be.' Oh dear, I was very near the tittering stage. 'On the front row ladies and gentlemen,' I heard Eamonn say, '. . . . we have the King of Satire, David Frost.' (Loud applause.) 'The Queen of Comedy, Thora Hird.' (Quite loud applause.) 'And Britain's most beautiful film star, Janette Scott.' (Whistles and applause.) He looked at David and said, 'Did she have a lot of trouble getting you here tonight,

David?' indicating me. 'Well, er, yes – quite a bit, really,' replied David. 'Oh well, never mind,' said Eamonn, '. . . the most important thing is that she got you here, because now we are able to say, *This is Your Life*!' And at this point he sort of showed the big red book to David, and then moved it over to me, as he concluded, 'Thora Hird!'

'No, it's not!' I argued. 'It's *his*!'

Talk about he who laughs last, eh? Scottie was *not* at a Masonic luncheon, he was at the studios waiting and *he* knew all about it; John Moxey, who had so willingly let me off rehearsals early, *he* knew. My brother Nev, who was brought down from the north (or up as the case may be), *he* knew; Jan, who was so nervous for me she suggested we had a drink, *she* knew; the Rev and Mrs Frost had been acting their socks off, *they* knew! and – from before the moment Jan had asked me if I could get David there – the King of Satire *knew*!

Do you wonder our country produces the finest spies and the most brilliant actors and actresses? Mind you – we do occasionally produce a real, gormless, egg-headed, dumb cluck – like, for instance, ME!

There was a smashing 'marble hole' under the street lamp opposite 6 Cheapside, Morecambe, Lancs, England, Europe, the World, and when the BBC made me the subject of *This is Your Life*, they and the Morecambe Corporation couldn't give me the marble hole but they did give me the street lamp! Honest!

'Meet the husband'

We were still 'laying schemes' to the best of our advantage when we took *The Best Laid Schemes* to
Bournemouth in 1964, for by then Freddie and I were
making a batch of *Meet the Wife* for television between
each summer season we played. In fact, 'Fraid' was
doing twice daily pantomime each Christmas as well,
and I'd do a television play. There really were so many
funny things that happened during *Meet the Wife*. For a
start, half the viewing public seemed to think that
Freddie and I *really were married* to each other. One
Sunday, this was during our season at Bournemouth –
Scottie and I had lunch out in a very old country pub
that was noted for its food, and we were having a drink
in the bar before lunch when it became obvious that
five ladies who were sitting round a small table, having
a drink, were talking about me. Anybody who appears
on telly will tell you that you have to 'behave yourself
in public because everybody knows you'. The Manager
of the pub told Scottie our table was ready and added
in a whisper, 'I know you want a bit of peace, Miss
Hird, so I'm not letting on who you are!' We moved off
towards the restaurant, which meant passing the five
ladies, and one of them grabbed hold of my hand.

'Eee-eee!' she verbally grinned. I grinned back, I mean
let's face it the viewers and theatre audiences are our
bread and butter, aren't they? I mean that sincerely.
'Eee we were just saying . . .' At this point all five ladies
burst out laughing. So I laughed – Scottie had not seen
the hand grabbing and was by now standing by our
table in the restaurant. 'Eee – we were saying – weren't
we?' She turned to her buddies for confirmation.
'Who's *he* then?' and with this she nodded her head
directionally towards Scottie. 'Oh,' I said, '. . . that's my
husband!' The shrieks of laughter were like an explosion! I tried to move away but unfortunately lady
number one still had my hand in the famous 'Indian
toe hold'. 'Now come on, darling, we're not going to
say nothink to nobody – yer boy friend is it?' enquired
lady number two. More uncontrollable shrieks!
'Naughty girl, I'll tell Fred,' added lady number three.
'Oh I do hope you won't!' I implored as I escaped to
join Scottie.

We had a good lunch and, as we came out of the
restaurant, I didn't need to *see* the five ladies, I could
hear 'em! A few bottles of Guinness and a few gins had
worked wonders. 'Hey, come here a minute, Thora!'
one of them bawled as I passed. Not wishing to be rude
I enquired, 'What is it?' 'Well,' said one of the five, 'she
didn't mean what she said about telling Fred. Don't
you worry, Thora, just go and enjoy yourself, he
(meaning Scottie) looks smashing – you deserve it, you
work hard!' I thanked them very much and went and
joined my lawful wedded husband for a dirty
weekend.

And it came to pass that Henry J. Meyer did get his pen out and wrote a comedy equally as funny as *The Best Laid Schemes*. The fact that Freddie and I were so happily successful in *Meet the Wife* prompted us to entitle it *My Perfect Husband*. I mean, fair do's. In any case, as soon as we finished in Blackpool we were due to start yet another batch of *Meet the Wife* for telly.

Whilst I was playing that particular season I was asked to read a script of a play for the West End the following year. Felix de Wolfe, my agent, flew up to Blackpool with this particular script and said that I would either 'madly' want to play the leading part or I'd want to be sick! Well, I read it that night, in bed, and let's be candid, I felt a bit sick! However, to cut a long story short, the clever author, and make no mistake he *is* a clever fellow, re-wrote a lot of it for me and the second time I read it, I didn't even feel faint.

Now you must be wondering why I haven't mentioned the title of the play! Well, just hold on while I put you in the picture as regards what happened when we returned to London. As I've said, we ploughed into another happy batch of *Meet the Wife* and whilst we were doing them we were asked if we would like to be in *London Laughs* at the Palladium, opening the following May for thirty-two weeks.

I'll bet you are thinking that I jumped at it – I mean, let's face it, starring in a Palladium show with lovely Harry Secombe, Russ Conway and up and coming Jimmy Tarbuck, and for thirty-two weeks! Any artist who refused that would want his brains washing – eh?

Well, folks – believe it or not, I wanted to do the play. Oh yes, very much I wanted to do the play, but

I couldn't do both. I had to decide.

Have you ever looked at a child when it has been deeply disappointed? Of course you have – well – Freddie Frinton, bless him, looked about six years old when I told him I'd have to choose between the Palladium and the play. We were walking to our respective dressing rooms in red section at the TV Centre, having put yet another *Meet the Wife* in the can, when Freddie said, 'I wish you'd do it, Chuck! (Meaning the Palladium season.) I've never been in the West End.' Incidentally, he always called me Chuck. As he said that I *knew* what my choice must be. We played the Palladium.

There's a wonderful saying my Mother used to use, 'Cast your bread on the waters and it comes back buttered!' Well, that's a fact – no kidding. As I decided to take the Palladium I *knew* how much I wanted to do the play but what I didn't know was how much I was going to enjoy those thirty-two weeks. Bliss!

We would rehearse *Meet the Wife* in the morning from 9.30 to 2.30. Scottie would collect me from rehearsal in the car and we'd come home for lunch and then try and have a walk – otherwise I'd never have had any fresh air. I'd be at the Palladium for 5.30 and we'd play two houses nightly (three on a Saturday, because there was a matinee) and on Sunday we were in the TV studios all day recording the *Meet the Wife* we'd rehearsed all week. The only day we were free of *Meet the Wife* was Monday, and on that day I had a sound show which we did at the BBC studio on Lower Regent Street, and called *One Born Every Minute*. I was rather proud of that title because I thought of it – I thought it fitted the story line because I played a district nurse who delivered quite a few babies during the thirteen weeks it ran.

So there we were, working day and night as you might say, and getting very little of the 'spondoolicks' we'd earned because, to quote my auntie, the tax we paid was 'an imposition'.

Right, so you are wondering why I didn't mention the title of the play I couldn't do because it clashed with the Palladium! Well the reason is, one of our best actresses played the part I'd been offered wonderfully, and I honestly don't know if she knows it was offered to me first. I hope she doesn't because the first night of the play was during our rehearsals for the Palladium show and I was able to go to it. She was great.

Apart from the enjoyment of that season at the Palladium, and I *did* enjoy it, Freddie and I had a lot of laughs privately. We were always having laughs at rehearsals for *Meet the Wife*, but of course that was all helped along by our director, Robin (they don't come any better) Nash. Robin Nash could direct me through the back of my head. It's a fact. I would make a move during rehearsals, let us say, to the gas stove and although I would have my back to Robin I could 'feel' if he wanted me to change the direction and let's say, move to the table. It was incredible. I used to say that he was the youngest Svengali and I was the oldest Trilby in the business. Any artiste will tell you how very important the director you work with is. I mean they can make your work a joy or a misery. Robin Nash understood Freddie and me – he knew our way of working together – he knew our form of timing a comic line or situation – he knew we were disciplined and he knew we were fond of him and respected him. Do you wonder we were such a happy team? Of course we didn't always agree, we would discuss things but we never had a real blazing row and nine times out of ten we finished up laughing. One newspaper man wouldn't believe that we were as happy as we appeared to be and indeed printed that we weren't. I shall never forget, he came to the Palladium to see us in our respective dressing rooms. He saw Freddie first and then came to see me. The series we were making at that moment was our final batch of *Meet the Wife* and – not that any of you readers are interested but I'm going to inform you just the same – the reason I didn't want to do any more was, I wanted us to finish whilst we were still a popular programme, savvy? *Not* because I wanted to leave comedy series for drama series and start *The First Lady*. But this *gentleman* of the press insisted we had had a row and that was the reason we weren't doing any more – he even went so far as to print his story the following Sunday. Freddie and I were at the studios, and someone laughingly brought the paper with the article in it on to the set. D'you know, it really upset Freddie? It didn't upset me – it made me mad as 'ell! But remembering one of the 'twelve bits of advice' my father had given me, which was 'slow time 'em', I did just that.

It would be about four months later that Jan's husband, Mel Tormé, came to star at the Talk of the Town, and prior to opening he gave a cocktail party for the press at the Mayfair Hotel. Scottie and I were invited.

I saw Mr Prevaricator standing with a large gin in his hand and I thought, 'I hope you don't speak to me or I might be rude,' and *then* I thought, 'Hold on, Thor – it's your son-in-law's "do", you are only a guest?' However, a little later, when someone touched me on the shoulder, I turned round and it was 'his nibs'. 'Hello, Thora, how are you?' he asked, grinning with a five-gin flush. 'What do you want to know for?' I enquired very quietly. He ignored that and then said, 'Great isn't he – y'know – Mel?' To which, I replied, still very quietly, 'If I say he *is* you'll say I'm after him; if I say he *isn't* you'll swear I am trying to break his and Jan's marriage up – so just 'op it will you, "Mr Stranger-to-the-Truth?" ' All right, I'll admit it was childish of me, and I'm not proud of what I said, but I really did it for Freddie.

Needless to say he has never written *one* word about me since – true or false – but who cares? I've known a lot of pressmen for a lot of years and they are super. In fact, it has always surprised me that 'his nibs' didn't have his pressman's badge, epaulettes, and buttons stripped off by his fellow writers in the middle of Fleet Street to the roll of the presses!

1966 came to an end and it had been a most interesting and wonderful year. *Call my Bluff, Dixon of Dock Green, The Good Old Days, Jackanory, Late Night Line Up*, a quick visit to France, thirty-two weeks at the Palladium, a meeting with Andrew Osbourne about a drama series, a series on sound, *One Born Every Minute*, my advert for Biotex on telly. We finished at the Palladium on 17 December and on the 22nd Scottie and I flew to Beverly Hills to spend Christmas with Jan and

Mel. Sadly, Jan's first marriage hadn't worked and neither had Mel's . . . happily, they both knew that this one was going to.

They had married in May in Japan whilst all the blossoms were in flower, five days after I had opened at the Palladium – and once more I was unable to be at my daughter's wedding. Hard cheese, Thor! Never mind! I comforted myself with the fact that she hadn't been at mine.

'Wherefore art thou – Nursie!'

We returned from America early in the year and I was asked to play the nurse in *Romeo and Juliet*, a Play of the Month, on BBC TV. Any actresses will tell you that there are certain roles they would like to play and that there are certain roles that *other* people would like to see them play. The nurse in *Romeo and Juliet* came under the latter bit. It was amazing the number of times folks had said to me, 'Ooo, I would like to see you play the nurse in *Romeo and Juliet*.' I was flattered, of course, but never did I feel strongly enough about the part even to say to myself, 'Ooo, I *would* like to play the nurse in *Romeo and Juliet*.' Anyway, I was asked to play it. And I most graciously refused.

Stand easy and I'll tell you why. Because I wasn't sure if I would be up to scratch. I mean, just think who had walked away with the part in the past – Dame Edith Evans, Dame Flora Robson, to mention but a couple, and those girls know their Willie Shakespeare backwards, frontwards and sideways. Besides, I had another more important reason for refusing with thanks. Hold on a minute.

Cedric Messina, producer, and Alan Cooke, director, didn't accept my first refusal and a couple of days later asked me again. Upon my second refusal Alan Cooke invited me to lunch. As we took our places at the table in the restaurant, he laughingly said, 'Right – now just tell me the reason why you don't want to play the Nurse!'

'All right,' I said, 'I will – but please don't think I'm not grateful to you and Cedric for thinking of me, it's just that – well – I – er – ' 'What?' he questioned. 'Well, it's just that I can never understand why the nurse is played as an old woman, when she's supposed to have wet nursed Juliet only fourteen years before!' 'And is that the only reason you won't do it?' he asked. 'That and because I feel that I might not be very good,' I stated. He started to laugh.

'If that's your only reason you've lost the argument because we are altering the period slightly and playing the nurse as a woman of fifty!' he retorted, attacking his veal.

'Oh well – I mean – I'm glad you feel as I . . .' I never had a chance to finish. 'Good, so you'll do it then?' He said this without looking up from his plate. There was a short pause.

'I'll tell you what, Alan. At three minutes to ten in the morning I'll ring TV Centre, by the time I'm through to your extension it should be about ten o'clock, so if you could please be near your phone at that time, I will say either, "It's yes, Alan," or "It's no, Alan" – will that be all right?' He agreed.

The following morning I did exactly as I'd said I would do and when I had got through to Alan's extension he picked up the phone and spoke immediately.

'Thora? Well, is it my lucky day?' he asked.

I replied, 'Well, that's a matter of opinion – because I'll do it!' And I did.

Robin Nash asked me to do a comedy sketch with Wilfrid Brambell (Old Steptoe himself). It was about two public lavatory attendants and was called *They Also Serve*. Alan Melville had written it and it was in his programme. The difficulty *was*, it was during the rehearsals for *Rome and Jule* and I didn't want to trouble Alan any more. I felt I'd given him enough trouble before I'd said I'd do the part, never mind giving him any more now I was playing it!

Robin Nash was wonderful, as usual, and even suggested that Wilfrid and I rehearse at my home. I was itching to do the sketch, and I was practically at the scratching stage when Robin told me I needn't go into the studios until four o'clock on camera day. Oh mate, it was too good to miss, so in a diplomatic way and at what I felt was the right moment, I asked Alan would it be possible for me to finish on a certain date around three o'clock?

He was most accommodating. 'Certainly,' he said, 'I shall be doing the sword fighting scenes that afternoon anyway!' I felt, in all fairness I should tell him the reason I wanted off early, so I told him. 'It's just a little sketch I'm doing for Robin Nash,' and left it at that.

You've no idea the fun and pleasure I get out of doing a job like the lavatory attendant sketch. It means I can pop into Wig Creations, have a gab with Mr Brian, explain what I'm doing and then the two of us decide the kind of wig I should have. We have laughed our socks off many a time at some of the comic results. In this case, it was a black wig with a donkey fringe. Let me add quickly that Mr Brian and Wig Creations have been responsible for some very beautiful wigs I've worn as well – for instance the one I wore when I played Mrs Hardcastle in *She Stoops to Conquer*. However, I digress.

When we came towards the end of rehearsals for *Romeo and Juliet*, one day Alan asked me, 'What kind of a sketch did you do for Robin – what were you?'

'A public lavatory attendant,' I replied.

'He just laughed, I don't think he believed me. Then his expression changed to a rather, 'director of *Romeo and Juliet* – Play of the Month' one. 'Not really?' he enquired. 'Yes – really,' I replied, 'and don't look worried Alan,' I added, 'both the Nurse and the woman in the lavatories are *staff* – well aren't they?' He agreed.

I never saw *Rome and Jule* because by the time it was shown I was busy putting a *First Lady* in the can. I enjoyed playing the Nurse and I hope Willie Shakespeare and all the very clever actresses who have played the nurse before I did, will excuse and forgive me for making her 'wetnursable'.

46

'The First Lady

In August 1967 we were ready to start on *The First Lady*. We filmed exterior shots to cover the first four episodes in and around Barnsley in *Yorkshire*. We also used Barnsley Town Hall and Council Chamber. Although I am a Lancastrian right down to my cotton socks, I admit readily that the people of Barnsley and thereabouts were grand and showed me nothing but kindness. Be that as it may, there was nothing in the scripts of *The First Lady*, apart from my accent, to denote that I wear a red rose as opposed to a white one. So after a little chat with Robin Midgley, who was directing numbers one and four, we added six words and they explained everything. It was thus: in the first episode, I got on to the Council and one of the Councillors had to say, 'I don't hold with women on the Council,' and we added a reply from me, which was, 'Especially if they come from Lancashire!' Believe it or not, those six little words gave me a very comfortable feeling!

I really could write a whole book about the sad, funny, serious and dangerous things that happened during the life span of Coun. Sarah Danby. The letters I received were unbelievable – comic, romantic and some rather sad.

One letter requested: 'Please, Mrs Danby, could you have a sewer one hundred and forty feet long laid in our street?'

Another one read: 'I love your clothes, especially the navy blue suit you wore last week, I've got a navy hat and shoes and my daughter gets married in six weeks will you please send me your suit and gloves?'

And: 'When we bought this house the fellow left his pigs in our yard, I've bought his wife a box of chocolates but his pigs are still there, will you tell him to move them Coun. Danby please?'

Also: 'I love your nails and wedding ring, I'm getting married can you tell me where you bought your ring and do you do your own nails?'

And:

'Everybody says I am the image of you.'

'I am always being taken for you in the laundrette.'

'I was asked for my autograph in the grocer's, they thought I was you!'

'I think I look just like you, I think I am as clever as you but my bank account is not as big as yours.'

'I am a bachelor of fifty-eight and would love to take you for a drink in an ordinary pub because I'll bet you've never been in one!' (Author's note: He must be joking!)

'Please, Mrs Danby, *please* try and get us a council house.'

'Where did you get the wallpaper on your lounge wall?'

'Will you seriously consider putting up for our council?'

'Will you please send me a photo with your glasses on, I want to get some!'

And so on and so on. I had literally hundreds of letters from women saying they looked exactly like me or that they had been taken for me or that their husbands said they were the image of me. Eventually, on the back of a fan photograph, which they would always request, I would write: 'Never mind it can't be helped!' or 'Beauty is only skin deep!' or 'Sorry, love – there's nothing I can do about it!'

I shall never forget that one lot of location we did for *The First Lady* was at Castleford Rugby Ground. Storywise, some shots of myself and James Grout (smashing to work with), who played Alderman Kingston in the show, and Henry Knowles (equally smashing), who played my son, were needed, sitting in the crowd watching a match.

We were in the director's room of the club house during the morning, and the president (or whatever it is a rugby club has) and his wife were chatting to us. During the conversation he acquainted me with the fact that I was 'kicking off' the match that afternoon. Laughingly I acquainted him with the fact that I wasn't! 'You *are*!' he argued. 'It's in't programme – in *print*!' It *was*! I'll bet a lot of people in 'our business' will stick up for me when I say I was 'rather annoyed!' I mean, hecky plonk, I don't mind doing anything for anybody, within reason, if I'm told about it beforehand, but the first I knew about the kick off lark was at that moment, when a programme was passed to me. What can't speak can't lie – there it was – as his nibs had said – *in print*!

The match was to be televised in *Grandstand* that afternoon and, as Scottie is an avid viewer, I got to a telephone after lunch and warned him. Please understand that I didn't ring him up so he could *watch* me! Oh, no! I rang him up so that he'd know when he saw me do it there was no need for him to think, 'Wot the 'ell is she doing now!' D'you follow?

Now at this point I must explain about Rose and Lillian. Rose and Lillian must be, nay *are*, two of the finest dressers the business has ever known, added to which they both are blessed with a fantastic sense of humour. Rose can make *me* laugh more than I can make *anyone* laugh – she's cockney, comic, kind and conscientious; Lillian was a dancer in variety and always 'did me a few bars of the Sailor's Hornpipe' to wish me good luck before I did a show. She's softly spoken, affectionate, knows her job and, like Rose, is now retired. It's the BBC TV's loss. I miss 'em at the studios.

On this particular location Rose was dressing me. Paul, the director, wanted me to walk up the grandstand steps and go and sit with Jimmy Grout and Henry Knowles and that was all in that shot. The camera was at the top of the steps in the grandstand, and the idea was to pick me up on film as I ascended the steps with the normal rugby fans as they filed in. Paul wanted to shoot on the crowd arriving and me amongst them. He was then going to pan over as I found my seat and sat down. Piece of cake eh? Well not really. You see all this was a few minutes before I was going to kick off! For the shot I have just explained to you, I was wearing a pencil slim tweed skirt and a sheepskin jacket. No complaints about the jacket – but the skirt – oh mate, it was difficult enough to sit down in it never mind about cock me leg up and kick a ball! Imposs! It was at this point that Rose took over. With my slacks over her arm she informed me that there was no need to worry as she had found four dustbins!

Taking me by the arm she propelled me towards the back of the stand. True enough, near one of the entrances to the stand were four dustbins. She then explained all the details of the operation. 'Now y'see, Miss Hird, you can do the shot with the crowd going up the steps in your skirt and brogues – right? Then nip down here quick, change into your slacks and boots behind these dustbins and then go and kick off – right, gorrit? When you've kicked off, nip back quick round here and I'll be waiting behind these dustbins with your skirt and brogues for the next shot you have to do up in the stand. All right, gel – gorrit?' I assured her I'd gorrit. We did the first shot in the skirt and brogues with the crowd – it had to be a 'one take'.

Rushing back to Rose and the dustbins I took my skirt off and then my brogues – I couldn't put my boots on next because I couldn't get my narrow slacks over 'em – I sat on one of the dustbins until I'd pulled my slacks on sufficiently for my feet to pop through. I was then able to pull my boots on and stand down on the wet ground. I pulled my slacks up over my bottom in a sort of bent double position so as to try and keep out of sight.

It was bitterly cold and wet and I pulled my mink coat on as I ran to join the two teams and the referee under the tunnel thing.

As we marched on to the ground I could hear Eddie

Waring announcing me. It's as well he did because nobody could see me in the middle of those giants! As I took big strides to try and keep up with them my boots sunk into the mud about four inches with each step and as I endeavoured to release each boot a loud squelch accompanied my frenzied effort. I reckon my walk on to that field (sorry, ground) was the funniest walk I've ever done and it hadn't been thought out, it was force-work!

I'd been advised to kick the oval ball rather to the side of it and to give it as hefty a wallop as I could because unless it travelled a certain number of feet or yards (I've forgotten which) the game couldn't or wouldn't start.

Taking off my coat I put it over the ref's arm (to the delight of the crowd). I didn't do it to get a laugh, I did it because it had suddenly dawned on me that as I ran to 'kick off' I might slip. *I* didn't mind slipping in the mud myself, but I didn't fancy my coat covered in what looked like brown chewing gum. I must admit the ref looked very surprised as he stood there with his whistle in his mouth, his eyes wide open and my mink coat over his arm!

The whistle blew – bluddy 'ell – I nearly jumped out of my skin – the captains of each team were crowding me a bit so I linked arms with each of them (it was their turn to be surprised) and the three of us set off at a run and I walloped the ball as far as I could. What a blessing I did hold on to the giants because by the time I had got over the shock of the piercing whistle blowing I realized that I had nearly sunk to Australia. The giants took off with me hanging on to them and literally pulled me out of the ground as they did so, to the accompaniment of an almighty squelch! I had to do the comic knees-up run again. To tell you the honest truth, those mighty men were so strong they nearly frightened me to death. With my boots sticking in the mud, my first thought was we've left my boots, feet and legs behind, they've pulled the top half of me off.

By now the game was 'in play' (did you notice that bit? 'In play?' I rather liked writing that, it sounded as if I know what I'm talking about!) Have you ever felt you weren't wanted? By then, I couldn't have been of less importance. The giants were attacking each other, the ref was running about after them with my mink coat on his arm and I was running about with my knees up trying to pull my squelching boots out of the ground and trying to retrieve my coat from the ref who was doing his best to get rid of it.

Eventually I squelched off like a cat on hot bricks to find Rose and the dustbins.

Faithful Rose – there she was at the side of the ground, tears running down her face she'd laughed so much at my pathetic attempt to kick off and the 'couldn't-be-helped' comic run.

We made our way behind the dustbins, which, let's face it, only came up to our waists, and Rose endeavoured to pull my muddy boots off – because until she had done so we couldn't get my slacks off. Lifting one of the lids off the aforementioned dustbins, we discovered a discarded newspaper which we wrapped round the muddy boots. When we'd got one boot off, we put one brogue on which enabled me to put one foot down on the wet and muddy concrete. It was as I stood in my Marks and Sparks floral elastic knicker roll-ons with one brogued foot up on a dustbin lid whilst I fastened my shoe lace that the belated coach-load of rugby fans passed. 'Good old Thora!' 'I see you've got 'em on.' 'What time is the strip club open?' 'Only a rose I give you!' 'Get 'em off!' etc., etc. I mean, what can you do in a case like that? I know one thing you can't do – you can't win!

47

Tribute to Cheapside

It was August 1970. Scottie and I had returned to the North on business, but we intended to make it a nice long weekend – for my sake. We stayed at our usual hotel in Blackpool. We know 'it' and 'it' knows 'us' and I can ask for toasted *brown* bread, instead of *white* – and I'm not regarded as an eccentric.

It's of no interest to you that my brother Nev's birthday was in August, but it was to me, and of course it does fit in with the bit I wrote about my mother's in April, mine in May, my dad's in June, my sister's in July and my brother's in August! Remember the phenomenon I swanked about at school?

Although we were in Blackpool on the day of Nev's birthday we intended to celebrate the occasion on the following day in Morecambe. Nev and his wife, Lily, picked us up in their car at our hotel, and the four of us set off. We left it entirely to Admiral Hird of the Iron Duke as to where the 'Mystery Tour – back for tea' would take us, but of course I knew the 'big finish' would embrace a view of the Central Pier, the Alhambra, the Royalty Theatre and Cheapside, Morecambe. *En route* I soon discovered that we were driving along country lanes and roads that have now recaptured their former beauty and glory, due to the opening of motorways. These roads and lanes have been quietly pensioned off and are not used now as much as they were. It was all marvellous.

It was a journey of happy memories and exclamations such as, 'Oh, Nev, this is Garstang isn't it?' I remember that little bridge – and us coming here from school to do some folk dancing at a gala – and dancing Helston Ferry all along that road and over the little bridge, accompanied by the local Brass Band playing 'The Floral Dance!'

It didn't seem long before a signpost informed us we were on our way to Wray and Wennington. 'Hey, d'you remember the school nature-study class had a picnic here?' Immediately, my mind flew back to the morning of that picnic. I had implored my mother to pack my picnic lunch in an empty strawberry basket the greengrocer had given me, instead of in a paper bag. And I asked for a little white linen serviette from my mother to cover the food. I was only about eight years old – so I suppose I was pretending to be Red Riding Hood or somebody. I vividly remember I had sixpence to spend and that, after eating the picnic banana sandwiches, the huge wedge of cake and an apple, I had visited the tiny village shop to have a look round and select presents to take back – we always did that. It was easy to decide on my dad's gift – five Woodbines in a little paper packet, *twopence*! My present to my mother was a bit more difficult and a great deal of lip chewing took place before I took the plunge. On the short wooden counter in the village shop, along with the strings of Spanish, sugar mice, kahli suckers and other tempting goodies, was a box of necklaces, made of white celluloid. The chain part of the necklaces was stamped out of celluloid and from it hung a pendant. It was the choice of the pendant I found so difficult as there were quite a few designs with different hand-painted pictures on them. At long last – and I swear no customer buying diamonds in Asprey's or Cartier's chose with greater care – I decided on a small oval pendant that had a little cupid painted on it. The only drawback about the Cupid was that one of its eyebrows was very high up and the other one very low down, giving it a perpetually quizzical look. However, it was the best of the bunch, so I bought it – *threepence*!

I only had a penny left out of my sixpence, so Nev had to be satisfied with a *real slate* pencil, which was a halfpenny, because I rather fancied ten aniseed balls to suck on the way home in the charabanc.

I'm off again about the nice things my mother did. Listen. On the Friday after my gifts had been given and received with great pleasure, my parents were invited out to dinner by some friends, who were called Rawbottom. (It *is* an unfortunate name, isn't it? I spent a lot of time as a child wondering why the very first Rawbottom had been called that – I had my own answer.) When my mother was all dressed and ready to go, she came upstairs to kiss us Good night and God bless. (We had a splendid 'help' at this time and we were never left alone on the rare occasions our parents had an evening out.) When my mother leaned over to kiss me as I lay in bed, something lightly tickled my chin – it was the pendant! She was wearing it! My present! Bought with my threepence! I also remember thinking how *nice* she looked in her lovely brown crêpe-de-chine dress and her tiny pearl earrings.

'Do you think everybody will like it?' I enquired – meaning the chain and pendant. 'Like it? I'm sure everyone will envy me,' she assured me. What a brave woman, a lovely dress and a threepenny pendant! I don't wonder the cupid looked worried!

What I've just told you all went through my mind as we drove through Wray village, August 16, 1970. Isn't it strange? The older one gets, the clearer the memories of childhood seem to become.

After a good few miles of reminiscing we approached Morecambe proper, the feeling I always get on these occasions started at the pit of my stomach – I can't describe it.

'Prepare yourself for a bit of a shock, our kid!' Nev warned me.

'Oh, it's all right!' I said. 'I mean – I know it's not there, is it? I mean, Cheapside, the Royalty, the bottom of Euston Road – it's *all gone*, hasn't it?'

'Yes,' Nev said, looking straight ahead as he drove along. 'It's all gone.'

Quite honestly, we were upon the scene of devastation before I realized it.

'Hey! Just a minute love, go a bit slower please – what was here?' I enquired of Nev. 'Tunstall Street and the bottom right hand side of Euston Road,' Nev informed me. I was ashamed to have to be enlightened. Tunstall Street! In my very early childhood it had been called Back Pedder Street, and the residents of the small cottages had taken umbrage and had it renamed

'Pilling Street'. Apparently, as the years passed by, someone else had got the needle at *that* title, and it was eventually called Tunstall Street, which it remained until the great invasion. When I was cashier at the Co-op, Queen's Square Branch, I used to pass the end of it six times a day: on my way to work in a morning, home to lunch, back from lunch, home to tea, back from tea (when there was always a lovely smell of kippers frying in Tunstall Street) and home again after my day's toil!

And now, it had all disappeared! One side of Tunstall Street backed on to the bottom of Euston Road – and one side of Euston Road backed on to Cheapside – and one side of Cheapside backed on to Sun Street and – what am I bothering to tell you all that for? There was nothing left of any of it!

All I could see was a vast open space. Where was I? On the Sahara? In the desert at Las Vegas? How could I imagine where any individual house or shop had been? It was all a great big nothing! Yes, that's what I was looking at, a great big plateau full of nothingness!

'Pull yourself together, Thora! – don't be sentimental, this is all under the heading of Progress, and you've a bigger shock to endure in about four seconds!'

I got out of Nev's car at the top of Euston Road – they'd left the top half. It was quite blustery, the wind coming from the sea. As I approached the corner of Market Street where Martins Bank, defiantly and proudly, still stands, I started to put my headscarf on – by the time I had tied it under my chin and raised my eyes, I was once again looking at nothing.

Well, not quite *nothing*. I was looking at, first of all,

where Houghton's greengrocery and butcher's shop had once stood. Mind you, to be fair, Houghton's had been replaced long before I left Morecambe, by a smart, modern impersonal Fruit Store, but it wasn't the smart, modern, impersonal Fruit Store that had disappeared in my eyes – oh no, it was Houghton's.

'Please may I have a cut apple for this bucket of peelings, Mr Hadwen?' I wonder which bit of rubble the 'cut apple' bucket used to stand on?

I looked amongst the stones and grey dust and tried to visualize where the entrance to the Royalty Theatre and Opera House started and Houghton's finished. Four more paces and I knew, I just *knew*, I was standing where the entrance to the Royalty had invitingly and proudly stood:

'A compact, comfortable and well appointed place of entertainment, lavishly decorated throughout and one of the most comfortable outside of London, a handsome stone structure, in the classic style. Designed by Frank Matcham. First opened April 4, 1898.'

Finally closed – demolished and erased (when the dust settled) on the morning of Monday, February 23, 1970!

To quote Howard Reynolds, who is so splendid a writer and has a brilliant command of words:

The bulldozers moved in, their steel jaws aided by hawsers which literally tore the place apart. The event lasted over several days and lunchtime crowds gathered, obviously for many reasons, in a sort of Requiem for a Dead Theatre. The walls came tumbling down, briefly exposing the interior, before that, too, vanished behind the dust and before the onslaught of men and machines.

I doubt not that several people who were present had hoped one day to see a show which would bring the house down; on this occasion the fulfilment of their hopes must have been somewhat bitter – I only went once – and that was enough. Seeing the inexplicable replaced by the ineffectual is an experience I don't cherish.

Thank you, Mr Reynolds – you clever writer!

Well, Mr Matcham, the theatre you so diligently designed in the classic style disappeared in less time than you sat at your drawing board. Three score years and ten is the expected life span, isn't it? Your theatre – gallant lady that she was – held her head high two years longer than that, Mr Matcham.

Of course, only those who had a sincere affection for her could remember how really magnificent she used to look when she was young. She wore her deep red velvet drapes and gilt ornaments so beautifully – everyone used to pass flattering remarks about her, Mr Matcham; she was, without doubt, the toast of the town! It was heartbreaking to see the state she had fallen into in her later years – of course she had no one to care for her – nobody was interested – d'you understand, Mr Matcham? And although she still flaunted her original style of dress, the red velvet drapes were black with neglect and dirt, her gilt ornaments sadly tarnished. That was the sad part, Mr Matcham, to see her so neglected and uncared for, through no fault of her own, let me add. Our apologies, Mr Matcham.

Please forgive us, Mr Matcham. Progress you know!

I made to move off, but stupid as it sounds, I felt as though the empty site of the Theatre was beseeching me, 'Don't go yet, Thora – stand and look at me for just a bit longer!'

I did so – and then I moved slowly on, past what had been the sweet shop, one window of which had always displayed 'Photographs of the Artistes'.

I had known it before it was a sweet shop. During my school days it had opened as MacGregor's – Herbalist and Drug Store. *Drug Store*! Get that bit – how American. Sure, Baby! I remember I thought it was wonderful. There were always silver and gold pills in glass bottles in one window. I was always asking my mother why I couldn't buy some as sweets and I recall I was always put off with a smart reply of, 'Because you can't – they are not for children!'

Unbelievable isn't it? – in this day and age of 'the pill' and all that! All the same, I got a lot of pleasure from looking at them as they glittered in the window. Thank God I never needed them!

Wait a minute, though – before it was the Drug Store it was Johnson's, High Class Fishmonger and Poulterers. Yes, of course it was. As I stood there I could hear myself, as a child, saying, 'May I have four nice pieces of halibut, Mr Johnson, please – and my mother says will you put in a sprig of parsley, please?'

Before I moved from the spot I was concentrating on what else I used to go into Johnson's for. Oh yes – I remember. 'Fresh garden peas – shelled on the premises.' And what else? (Oh, *do* let me think of something else because it will at least postpone my looking

at the wide open space that was Cheapside.) Oh yes –
of course – over the sweet shop that used to be
MacGregor's Drug Store, that used to be Johnson's
Fishmonger and Poulterers – were two floors of rooms
that belonged to and were part of the theatre. They
were rented out to various business people – Tommy
Burton, the Bookie (sorry, Turf Accountant), had his
office up there and Withers, the Signwriter, had his
workshop up there. His slogan was: 'I made signs
before I could talk!'

Oh, and the man who informed me that my mother
obviously didn't object to me putting my hands in a
bucket of diluted dog shit, he had a room up there as
well – up where, Thora? There wasn't anything there
any more! There's no point in your looking up there –
it's all been knocked into oblivion by a dirty great bulldozer! By now, Neville had assumed the guise of a
guide on a conducted tour: 'And here we have –
Cheapside!' he announced. I looked in front of me at
another expanse of nothingness. 'Hello, Cheapside that
was – and now isn't!' I breathed. But just a minute! I felt
it *couldn't* be Cheapside. Cheapside was never a *little*
street – was it? I looked carefully – it *can't have been*
Cheapside! It all looked so little. If you knock houses
down to ground level and clear the rubble away, it
should all look so much *bigger*, shouldn't it? – like a
room does when the furniture has been moved out
whilst you spring clean or decorate? But even the
roadway – that has escaped the bulldozer – is *only little*!

No, it can't be the remains of Cheapside – can it?
Thora Hird, 6 Cheapside, Morecambe, Lancashire,
England, Europe, The World! All gone. No, hold on a

minute, be fair – not *all*. Be grateful, they've left the roadway of 'our street', the part where the tram lines used to be – the best repository for horse manure, the part I learned to ride my two and sixpenny Rudge Whitworth bike on (which I painted myself but forgot to sandpaper the already existing chipped enamel of, and consequently after painting over the humps the end product looked rather like a gnarled old tree or someone with varicose veins) – the part I ran across to take the meals to the young mothers that had given birth to brand new babies. They'd left that! – *or it had refused to be moved*!

I wanted to walk down the middle of our street. Wait a minute! what was this? A railing across the top of Cheapside – and worse still, a notice which stated very definitely in red print: NO THROUGH ROAD. Never mind; perhaps one could get in from the far end of what once had been Cheapside – oh no! the notice *there* was even more forbidding: DANGER – PUBLIC ACCESS PROHIBITED. '*Public access prohibited*? No entrance into Cheapside? But everybody used to 'enter' Cheapside, they were either going up Cheapside or going down Cheapside, *to* somewhere or *from* somewhere, or like me and many more they were *living* in Cheapside, having brand new babies in Cheapside, living happy unsophisticated lives in Cheapside – entering and leaving the stage doors of the Royalty in Cheapside! being ill in Cheapside, dying in Cheapside. 'Access Prohibited' to Cheapside because it *wasn't safe*?

Don't be ridiculous! *It was the safest place in the world*! Wasn't our front door open from morning 'til night?

Wasn't I always swanking about Number Six? Weren't all the front steps scrubbed and 'rubbing-stoned' individually and to perfection? Weren't all the grates black-leaded until they shone like diamonds? Hadn't I learned what 'arse' meant in Cheapside? Hadn't I gone to school from 6 Cheapside? Hadn't I been ashamed of the front door key of Number Six and then been more ashamed of myself for being ashamed of it? What about the gold bracelet I won, hadn't that been hidden under my pillow in the front bedroom in Cheapside?

The front bedroom! Hadn't it boasted oil paintings of bullrushes and birds in flight and irises on the panels of the door? And hadn't I come out of the front door of Number Six as a virgin bride to go the Wesleyan Chapel to marry Jimmy Scott? *Access Prohibited – No Through Road.* That's what the 1970 notice on the railings said – KEEP OUT! that's what it implied – KEEP OUT! I stood there, *barred* from my street of happiness and memories. The voice in my mind said, '*Can I come in for a minute, Mrs Hird?*' NO! – NO! – NO: – nobody can come in – keep out! Blink your eyes, Thora – remember you've got your false eyelashes on – push the tears back, love!

'I see the cellar is still there,' comforted Scottie. The cellar – my memories were nudging me again. 'It's your week to bring the coal up, Nev!' 'Have you brushed the cellar steps down, Thora?' 'Let's play in the cellar – you can tie me up with orange box rope and I'll pretend I'm Pearl White in *The Lightning Raiders* and escape – go on, our Nev!'

I could see there was still whitewash on the cellar walls – I wondered how many coats of whitewash had been added to where our last artistic effect adhered.

'Remember our back yard, Thor? Look it's still there!' added Nev.

'Yes, yes, there's our own back yard – no walls left to call over to Mrs Houghton, just the stone base, the part we swilled and then "did" with a yardbrush – they've left that.'

Hey, there's where the 'lav' was! *'Neville, will you fold and cut some newspapers and string them for the lav, please?' 'Did you scrub the seat well with disinfectant, Thora, love?' 'Hey – you needn't sit out there on the lavatory any longer, you can come back in – I've washed up!' 'Neville, come here – have you been smoking in the lavatory? Now look at me – have you? Well, you'd better go and empty some Izal down the pan, before your Dad goes in, because if he smells you've been smoking, he'll go mad!'*

Just the ground left – that's all. Looking like an empty tray, a lonely plateau.

Wait a tick, though – what's that? There! Over there where the orange box full of soil used to stand under the window in the back yard. *That over there!* Growing in our back yard! Can you see what I'm pointing to? Scottie and Nev looked in the direction of where I was pointing.

A bush of weeds had bravely pushed itself through the grey dust and was waving in the breeze – just as though it was beckoning or trying to attract our attention. It couldn't be – surely it couldn't possibly be the *Polygonum Cuspidatum* alias the *Reynoutria Japonica* – defying all adversity? Had it, after years of limited sunshine, burst forth in all its glory in its now wide-open and unlimited space? How marvellous! Long live our back yard! 'Well – 'as my mother would have said, ' – 'it's a nice bit of green and it isn't hurting anybody!' Hurting anybody? It's a crumb of comfort! It's soothing me!

I'm quite sure – or nearly sure – it wasn't our *Polygonum Cuspidatum*. On the other hand, I wasn't near enough to find out, so I'll pretend it *was*. It was on the very spot where our 'nice bit of green' had been. So what matter?

One thing is sure, whichever it was – it will have to go when the new buildings go up. There will be no place for it in the new scheme of things. Mind you, if you *are Polygonum Cuspidatum*, little bush, they'll have a job to get rid of you! When you start to seed in a few weeks' time, I wonder where your seeds will float and eventually come to rest? Please don't float as far as our cottage garden – not even out of affection!

Well, it's no use standing here any longer, just looking and reminiscing.

I wonder what will be built on where Number Six stood? Whatever the end product is, I hope it will contain as much happiness and love as our house did. I hope whoever lives or works on that little area will be as gay and have as big a sense of humour as the Hirds had. Yes, I think *that* will be the best thing I can wish the progress marchers – a sense of humour. They'll probably need it!

'Come on, love,' said Scottie.

'Yes – let's go,' said Nev.

So long, our street. Thank you for everything that stemmed from your having been there, my very happy and colourful childhood, the loving and unforgettable home life that you embraced.

Cheapside! I salute you!

On 28 November 1972, I opened the Arndale Centre, Morecambe. It stood on, what had been, one side of Cheapside (the one step and ordinary flat window side), Sun Street and part of Market St. 'Our side' of Cheapside still remained an undeveloped plateau. The main doors of the shopping centre were graced by two large brass handles. By the time the opening ceremony was completed the same handles had been mounted on to a polished wooden plaque . . . duly inscribed, and presented to me by S. H. Chippendale Esq., of Town and City Properties. You've guessed haven't you? They were the 'solid gold' handles off the mansion doors of one of my childhood fantasies. *The Royalty Theatre dress circle door handles!!*

48

'Round the World in 140 Days'

I'd often thought how nice it would be to be able to go to Australia under the banner of doing a job there. Well, it happened when I was invited to star at the Theatre in Perth, during the Festival. The tempting tit-bit about the invitation *was*, that I was to rehearse three weeks and play four weeks. The reason I mention the tempting tit-bit is that I had previously been invited to work in Australia – on about six occasions – but the periods of work they offered had always been a year or six months and I'd been unable to accept because I never seemed to have that amount of time free – consequently when I was invited to go for a seven week visit, I was delighted.

You are already aware – well I think you are – I'm sure I've written it somewhere in the book, that Scottie and I are both 'travel mad!' So as soon as it was decided that I would accept the Perth Festival job, one could *see* the wheels beginning to turn in Scottie's brain regarding something we had always wanted and intended to do.

'Well,' he began, 'it would seem to me to be a wonderful opportunity to go around the world! Aye? What do you think?' I opened my mouth to answer in the affirmative, but I didn't get the chance. It was one of those odd moments when my quiet Scot's husband was carried away with enthusiasm. 'I mean,' he continued, 'we're half way round the world when we get to Perth, then after you've finished your work there we can fly to Melbourne and then Sydney and then we can fly to Fiji and see the Hacketts, then we can fly to Hawaii and then . . .' 'Hey, hold on,' I interrupted, 'where's Singapore? I've always wanted to stay at the Raffles Hotel.' Scottie kindly told me where Singapore was, and assured me that on our flight out to Perth we could break our journey at Singapore for a couple of days and we could stay at the Raffles Hotel. We did.

Oooo Mate, it's places like the Raffles in Singapore, Reid's Hotel in Madeira and the Fairmont on Nob Hill in San Francisco that convince me I have been here before. Raffles Hotel thrilled me pink! *Full Somerset Maugham period!* I was humming the theme music of the Somerset Maugham television series all the time we were there. For instance, the *hall* of our suite was bigger than most modern hotel rooms and the bathroom was as large as a flat.

And before anyone reading this remarks, 'Ridiculous!' let me add, 'Yes – it is – *these* days – because not many visitors want that kind of place, either the style or the price – but when Raffles was built the life style was very different and believe me or believe me not there's still a great atmosphere of the turn of the century there and I loved it.' Thank God I can still get a lot of pleasure out of what, to some folks, would seem unimportant things. When I looked at the pale grey linen note paper on the beautiful desk in our lounge at Raffles, I saw that under their own crest, which topped the sheet, was Thora Hird printed in gold lettering and on the other side of the desk another batch of note paper bearing the name James Scott. All right, I know we were paying for it – but I was real chuffed and I don't care who knows it.

In the Street of Fame (or shame!) we saw – and I'm not exaggerating, the most beautiful, sequin-gowned, elegantly wigged and made-up women!!! Pardon the expression! The driver of our Trisha, a quaint bicycle with a sidecar for two and a cheerful driver to pedal you around, started to nudge me as he grinned all over his face and nodded his head in the direction of 'the beauties'. He nudged me so much that eventually I had to admit to him that I *knew* they were fellers – mind you, their make-up was smashing and I could have wished for a closer look – and, indeed, nearly got it because one of the 'gorgeous slant-eyed beauties' approached Scottie and was about to offer his/her (delete whichever is not applicable!) wares, when our driver, 'the cycling terror of Singapore', known to his friends as 'the Reg Harris of the Chinese quarter', took off like a catapult. He peddled like mad, laughing his head off, all the way back to the Raffles. I was sorry to say good night to him, his shorts and shirt were spotless, somebody had been using the biological action, he only had the camera right hand side teeth left in his upper set, but this made his grin not only lovable but unforgettable. When Scottie tipped him the 'slice of melon' grin grew even wider and it was a happy man who threw his leg over the Trisha leather driving seat and peddled off – still grinning!

My engagement in Perth was enjoyable for many reasons. The very first morning we walked out of our hotel to go to rehearsal, a lady and gentleman walking along the pavement saw me, and with cries of 'Eee, is it Thora?' approached me with affection. 'Eee-ee-ee, well!' the lady laughed, 'we never thought we'd see you in Australia, did we Dad?' she said, nudging the gentleman with her. Dad agreed, I think he always did! When I remarked that she sounded as though she came from Lancashire, she informed me with glee that a lot of the immigrants in Perth 'were from the north! In fact,' she assured me, 'most of 'em!' And she was right.

Another reason for my happiness in Perth was that I was appearing in Walter Greenwood's *Saturday Night at the Crown*, the play I had appeared in hundreds of times. As a matter of fact, I played the part of Ada Thorpe for the thousandth time on my second night's performance at the theatre in Perth and a huge surprise cake, covered in lit candles, was carried on stage at the final curtain. But wait, I haven't finished about the happiness stakes yet. The director of the Perth Theatre, Edgar Metcalfe (what a clever director, and as nice a person as you would meet on a day's march!), extremely capable and, being an actor, and a good 'un, able to *show* members of the company how he wanted a line delivered. He not only got the best out of me but out of the rest of the cast, too. Steven Porter, who did all my publicity, was fantastic, and as Australian as a kangaroo. I've put that bit in on purpose because Edgar Metcalfe is English with grass roots in Lancashire, and I have no wish to sound biased about Edgar. Bless them for making our visit so very happy.

Another blessing was that my television series *Meet the Wife* and *The First Lady* had both been on the Australian television screens, so people felt they knew me.

One of the many functions we attended was in a sort of Assembly Rooms. Everyone there was British and by the time we arrived, after the show at the theatre, the guests were well into the Saint Bernard's Waltz.

As we approached the room by a long corridor, the MC spotted me – he rushed up to the orchestra waving his arms and silenced the lilting strains with a loud, 'Shut up – she's here!' Everyone stopped dancing as though they were playing 'Statues' or as though it was a spot dance. There were tables and chairs round the sides of the room where refreshments were being fully taken and enjoyed. I was bustled to the mike on the bandstand.

I started to make a very short speech, but there was something wrong with the mike (there so often is). So, using my 'back of the gallery' voice, I said I would go to each table for a chat. This was received with loud cheers. By now everyone was clustered round the bandstand with bits of paper and pens for my autograph. Bless 'em' all, but I've often wondered how many of the bits of paper, fag packets, serviettes and snapshots that folks like me so gratefully sign, are kept! And another thing that always strikes me as strange is, the person who asks for your autograph never wants it for themselves, it's always, 'Will you sign this for my niece', or 'Please – it's for my little grandchild!' or 'If you wouldn't mind, it's for my little boy, he always watches you on the telly!' Well, as I say, bless 'em all, the moment they stop asking us, we'll know we're out of work! As long as anybody is sufficiently interested in me to bother to ask for my autograph, I will be sufficiently interested in them to sign it!

Asking the autograph hunters very politely if they would kindly return to their various tables where I would sign my autograph with pleasure, I then moved away from the mike and made my way to the first table. I asked a lady who was sitting there if she was glad she had emigrated, and she replied, 'Oh yes, Thora love, y'see, we came here with our son and daughter and they have both married Australians and our grandchildren have been born here – so where else would we want to be?' I thought that made sense, all the family and loved ones together. At the next table I asked a lady, 'Are you happy here?' Like a shot from a gun she attacked me verbally. 'I 'ate it!' she exploded, 'I've 'ated every minute I've been here!' 'Oh dear – well never mind,' I said, as gently as I could, 'perhaps you'll be happier when you get used to it – how long have you been here?' She gave me a piercing look as though *I* had persuaded her to emigrate. 'Eighteen years!' she exclaimed. 'And I've 'ated every bloody minute!' I felt it was time I moved on to the next table.

We were shown great kindness in Melbourne and in Sydney, though how the 'ell either place knew I was there I'll never know because after we left Perth I was travelling as Mrs James Scott.

Our next port of call was Fiji.

What can I say about Fiji? Oh, mate! A couple of our dearest friends live in Fiji, Mr and Mrs Jack Hackett. It's a friendship that both Scottie and I treasure. I've known

Jack Hackett and his wife Lena 'forever' as you might say, in fact, it was Lena's bike I used to borrow when we were kids. I'll tell you why. You see, my bike, the halfcrown one, that I had black lacquered without rubbing down with sandpaper first, so that it looked like a jumble of black varicose veins on two wheels – you remember? – I told you about it earlier on in this saga – well, it was not as posh as Lena's – but I scored because I had a tennis racquet and four old tennis balls in a string bag. The bag, rather on the lines of the present-day net jobs that you buy oranges or apples in, *was* for tennis balls.

I would ride around Cheapside, Sun Street, Anderton Street and Moss Lane clutching the tennis racquet and string bag of balls across the handlebars and, in return for the loan of the bike, I'd lend Lena the racquet and the string thing with the tennis balls in for when she rode round. Incidentally, neither of us could or did play tennis – but that never came into it! It was merely that the racquet and balls added a bit of tone. I mean, if it so happened that anyone, seeing either of us riding along with the tennis racquet held with authority across the handlebars and the four tennis balls in their string thing swinging to the rhythm of the peddling, if they wanted to think we were either of us on our way to Wimbledon, that was up to them.

The bit that you might not understand, and come to think of it, neither can I now, so many years after – sometimes I would borrow Lena's nappa gloves that had a bit of beaver or some sort of fur, round the cuffs. Elegance personified eh? Cotton dress, short white socks, racquet and balls on bike – and fur trimmed gloves, on a hot day!! I wonder what a psychiatrist would make of all that. Ambition? Swank? Or being a bit loose in the lid?

Any road, Lena Hackett has remained just as good a friend and just as generous to this day. Jack and his brother, Desmond, used to be in the St Mary's School Concert, and 'our Nev' and I were in Miss Nelson's School Concert. When we were all school children, there was great rivalry in a friendly way, but even so, Jack and Neville became great friends as Lena and I have always been. I suppose 'Hackett' as I call him, is one of the most interesting and intelligent characters I am lucky enough to know. And I'm not saying that because he's an OBE and wears a pair of cuff links given to him by Her Most Gracious Majesty, in recognition of his splendid work. Good old Jack, you're lovely. (If you read this, Lena, so are you!)

Yes, we had an unforgettable time in Suva. One occasion would be impossible to forget. The 'Tabua' Ceremony, it was great! The 'Tabua' Ceremony, at which I was the guest of honour, is really a very moving and important affair and, although I cannot understand why they considered *me* important enough to bestow it on, it *did* happen and it's one of the times in my very happy and wonderful life that I shall be able to tell my grandchildren about without any exaggeration.

When Scottie and I and the Hacketts arrived at the appointed place, which was a thriving Sports Club run by Harry Charman MBE, an Englishman, I was presented with the most beautiful bouquet of small orchids in various colours, by a little Fijian boy. He was extremely handsome and was wearing his best clothes, western style. (I don't mean cowboy clothes, I mean the sort our little English lads wear.) He was also wearing a pair of well-polished leather shoes that should have had laces – but hadn't. He was about eight years old and a real little charmer.

After the usual introductions and photographs the ceremony began. It was all in Fijian but an interpreter, a Fijian headmaster, echoed the words for me in English. I wish I could remember every word that the ceremony embraces, it really was beautiful. They told me that they were not a wealthy race of people but, had they been, they would have given me pearls and precious things. However, they said they wished to bestow on me one of *their* most precious possessions – a Tabua – a whale's tooth.

The man who spoke the ceremonial words had a beautiful, soft voice and I sat there trying my best not to cry. As I looked at these wonderful people who were dressed in native costume – a sort of wraparound, brightly coloured skirt – I thought 'Eee, Thorird, this is all happening to *you* and you used to scrub and yellow stone your mother's front steps!' D'you wonder I felt like weeping?

They then presented me with the whale's tooth, which was hanging on a kind of mayoral chain made of very cleverly interwoven hemp of some kind. It's one of my many treasures and I look at it very often – with affection.

Incidentally, we had to get written permission from the High Commissioner to bring it from the island, or should I say, 'For it to leave the island'. That's how important a whale's tooth is.

Although we still had some travelling to do, I'd like to jump ahead to our return to England where we had to declare 'it' – the tooth – at Heathrow Airport Customs.

'Have you anything to declare?' the customs official enquired.

'Yes,' I answered, '. . . a whale's tooth!'

He was a very smart and good-looking young man and displayed a smashing set of teeth as he laughingly said, 'Oh, come off it, Thora – you're not on the telly now!'

When the time came for Scottie and me to leave Fiji and the Hacketts, we did so rather reluctantly because we were sorry to leave our good friends. I think as one gets older the 'Heart and Flowers' element creeps in and whether one tries to dispel the thought of, 'I wonder if we shall ever meet again?' or not – you *think* that. Don't you agree? Well, I know *I* do. But there again, I am what is commonly referred to as, 'a soppy 'aporth'.

In the case of the Hacketts, it's daft to think the above because they fly to England to visit their brilliant surgeon son almost as often as I go to Oxford Street. Come to think of it – their journey from Fiji doesn't take much longer than when I go to Oxford Street! And anybody who has waited for an 88 or 12 bus in the Bayswater Road will understand what I mean!

We were bound for Honolulu and we looked like a couple of sticks of liquorice, we were so brown. As the plane took off my excitement eclipsed any heartache, the reason being that our daughter, Jan, and our three-year-old granddaughter, Daisy, were to join us in

Hawaii a couple of days after our arrival.

I think I'm pretty safe in saying it is almost impossible to be bored in Hawaii. Even so, like any mother or grandmother, I was ticking the hours off with loving impatience until their arrival.

Scottie and I arrived at the airport to meet them (much too early – of course). I stood with a couple of heavily perfumed 'leis' hanging from my arm, champing at the bit and ready to fling a lei round their respective necks as I greeted them with the word 'Aloha!' (Oh, Dorothy Lamour has nothing on me, when the mood takes me!) The planes from Los Angeles were touching down like a hail storm, there were so many, and quite honestly it wasn't until a little vehicle, rather like a dodgem car, carrying an airline official, stacks of luggage and our two favourite girls, was under my nose, that I saw it! Even then I'd have missed the joy of the last two yards of their approach if a little voice hadn't called out rather shyly, 'Hi! Ganny! Hi! Popa!'

How in the name of goodness can one write about moments like that? Well I'm not clever enough to do so, and that's for sure. I forgot the leis, even though I had cramp in the arm they were hanging from, I forgot the 'Aloha bit!' (sorry, Miss Lamour) and as I crushed first Jan to me and then Daisy, I crushed the flowers in the leis as well, but I didn't give a damn. We were all together safely and that's what mattered. You can't buy moments such as those, can you? It's a good job really that affection costs nothing. If it did, with inflation as it is at the moment, nobody would be able to afford it! Wouldn't life be awful if we couldn't show a bit of love now and again?

Eventually, after a couple of choruses of 'Goodbye Hawaii', Jan, Daisy, Scottie and I flew off to Los Angeles. Scottie and I of course stayed with Jan and Mel in their Beverly Hills house. Every time we visit them it's lovable and interesting but on this particular visit there was an added enjoyment because we didn't really know how long we were staying. I don't mean we intended staying for ever, I mean we had no idea whether our visit would be two, four, six or eight weeks. Every time Scottie and I opened our mouths to say, 'I think it's time we were thinking of . . .' Jan would throw up her hands and say, 'If you are talking about going back to London, *don't* tell me, I don't want to know until just before you leave for the airport. I can't bear the unhappiness of that "last day you're here bit!"' It's nice to be loved, isn't it? I mean, it's nice to be loved dearly by your daughter, and it's an added bonus when your son-in-law loves you as well. And it's quadruple green shield stamps when *you* love *them* in the same way.

It was during that particular visit that Scottie and I were taken to the theatre by a couple of very good friends of ours, Bunny and Maurice Charles. It's extraordinary how many friends we have accumulated in Beverly Hills, all of whom willingly go out of their way to give us a good time. Thank heavens most of them visit England, which gives us a chance to reciprocate. On the night I'm talking about, Bunny and Maurice were taking us to see *No, No, Nanette*. We had a splendid dinner before the show, in the theatre restaurant, the food was super, the wines excellent and, add to that, the head waiter was from Preston, Lancashire,

England. 'Nuff said! Well, there's nothing more *to* say, is there?

The production of *Nanette* was very good, and we all enjoyed the show, so you'll gather that by the time we were having coffee and a liqueur in a Mexican coffee house, we were all in a happy mood. And, as my mother would have said, 'We weren't hurting anybody.'

My husband has quite a few traits like my dad and one of 'em *is*, that he has never *ever* said to me with regards to my work, remarks like, 'Oh you *were* good!' or '*You* were the best!' or 'I think you are *marvellous*.' He'll criticize me now and again, and I'll take it because nine times out of ten he's right – the tenth time out of ten, he's wrong, and that's when I argue! However, I have my own way of knowing when he thinks I'm 'not so bad', 'all right', 'competent', or 'a touch of the professional', – he says nowt! I understand him very well.

On the particular evening in Beverly Hills I've just been talking about, as we came out of the theatre Scottie slipped his arm through mine and said, without any emotion, 'If they ever put *No, No, Nanette* on in London, you could eat the part of the maid!' And that was that. I never even answered him.

We eventually arrived back in London after a fantastic holiday. It was only a few months after we returned home that I was asked to play Pauline, the maid, in the London production of *No, No, Nanette* at Drury Lane. Once again, being under the Gemini sign, I had to decide which of two jobs I wanted to do – I couldn't do 'em both – it was a case of telly versus stage. I was inclined a little towards 'the job on the box' but both Felix de Wolfe and Scottie (who, in fairness, I must say, never persuades me against 'my witch's water feeling' – if I feel it strongly enough) advised me to go back into the theatre, especially in the part of Pauline. I did, and I'm happy to say they were right.

There's one little story I'd like to recall. It happened on the last night of the run of *No, No, Nanette*. I was sitting in Annie Roger's dressing room, we'd had a matinee and we always had tea in Annie's room, because we're good friends and enjoy each other's company.

Just before 'the half hour' was called, my dresser came into Annie's room and said there was a lady to see me. I was expecting a lady friend so I set off for my dressing room. *En route* I met Scottie, who was coming to see the last performance, so we both made our way to my dressing room. This little story took place during the SOS ('Save on Something') electricity shortage period, so, of course, I had only left a very small light on in my room.

As Scottie and I entered my dressing room, what we saw in the shadows was a young woman with her arms full of long-stemmed deep red roses and white lilies (I don't mean funeral lilies, I mean the other sort).

I said 'Good evening' to her, and as I did so, she burst out laughing. I knew that laugh. So did Scottie, who at that moment was switching my dressing table lights on. I can remember thinking during the second before the lights came on, 'That sounds just like Jan!' The lights came on – and – it *was* Jan! Honest to God, I've never had such a wonderful surprise in my life – I stood there as though I'd been turned to stone – it sounds silly to say that, but it's true. Jan's voice brought me back to life, she just stood there holding all the lovely flowers and said, ever so quietly, 'Did you think I'd let you fold at the Lane without seeing you?' She'd flown from Beverly Hills, nearly six thousand miles for *one* day just to watch her mum 'having a go!' I reckon her seat for the play was the most expensive ever sold at the Lane, eh? It was a great night for me, I must say – I don't mean *I* was great, I mean the whole evening was great! Where I had to do a little tap dance in the show, the orchestra had prepared a 'farewell surprise' and instead of playing the usual music they broke into 'The Stripper!'

All right then, the London production of *No, No, Nanette* wasn't a roaring success, but *I* enjoyed myself, and as far as (to quote Scottie) 'eating the part of Pauline' went, I perhaps didn't do that – but I spread it on my bread as artistically and professionally as I could!

49

Ours is a nice house . . .

I have a lot of faults. I don't mean evil, wicked, sinful faults, I mean little, everyday, not very clever, 'you'd hardly credit it' faults. I am also incapable of doing a lot of little ordinary jobs that women friends of mine take in their stride.

For instance, I can't mend a fuse, I can't read a road map correctly, I can't drive a car, which is perhaps just as well as I can't read a road map. I have no sense of direction and I am still trying to work out how, when I press a switch, the room fills with light! I should give up trying to work out how, when I lift the telephone receiver with one hand and then put the index finger end of the other hand into a series of little numbered holes which enable me to turn the dial to any number I so desire, in no time at all my daughter's voice in Beverly Hills says, quite clearly, 'Hello, is that you, Mummy?' (I haven't even worked it out how it happens when I ring my next door neighbour!!) As for a gramophone record, radio or television – nuff said!

I was thinking of letting you know that I'm not so bad at pressing flowers, flower arrangement, writing poetry. I'm very good at cleaning of all descriptions, including brass, copper and silver (and I don't leave any deposits of Brasso, or Silvo in the crinkly bits). I'm excellent at washing up, which Scottie says I always make into a production because I always wash behind and round the taps, the top of the cooker, the top of the 'fridge, wipe any splashes off the kitchen cupboards and then wash the washing up bowl and dry it, having poured the soapy water out of the bowl into the sink so that I can wash round the sink with a final flourish! And all that is at each washing up session! Sewing, not bad, not good! Knitting, pathetic! Darning, very good, but nobody does it anymore. I can boast about two things (and don't misunderstand that remark, although I do wear a 38" bra), my handwriting, and my figures – not my own figure, I'm not talking about that, I mean, *fig–ers*, sums and keeping an eye on the building society books!

My husband tells me, and he'd tell you, I am interested in money only to the extent of keeping out of debt. It is due to his enquiring as I go out, 'Have you got some money on you?' that I ever have.

When Scottie is doing jobs such as laying stone paths in the garden at the cottage, a spot of carpentry in our Mews house, or anything of that nature, I am a competent labourer. I know a gimlet from a screwdriver, and a screwdriver from a brace and bit or a bradawl. It is yours truly who holds the bucket of Flash when himself is up the ladder washing anything I can't reach. Oh, and that's something else I'm no good at, going up ladders. Only the other week, I was using the step ladder – I wanted to wash some old fashioned stew jars I have 'on show' on top of a kitchen cupboard. All of a sudden, I cried out, 'Scottie!' He flew into the kitchen and in an alarmed voice enquired, 'What's up?' I replied, '*I* am – and it's making me feel dizzy!' He was most relieved that nothing was really wrong and burst out laughing. 'Dizzy?' he said, 'you can't be, you're only up three treads!'

In other words, though not indispensable, I am quite useful in my simple way and I am always there 'to take it out on' if anything goes wrong, whether it's my fault or not, which does happen occasionally. Every wife must know just what I mean. Credit where it's due – he's the engine driver and I'm the oilrag!

And while we are on the subject of 'things I'm not good at', I'll just tell you a little anecdote which unfortunately was one of those incidents that couldn't be helped. Well, perhaps, it could . . . but let's see what you think.

I'm rather fond of milk-chocolate-covered raisins and I'm more than rather fond of nibbling a few when I'm in bed at night, reading, before I drop off. I don't mean every night, I mean just odd nights. No I *don't* mean 'odd nights', as used in the expression 'What an odd sort of carry on!' I mean, odd, not exactly divisible by two, casual, out of the way, apart!

One day I was in the toffee shop with the intention of purchasing a quarter pound of the little brown beauties, when suddenly I thought, 'Oh, blow the expense, I'll get a pound while I'm here!' (I was in a rather reckless spending mood because I'd received a cheque that morning from the BBC covering a *Meet the Wife* tenth repeat, in some far off Zululand, or some such place. It was for 27p!)

We sleep in a fourposter bed and the head of same is

in front of many rows of bookshelves – are you with me? Well, listen carefully or you won't be. When one is in bed, the most accessible shelf holds a telephone, a radio alarm, the books we are currently reading, a few throat sweets, and some indigestion tablets. It *had* also held, on quite a few occasions a little paper bag with my quarter pound of milk-chocolate-covered raisins in it. Often – as we lay on the love couch, Scottie, my romantic husband, the gay galliard of *my* life, has said to me, 'You're not going to ruckle that paper bag half the night, are you?' or, 'What are you eating?' or, 'Oh, hell, are you going to read and eat chocolate-covered raisins until the early hours?' Now fair do's – he'd every right – because each time I raised my arm and hand over my shoulder to reach the little paper bag, I pulled the bedclothes off Scottie, *nearly* waking him, and the noise of my hand delving into the paper bag *completely* waking him! And he didn't like it . . . Well, he wouldn't – would he?

It was the night of the day I had splashed out on the whole pound of chocolate-covered raisins that a very good idea struck me. This was it. If I put about a dozen milk chocolate raisins in a soft 'rustle-less' face tissue, I could then lay the silent tissue in a small indentation in the duvet and, without a sound, read as well as have my midnight feast! I mean, let's face it, it was the least I could do, as I did not wish to disturb, annoy or hurt my beloved spouse in any way.

Unfortunately, 'the very good idea' did not dawn on me until after I was comfortably and snugly settled in the four poster. To try and see *me* under a large duvet is almost impossible and a sight for sore eyes, because I only use one pillow; so consequently I sort of dissolved into the bed. (Years ago, when we first acquired a duvet, Scottie got into bed one night and as he lay down he nearly jumped out of his skin. *He didn't know I was already in bed until a cold toe touched his calf!*)

Any road, on this 'good idea' night, Scottie was sound asleep so I carefully raised my arm above my head and my hand groped along the shelf for the pound of milk-chocolate-covered raisins. My body remained immobile, like one of the stone effigies you see on top of ancient stone coffins. Only my hand and arm were active, silently slithering along the shelf like a well trained snake. Ah! A finger tip touched the paper bag! Sh! Now all I had to do was to get my hand in the bag, silently, and procure about a dozen tempting morsels. I honestly never intended what happened next but there was nothing I could do to stop it! Like a drip from a tap, two or three milk chocolate raisins dribbled out of the bag – and then – the whole pound cascaded out of the bag like a thundering waterfall – all over Scottie's face! It was like a brown hailstorm! I'm laughing now – come to think of it, I laughed *then* – but Scottie wasn't laughing – I mean, fair do's, what a way to be woken up!

It took us quite some time to find and gather in the pound of milk-chocolate-covered raisins – there's a lot in a pound y'know. Upon Scottie's startled awakening he had jerked up into a sort of sitting position, and the MCCRs had found their way into the bed, the duvet was sprinkled with 'em and a few had been squashed into the carpet after we had sprung out of bed. I won't record the dialogue of the next ten minutes. It's private!

I didn't drop anything on Scottie again – well – not for seven weeks I didn't. And then, one night, putting the book I was currently reading back on the aforementioned shelf without looking what I was doing (I was using the well trained snake method again) *my* book caught *his* book and knocked it off the shelf and *his* book fell on his face. Needless to say it woke him up . . . Well it would. It was Tolstoy's *War and Peace*!

Sometimes, now, when I'm reading a big book, like, let us say, Antonia Fraser's *Mary, Queen of Scots* I sleep in the guest room!

Well, you can't blame him for making a little request like that, can you?

I'm not going to tell you that once we were in Scarborough and I moved the reading lamp from the bedside table on my side of the bed, and balanced it on the rather wide mahogany bed-head so that it was between us and we could both read. It fell. Not on me . . . On Scottie . . . But I'm not going to tell you that!

My brother Neville . . . 'Our Nev' . . . 'The Admiral', died in May 1975. A piece of the happy and loving pattern of my life snapped off and was lost forever.

Nev died on a Saturday, and I was opening in a new play, at Brighton, on the following Monday, the dress rehearsal for the show was on the Sunday evening, the play was a comedy. I'm grateful it was. I'm not a stupid woman but as I stood in my dressing room putting my make-up on, I felt . . . somehow . . . I could imagine Nev saying, 'I'm sorry this has happened just before your first night our kid!' For the very first time during all the many plays I have appeared in, I was 'off', so that I could travel to Morecambe in Lancashire to the cremation. My capable understudy took over.

It was a beautiful sunny day, as the sad cortége made its slow way to the crematorium, men who had worked with and had been friends of Nev, respectfully walked on each side of the hearse. I found myself thinking '. . . they've all put their best suits on and a clean white shirt and a black tie!' It's ridiculous to say that a dark suit, a clean white shirt and a black tie looks sad because I don't suppose it really does . . . but . . . well . . . I thought even their well polished shoes looked sad. The amount of people that had congregated at the crematorium denoted that many, many others had respected and loved Nev.

When we were kids, there was a joke that many comedians used, it went something like this: 'I was having a bit of a walk round the cemetery the other day, I'd gone to collect a few jam jars because my mother was going to make some jam!' That's *it*! I mean, that's the joke . . . and it always seemed to get a big laugh. When Nev and I were young there weren't any granite or marble vases on graves, the popular receptacle for flowers was an empty jam jar . . . usually pressed well into the soil of the grave top so that the wind wouldn't blow it over! The aforementioned 'joke' was usually performed by Neville if, when we were children, we ever walked past a cemetery. Do you know? That old gag came into my head as we got out of the car at the crematorium . . . right in the midst of my numb grief. I wondered for a moment, if Nev had made me think of it! *I* think he had.

Ours is a nice house . . .

The service was over. As we got back into the car a tall, distinguished looking man took my hand and gave it a gentle understanding squeeze, his eyes were full of sadness and they looked straight into mine. We didn't speak. The car moved off and had only gone a little way when I realized who he was . . . 'ELOPYAM!', our Nev's best friend when they were lads! Reg . . . who used to work at the MAYPOLE . . . hence his nickname. I hadn't seen him for thirty years. There were neighbours there 'from our Cheapside days' who had attended out of love and respect. Yes . . . they were all there . . .

50

'All down for the finale – please!'

It's over twenty years ago that I spoke at a luncheon at the Piccadilly Hotel for some charity or other, and the gentleman who was sitting on my left was in quite a comfortable position on *The Empire News*. Don't you love that expression, 'in quite a comfortable position!'? Well, never mind whether you do or do not, he turned to me and without any preliminaries, stated, 'Thora – you should write a book!' Please note, I have just mentioned a bit of history. I don't mean the chap who was telling me I should write a book – I mean mentioning *The Empire News*. There's no *Empire News*, full of juicy bits of news of the empire, any more – dead as a dodo – just as there is no *Sunday Chronicle* – which my father swore by! Now there's another marvellous expression, 'swore by!' Swore what by? The times I have heard friends and neighbours in the north use that expression when they have been giving someone a cure for a complaint. They would always end up by saying, 'Well, you just try that love – it'll do the trick, my mother swears by it!' Actually in that last statement you've got 'two expressions for the price of one', because 'do the trick' is another one often used, meaning 'to cure', 'do the job', or 'fix it'.

Any road up, let's get back to the fellow in the *Empire News* who was in quite a comfortable position. He wasn't the first person to have *told* me I should write a book. There had been quite a little band of folks who had *told* me I should. *Asked* me, 'why don't you?' or *enquired*, 'have you ever thought of?' Well, I had 'thought of' – quite a few times, but then I always thought just as quickly, 'who'd want to read it?' Anyway, by the time I had decided to have a go I was always too busy, which stresses once more (with feeling) how very lucky I have been and am, to be employed so much in the kind of work I enjoy.

All right then, about ten years ago I started to make a list of incidents to do with my childhood, but quite honestly, that was about as far as I got! Once again my work, especially on television, really *did* occupy every moment of my time. Rehearsals, learning the words, dress fittings, opening a fête here and a bazaar there. Add to that the fact that I am a housewife as well – and it doesn't leave more time to try and write a book does it?

The bit of paper with the list of childhood incidents written on it got pushed to the back of a drawer.

Six years ago, our daughter Jan gave birth to a baby girl, Daisy Ann Tormé – a golden-cum-marigold-cum-carroty-haired little smasher! You would, of course, expect me, like any other red-blooded grandmother in the world, to rave about her, to tell you how very clever she is, and that her IQ is far and away beyond the average. You would also expect me to say that she can execute a little number like, 'Don't jump off the roof, Dad, you'll make a hole in the yard!' with professional expertise. You would agree, I think, that as a loving grandmother I have a right to think and say, 'She's wonderful!' Well, you would wouldn't you? And you'd be right! I *am* saying and thinking and raving because – well – she's our grand-daughter, isn't she? Bless her little heart! 'Nuff said, Thor – do shut up! The dictionary (my constant companion) says, '*Grandmother, a father or mother's mother*,' and the next word is '*Grandmotherly, like a grandmother, over anxious, fussy!*' Need I say more?

Two years ago, our grandson, James Scott Tormé, practically marched into the world to the swirl of bagpipes! He's a real handsome lad, and no mistake, but don't worry, I'm not going to start on about him. One thing I will say, if you'll allow me, he's the spittin' image of my husband. (That's another of those expressions I heard so often during my childhood. According to the dictionary it means, 'an exact replica, the exact likeness of, as like him as if he had spit out of his mouth.' Well perhaps the expression isn't too savoury but it's descriptive enough. He's named after my husband, James Scott – or to put it more correctly: 'whose namesake he is!' Isn't nature wonderful? Especially the hereditary bit? Young James has the same sort of ears as Scottie, same sort of nose, same sort of little cleft in his chin and the same sort of expressive eyes as his mummy and Scottie. It's fantastic isn't it?

Any road, there's your hereditary bit for yer! James Scott Tormé, the spittin' image of Scottie, his grandfather: Daisy Ann, the spittin' image of her daddy, Mel Tormé; Jan, our daughter, the spittin' image of her daddy, my husband; but – hold on, nobody, but

nobody, is the spittin' image of yours truly, me (and
you can't blame 'em!), except the thousand women
who all claimed they were the spittin' image of me
when I was doing the *Meet the Wife* and *The First Lady*
series! But of course, they weren't relatives and could
afford to risk what folks might say.

So, patient readers, after various anecdotes and
going off the subject and back on to it many times, here
I am, telling you that it is for our two grandchildren
that I have recorded some of the events of my wonderfully blessed happy and loving life – up to now! You
see, because Jan and Mel and the grandchildren are
domiciled in Beverly Hills, USA, and although we nip
over there as often as possible, it isn't as if they lived
in the next street. (And with inflation as it is at the
moment, who the 'ell would *want* them to live in the
next street?)

What I mean is, Scottie and I can't take Daisy and
James out for tea or take them into a toy shop or into the
park each week, thereby being able to bore 'em stiff
with the remark, 'When I was a little girl . . .' (Of course,
Scottie wouldn't say 'girl' – well, it's to be hoped he
wouldn't.) I was only kidding about the 'bore 'em stiff'
bit, because we all know kids love stories about yester-
year, hence the popularity of fairy stories. Not that I'm
suggesting that our three front steps in Cheapside were
ever likely to turn into a golden coach! But just a
minute – did they? That's quite debatable really, when
I consider what a happy life I lead.

It dawned on me that my young grandchildren
would never *really* know me, I mean the *real* me. All
right, they know *me* well enough as Ganny from

England where the Red Buses come from and as the Ganny they come to see in London because it's great fun and there's a musical toilet roll in the 'loo'! Even so, I wanted them to know I wasn't always a 'star' of the theatre and television. (Excuse me using that four letter word, but it was unavoidable in that context.) And it was with that thought in mind that I rescued my list of childhood incidents from the back of the drawer.

I would try and write a book – not for publication – but for James Scott and Daisy Ann.

I want them to know how much I enjoyed my childhood and to let them know I wasn't always a grown up Ganny – like I am now. I want them to know that my childhood with 'our Nev' was really no different from theirs as far as happiness and love and the feelings of joy and sorrow are concerned. I want them to know that although I scrubbed and yellow-stoned 'our front steps' and blackleaded our coal hole and grates when I was only a little girl, it wasn't because I was badly done by or that I had cruel parents. It was to make me capable of running a home and to give me a sense of responsibility when I became a housewife (always providing that some day someone would pop the question!).

I want them to realize that 6, Cheapside, was more than just part of a street, and hecky plonk, were we proud of it. We didn't have electric light (although we all wanted it and eventually had it installed), the houses had gas brackets and gas mantles and we all rather tried to outdo each other with our glass shades that surrounded the gas mantles. I want them to realize that, although we were doing our homework by gaslight and there was no magic tap which when turned produced hot water, we weren't living in the squalor of the Dickensian period and I wasn't going to school in a crinoline. In fact, I would *like* them to know that my knicker legs – with the needlework trimming and either blue or pink baby ribbon threaded through – were the shortest knicker legs in our school! Which goes to show I measured 'em during needle work class with my linen tape measure against some of my school pals' knicker legs! Proof positive that I was blessed with a mother who was a good thirty or forty years ahead of her time.

It will be nice for them to learn how much happiness and love their own mother had given and does give to Scottie and me. They will be wise to listen to their Sunday School teacher, who also happens to be their loving Mummy, and not only listen, but digest. By the time they are old enough to read and understand this book I feel almost sure they will have been taught by their parents that, although a lot of the best things in life are free, there are lot of things that are not – therefore, anything they want badly enough is worth working, saving and waiting for!

I want them to know how much I enjoy, early morning on a beautiful summer's day . . . flowers, wild or cultivated . . . the smell of newly cut grass . . . arriving home after a walk on a frosty autumn afternoon just in time for toasted brown bread and honey, and freshly brewed tea . . . and the scent of chrysanthemums around. I want them to know how much I have always detested hypocrisy, dishonesty, cruelty in any form; liver, kidney, sweetbreads or offal of any description.

I'd like them to believe that if they cast their bread on the waters it invariably comes back buttered. I want them to know how dearly they are loved by their mummy and daddy and that the 'bonus in the love stakes' is because, added to the joy of their existence, they are part of their Mummy, who in turn, is part of us. I want them to know that I am called Ganny because on the first little card Daisy sent to us, announcing her arrival when she was about one hour old, was written 'To my Ganny and Popa'. (Extremely *well* written, I thought for an hour-old child!) I don't really want them to know that their dear mother had missed the 'R' out of 'Granny'. And who could blame her? When only one hour before she'd given birth to, quite probably, the first Lady President of the USA! So Ganny I've remained. There's nothing the matter with a moniker like that is there? Well *I* like it!

Before long, Scottie and I will be with them once again, staying in the lovely little cottage which Jan and Mel gave to us, and which is in the grounds of their house. I won't bother them with any of the details of this effort of mine because we shall be too busy listening to the description of all the things that have happened since our last visit, three months ago. Daisy will fill us in with all her school news, and tell us how many more widths of the pool she can swim. Young James Scott will be looking forward to another birthday, to the accompaniment *not* of one of his daddy's brilliant arrangements, but of his four proud grandparents 'ooooing' and 'Ahhhing'. Mel's parents will be proclaiming 'Oh, Gees, – he's the greatest!' and 'Oh, Gard – look at him'. Equally proud and just as barmy or daft, will be Scottie and me exuding (I think that word's wrong) praise – 'He's really very intelligent!' 'Oh – look!', 'Oh, isn't he bonny?' and 'Bluddy marvellous!' 'Twas ever thus! All these things have the importance of the moment and make anything I have to tell them unimportant until they are old enough to read and understand what I have written with truth and affection.

In any case, on the next trip, Daisy and I will be preparing yet another big production – an extravaganza starring: 'Your own, your very own, Miss Daisy Ann Tormé, who will now sing for you, "Your baby has gorn dahn the plug-ole!"'

I shall buy a copy of the book and send it to them. (My brave publishers who have faith in me needn't worry unduly – because I know somebody else who is going to buy a copy as well – so that's *two* for starters!)

There are many more happy, comic, sad and illuminating moments of my life up to now that I haven't recorded in the book – whether I have chosen what I *have* recorded wisely or not – I don't really know. I hope I have.

Please believe me that, as I write this, the church bells are ringing. It must be practice night for the bellringers. Any road up, they are ringing – like mad!

And that's how it all began.

BOOKS BY

THORA HIRD

HarperCollins publish the
following books by Thora Hird:

Is It Thora?
My Autobiography Volume Two

✳

Happy Days!
Daily Readings

✳

Thora Hird's Praise Be! Notebook

✳

Thora Hird's Praise Be! Prayer Book

✳

Sing With Praise

and

Thora Hird's Little Book of Home Truths

Is It Thora?

———

My Autobiography
Volume Two 1975–1995

This eagerly awaited second volume of Dame Thora Hird's autobiography takes the popular actress and television presenter through a mesmerizing past two decades.

From the huge success of the television comedy 'In Loving Memory' and its sequel 'Hallelujah', to her BAFTA award-winning performance in Alan Bennett's 'A Cream Cracker Under The Settee', Thora found her acting career reach new heights as it moved into its sixth decade.

These years are recalled by Thora with fondness and great humour, spiced with fresh recollections about her childhood.

Is It Thora? is sure to become an enduring testament to one of Britain's best-loved personalities.

Happy Days!

Daily Readings

"I nearly always put 'Happy Days!' before my name when giving an autograph. It exactly describes how I feel about life.

"This little book is a 'thought' for every day of the year, and on some days I've included stories and memories of incidents from the past that have gone to make our family life so joyous.

"I hope that for you as well as for me, they add up to a year of 'Happy Days!'"

DAME THORA HIRD

Thora Hird's
Praise Be! Notebook

—

Thora Hird's Praise Be! Notebook is
a selection of the hymns requested by
listeners to the programme that is presented
by Thora Hird. Listed alphabetically, each
section also includes thoughts and ideas that
have gone into the making of the
programme over the years. A book I think a
lot of people might enjoy

EUROPEAN CHRISTIAN BOOKSELLER

Thora Hird's
Praise Be! Prayer Book

———

Viewers of the popular BBC television programme,
Praise Be!, presented by Thora Hird, will need little
encouragement to buy her latest book.

She has collected together favourite prayers (a
delightful mixture of old and new) and interspersed
them with touching and amusing anecdotes from
her own experience.

She chats as easily with the written word as she
does with the spoken word on television. All this
goes to make up a super little book to buy for
yourself or to give to a friend.

CHRISTIAN HERALD

❁

For 15 years a regular five million viewers have
made *Praise Be!* one of Britain's best loved
television programmes. And there is no secret to its
success – presenter Thora Hird lets all the viewers
know they are special, but that their moments of
sadness and joy are shared by many others.

In *Praise Be! Prayer Book* she has collected her
favourites – old and new, written by the famous and
the forgotten and even some sent by viewers. It is a
book that cannot fail to bring comfort in times of
trouble and help the reader to give thanks for
blessings in times of joy.

METHODIST RECORDER

Sing With Praise

Hymns, Prayers and Readings
for Help the Aged

This delightful book has been produced for the
friends and supporters of one of Thora's favourite
organizations, Help the Aged.

It brings together a selection of Thora's most-
loved prayers, hymns and readings, all introduced
in her inimitable and amusing way.

Sing With Praise also includes new hymns written
by readers of Help the Aged's associate magazine
Yours, many of which are published here for the
first time.

With a special emphasis upon the ups and downs
of life as an elderly person, *Sing With Praise* has
been as warmly received as Thora's previous
books.

Thora Hird's
Little Book of Home Truths

––––––

"I've realized that I am one of those lucky
people who received a double blessing when
I was born: first to grow up in the North of
England, and second, to have had two of the
best and wisest parents in the world.

"This book is a collection of things I
was taught as I was growing up in
Morecambe. And some of them are things
I've learned for myself over eighty years. I
don't suppose they are going to shake the
world – but who knows? The may make life a
little happier for someone."

DAME THORA HIRD